Power Tool Woodcarving

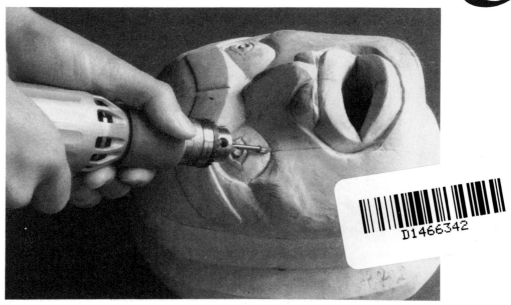

Alan & Gill Bridgewater

STERLING PUBLISHING CO., INC.
NEW YORK

Acknowledgments

We would like to thank all the manufacturers and suppliers who helped us with this book. One and all, they have been wonderfully generous with their time and expertise. We asked and they gave—we questioned and they answered—we stumbled and they helped us on our way.

Tim Effrem—President, Wood Carvers Supply, PO Box 7500, Englewood, FL 34295-7500 USA.

Peter Appelby—Director, Pulsafe Respirator, A & H Supplies, Compass House, 3 Lewis Rd., Sidcup, Kent, DA14 4NB UK.

Roger Buse—Chief of Sales, Hegner UK, Unit 8, North Cres, Diplocks Way, Hailsham BN27 3JF UK.

Jim Brewer—Research and Marketing Manager, Freud, PO Box 7187, 218 Feld Ave., High Point, NC 27264 USA.

Michael Brainerd—Marketing Services Manager, Dremel, 4915 21st Street, Racine, WI 53406-9989 USA.

Willard Nelsen—President, Foredom Electric, Bethel, CT 06801 USA.

John P. Jodkin—Vice President, Finance, Delta International Machinery Corp., 246 Alpha Drive, Pittsburgh, PA 15238-2985 USA.

Jody Garrett—Director, Product Development, Woodcraft Supply Corp., 7845 Emerson Ave., PO Box 1686, Parkersburg, WV 26102-1686 USA.

Cays Thomas—Plasticine, Blue Bird Toys, Swindon, UK.

Glen Tizzard—Draper Tools Ltd., Hursley Road, Chandlers Ford, Eastleigh, Hampshire SO5 5YF UK.

Library of Congress Cataloging-in-Publication Data

Bridgewater, Alan.
    Power tool woodcarving : projects & techniques / Alan & Gill Bridgewater.
        p.   cm.
    Includes index.
    ISBN 0-8069-8710-3
    1. Wood-carving—Technique.   2. Power tools.   I. Bridgewater, Gill.   II. Title.
TT199.7.B747   1994
745.51—dc20   93-41044
                                                              CIP

Edited by Rodman P. Neumann

10   9   8   7   6   5   4   3   2   1

Published by Sterling Publishing Company, Inc.
387 Park Avenue South, New York, N.Y. 10016
© 1994 by Alan & Gill Bridgewater
Distributed in Canada by Sterling Publishing
% Canadian Manda Group, P.O. Box 920, Station U
Toronto, Ontario, Canada M8Z 5P9
Distributed in Great Britain and Europe by Cassell PLC
Villiers House, 41/47 Strand, London WC2N 5JE, England
Distributed in Australia by Capricorn Link (Australia) Pty Ltd.
P.O. Box 6651, Baulkham Hills, Business Centre, NSW 2153, Australia
Manufactured in the United States of America

Sterling ISBN 0-8069-8710-3

Contents

Color section follows page 64.

Preface

Our intention with this book is to explore and demonstrate the use of power tools for woodcarving. By power tools we don't mean chain saws—although some idiosyncratic souls do "carve" with them. What we do mean are small, handheld rotary and reciprocating tools that use power to closely mimic the natural motions used in traditional folk art woodcarving.

When we first became interested in woodcarving—quite a few years ago now—we were somewhat puzzled and overwhelmed by the sheer weight of technique and jargon that seemed to bear down oppressively on most aspects of the craft. For example, there were hundreds of gouge types that might or might not be used. And then again, the subject of tool sharpening was horrendously complicated. All things considered, there seemed to be a wall of technique between us and just about every area of the craft.

Okay, so the tools do need to be sharp, and the wood must be chosen with extreme care; but that apart, all the rest can be summed up by the old adage "If it works for you, then it's the right way forward."

This brings us very neatly around to the somewhat contentious subject of power tool woodcarving. We use the word contentious advisedly, because there are still one or two traditionalists out there, who are undecided as to whether or not power tools should be used . . . ever!

When we first saw a reciprocating carver, we just couldn't believe that it would work. The moment we switched on the power, the whole thing would surely start leaping about, or so we thought. And then again, we couldn't see how rotary tools could possibly produce small, highly detailed carvings. We were as apprehensive as anyone—let's stick with the well-worn mallet and gouge.

The wonderful, joyous, enlightening news is . . . that power carving tools are so efficient and easy to use that, perhaps for the first time, there are almost no barriers to anyone becoming a woodcarver. No longer do you need to be physically strong—in the sense of being able to lift a mallet and work for long hours sawing, heaving, and thrusting.

Reciprocating tool. When the blade is pressed against the workpiece, it starts to vibrate and cut at high speed—no leverage is needed.

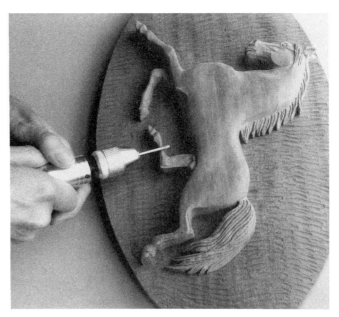

Rotary tool. Hold the tool at a low angle to the workpiece—it is the side of the bit that does the carving.

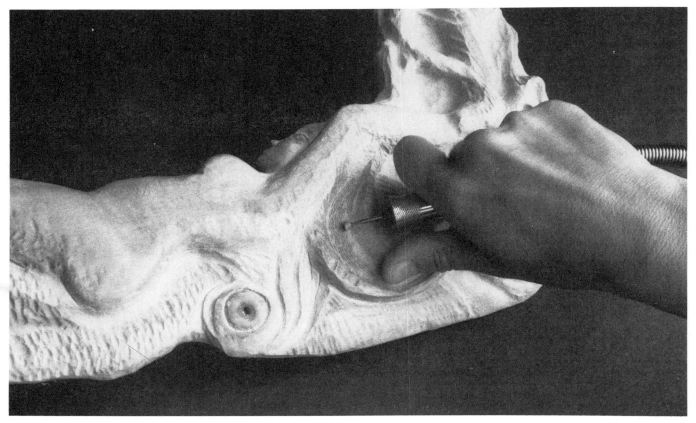

Use an aluminum oxide point/bit to create superfine lines and textures.

Use a rotary saw to set in—cut around—the lines of the design.

If you are young and fit, then so much the better; power carving tools are going to get you there faster. If you are not so young and perhaps more fragile than you used to be, then power tools are going to let you have the pleasure without the pain. Any age, physique, or gender—power carving heralds a woodcarving renaissance!

Just as with hand tool woodcarving, power carving is still the pleasuresome experience of sweet-smelling wood, shavings, and of following the undulating grain with hands, eyes, and senses. Nothing has been taken away—everything has been given! Now, at last, we can all get on with carving without being loaded down by "technique." The pleasures and challenges are still there, and of course the projects are just as exciting as ever. The true meaning of power tool woodcarving is that you can now work the wood with fingertip sensitivity, where you once worked with the brute force of muscle power.

Okay . . . so we suspect that some doubting traditionalists still have in mind that power tool woodcarving is about chain saws and free forms, but not a bit of it. Power carving systems are as sophisticated and as much removed from chain saws and the like, as, say, a steel chisel is from a stone axe.

There are reciprocating tools that imitate—and improve—the cutting action of a mallet and gouge. There are rotary tools that are as delicate and as sensitive as the point of a dentist's burr. And there are many options in between. As for tool bit/blade types, there are gouge blades and chisels that slice and cut, coarse structured tooth burrs that shape and abrade, ruby points that are able to touch and stroke the wood to a fine finish, and diamond points that can carve just about anything from a delicate incised line through to dips, ripples, and hollows.

As to the scope and range of power carving, one swift look through the book will show you that you can carve just about anything and everything, from cigar-store figures, duck decoys, and dough bowls, through to butter stamps, flower carvings, and hand-sized miniatures.

Being mindful that our intention is to explore and demonstrate, we have used as many power tool systems, to carve as broad a range of projects, in as many ways as possible. In so doing, we have named the tool system, its manufacturer, and its number in the caption below its photo for each project, as well as defined and described the function of the various systems. This is not to say, of course, that we expect you to work through all the projects using different tools. Our hope is, that by reading through the projects—learning something about the various options along the way—you will be able to make a balanced judgment when it comes to buying your own power carving system.

Touch carving. In the technique known as touch carving, each tool is touched down on the workpiece and allowed to make its characteristic mark.

Whether you are a raw beginner to woodcarving or an experienced woodcarver who is looking for a better way forward, you're going to be in for many, many pleasant surprises! Best of luck.

Alan & Gill Bridgewater

Power Carving Basics

Tools, Tips, and Techniques

What is power carving? Or, to be more precise, what is power tool woodcarving?

Well . . . power tool woodcarving is a technique of woodcarving that uses an electrically driven system as the prime mover. No more handheld mallets and gouges; no more reliance on muscle power; these are all put to one side in favor of the latest in reciprocating and/ or rotary power tools.

There are two basic types of power carver: the reciprocating system that imitates the traditional bang-and-cut, in-out-in-out working action of a mallet and gouge; and the rotary system that uses various chuck-held burrs and cutters—similar to an electric drill. The reciprocating tools slice away the waste as chips and curls, whereas the rotary tools turn the waste into dust.

Within these two primary systems, there are many secondary types. Some of them are so small and self-contained that they can be held easily in the hand—like an electric razor—whereas others have more bulky control boxes linked with flexible shafts to any of a number of quite different tool-holding handpieces. You will have

to decide which system is best for you, but let us help by describing the major types and by explaining their differences.

RECIPROCATING CARVING SYSTEMS

Reciprocating Self-Contained Handheld Carver
A self-contained handheld reciprocating motor unit system can easily be recognized because the whole works, the total unit—the motor, tool, and chuck—can be held in one hand with the only link-up being a thin, flexible power cord going back to the electric socket. The unit is so small, lightweight, and maneuverable that it can be used without regard to the power cord.

One particular handheld reciprocating carver, the Automach, comes complete with a single spanner and five blades. In use, a chisel or gouge-like blade is selected, a single nut is undone, the blade is set in place in the chuck, the nut is retightened, and the power is switched on. And, just in case you think that, once the

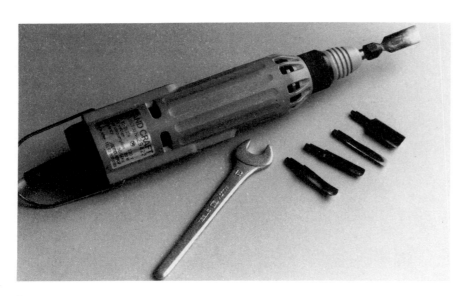

The Automach is a self-contained, handheld woodcarving system fitted with the reciprocating headpiece. Supplied by Woodcraft Supply Co. USA.

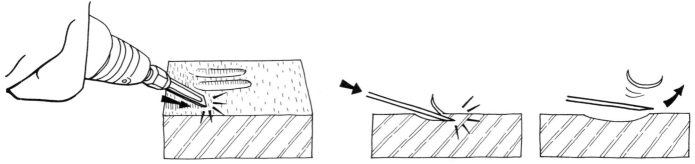

The Automach, running at high-speed reciprocation of 10,000 blows per minute, is able to slice through even the hardest wood. (Middle) the rapid action means that you can "spoon" out the waste wood. (Right) the moment you break contact with the wood, the vibrations come to a halt.

power is on, the machine jumps about like a pneumatic road drill, it doesn't. Apart from a low hum and a small amount of vibration, the carver just sits in your hand . . . waiting.

When the blade is pushed against the workpiece, it immediately starts to vibrate in and out at very high speed—to reciprocate—with the effect that it effortlessly slices through the wood. And so efficient is the carver, that a great many of the rules and restrictions associated with traditional mallet-and-gouge carving can be disregarded. Perhaps, to say that a power carver cuts like a hot knife through butter is a bit of an exaggeration, but, certainly, you no longer have to worry quite so much about such stultifying details as the angle of approach, grain direction, and how to cut through a

tough knot. The vibrating blades cut straight on through such problems. For example, I found that I was able to slice straight across pitch pine end grain and through the hardest of knots without any trouble at all.

Better still, the cutting action is so safe and efficient that the workpiece can be held and supported in one hand, and the tool operated in the other. You don't need to be strong, and you don't have to have a huge range of expensive gouges. The design of the system is such that you can get on with the carving without worrying too much about technique. Certainly, you do have to spend time selecting, changing, and sharpening blades; but that apart, the system is as much removed from the mallet and gouge as, say, the word processor is from pencil and paper.

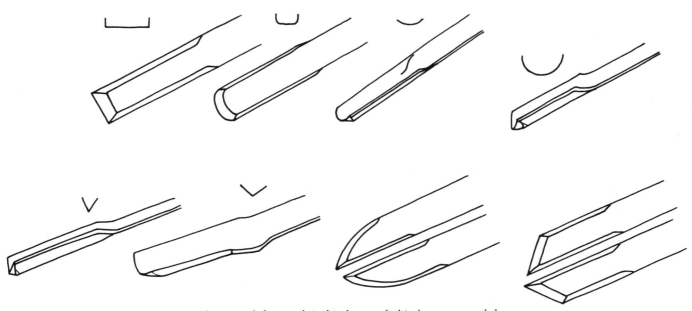

Blade shapes for the reciprocating tool—(top, left to right) chisel, round chisel, gouge, and deep U-shaped gouge—(bottom, left to right) deep V-section, shallow-V-section, left and right curved blades, and left and right skew chisels.

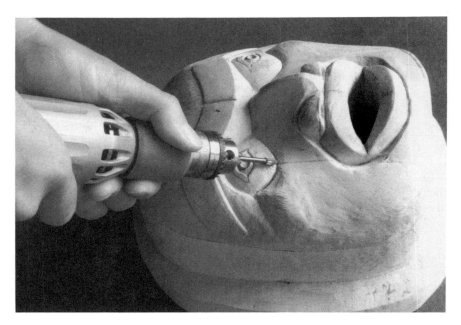

The Automach carver fitted with the rotary head option.

The Automach self-contained reciprocating carver we use has a quick-change head that allows it to be very swiftly converted to a rotary carver. The reciprocating head is unscrewed, the rotary head with the Jacob's chuck is screwed in place, a blade is chosen and fitted, and then . . . on with the job at hand.

Reciprocating Flexible-Shaft Carver

Reciprocating, flexible-shaft power carvers—sometimes called flex-shaft carvers—have a large, boxed electric motor that plugs into the power socket, a flexible shaft that snakes out from the motor unit, a handpiece that pushes onto the end of the shaft, and a separate foot pedal and/or a switch on a control panel. And, of course, there is also a selection of gouge and chisel blades.

Although flexible-shaft reciprocating carvers operate in much the same way as the handheld units—gouge-like blades only start to vibrate when they come into contact with the workpiece—there are important differences. First, they are much more powerful than the handhelds. Second, the push-fit design of the handpiece to the shaft allows you to choose any number of handpiece types. For example, you might fit a handpiece

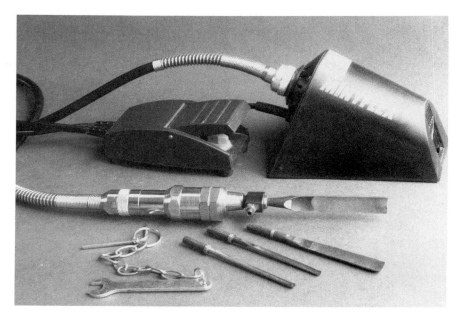

Minyflex power carving system—as supplied by Hegner UK/USA—with motor, foot switch, electronic speed control, reciprocating/percussion handpiece, and gouge/chisel blades.

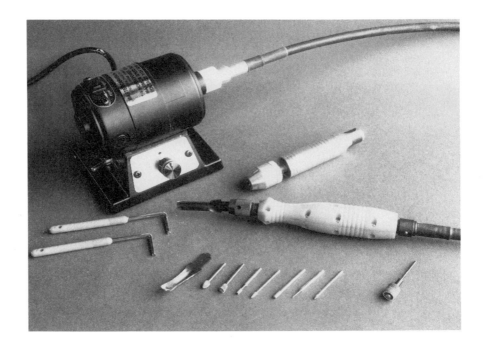

ABC Portable Mastercarver—as supplied by Woodcarvers Supply USA—with bench-mounted motor unit, and both a quick-change rotary handpiece and a reciprocating handpiece.

with a selection of collets; or you might prefer a handpiece with a Jacob's chuck; or one with a lock-and-turn grip; or one with a very small head and a flexible extension; and so on. The swift changeover of handpieces allows you to shape the system to suit your own woodcarving needs.

The boxed motor units also come in a great many shapes, types, and sizes. There are hang-up and bench-mounted units that run in both forward and reverse rotation, and units with a separate foot control, and so on. The flexible-shaft system allows you to pick-and-mix components—motor units, handpieces, and controls—so that you can build a power carver that best fits in with your way of working and with your workshop situation.

Many flexible-shaft systems are dual purpose, in that they come complete with both reciprocating and rotary options.

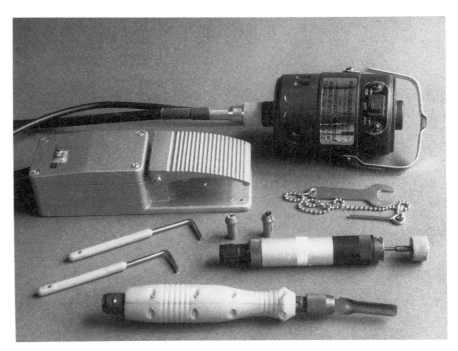

Mastercarver system with a reversible motor, rugged cast-metal foot pedal speed control, both handpiece options, and a set of collets. Note how the reciprocating handpiece is sheathed in a plastic stay-cool, good-to-hold handle.

When you fit a Hegner blade in the reciprocating hand-piece, all you do is slide it in place and tighten the allen screw and lock-nut.

Reciprocating Tool Type and Sharpening

Reciprocating carvers use chisel and gouge-like blades that variously fit into the handpieces. Some are held in place with allen screws and lock-nuts, whereas others are clenched in a collet.

Depending on your choice of system, the carver comes complete with anything from five to ten blades with a list of other blades available. For example, the Wood Carvers Supply handpiece comes with five gouge/chisel blades with another 18 available; whereas the Automach carver has four blades and 21 or more others available. The idea is that, if and when you feel the need to expand your carving options, all you do is order extra blades.

You can sharpen your power carver chisel and gouge blades in much the same way as with traditional tools, that is, by honing and stropping on a flat oil stone—I still sharpen my chisel blades in this way, but I now prefer to sharpen my gouge blades using a rotary tool. The procedure is beautifully simple. After fitting a fine-grade, drum-shaped aluminum oxide point in the rotary carver (and being sure to wear eye protection such as goggles), you hold the gouge blade up to the light so that you can clearly see the bevel, and then shape the bevel with the rotary point. Working in this way, you can easily dress and shape the angle of the bevel, and the inside and outside curves of the particular gouges, to suit your needs. If you want to go for a super-sharp edge, all you do is fit a polishing point in the rotary carver—felt or leather—add a touch of polishing compound, and buff, hone, and refine the cutting edge.

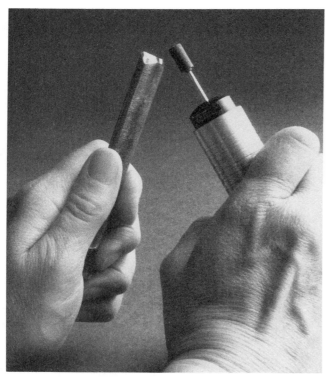

To sharpen the outside of the gouge blade, run the rotary oxide bit around the bevel

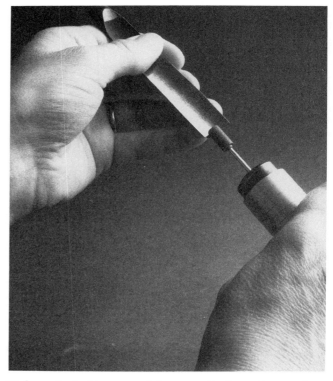

To hone the inside curve of the gouge blade, swifty run the rotary bit along the curve to remove burrs.

ROTARY CARVING SYSTEMS

Rotary Self-Contained Handheld Carver

As with the reciprocating carver, the handheld rotary carver can be most easily identified by being self-contained with its only link-up through a single power cord. That said, you do have to make a choice between a tool that is dedicated to being only rotary and one that can be changed over to the reciprocating option.

I have two handheld units: one that is primarily a reciprocating tool that can be converted by means of a rotary headpiece, and one that, although it is dedicated to being rotary, has a vast number of clip-on options that use rotary movement. For example, it can be used as a router, shaper, saw, drill, and so on. It can't be used as a reciprocating tool, but it can be used for just about everything else.

And then again, one of the units has a single speed, while the other runs at variable speeds.

Rotary Micro Carver with Control Box

Micro rotary carvers are a sort of hybrid between a self-contained unit and a system that is controlled through a pedal and switch. My particular micro carver has a control box with both a manual switch and a foot pedal; it runs in both reverse and forward rotation; it has a handpiece with a sophisticated snap-fit collet; and it has a coiled power cord link-up between the handpiece and the control box.

The Dremel Moto-Tool with variable speed control. Dedicated to the rotary option, this system has various attachments—a router, a shaper, cutter bits, etc. Note the shaft lock and the swift-change bit head.

All this adds up to a system that is both flexible and maneuverable. Certainly this system is dedicated to only doing rotary carving at a small scale; but, in the context of carving very small, intricate pieces, it is a wonderfully efficient quality tool.

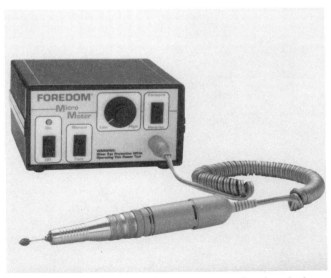

Foredom Micro Motor carving system 1035 fitted with the MH-135 handpiece. Note the handsome layout of the control panel and the sophisticated super-lightweight handpiece. The quick-change design of the handpiece allows you to swiftly change tool bits.

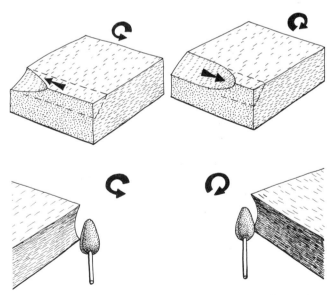

In the context of rotary systems, some tools have forward and reverse rotation. If it's not possible to turn the workpiece or change your angle of approach, all you do is switch to the reverse/forward direction so that, in effect, the spinning bit/tool has changed the direction of the cut. (Top) change the rotation so that the tool spins off the edge of the workpiece. (Bottom) change the rotation so that the direction of spin allows the bit to ride off the edge of the wood.

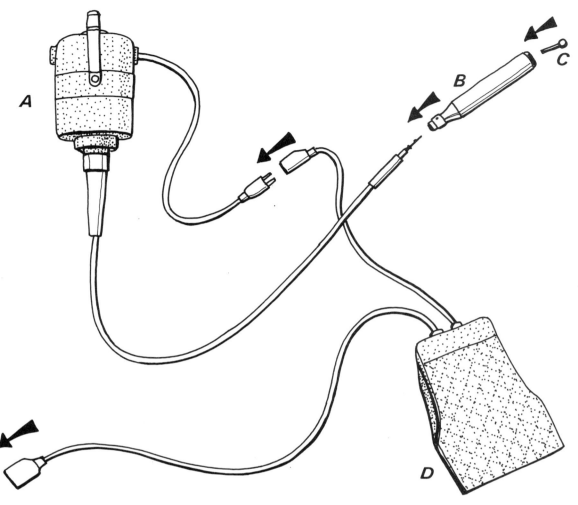

A typical flexible-shaft rotary carving system—(A) motor; (B) handpiece; (C) carving bit; (D) foot control. Note the various cables and shafts that link the system.

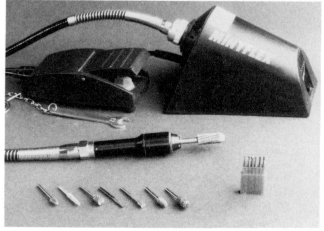

The Minyflex carving system—as supplied by Hegner— equipped with electronic speed control, three-jaw chuck, rotary handpiece, and spanner/wrench. Note also the selection of cutter bits, the micro bits, and the large cutter fitted in the handpiece.

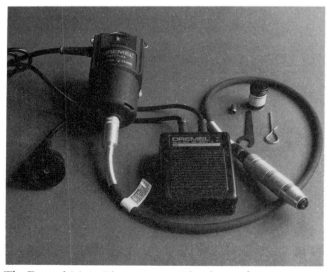

The Dremel Moto-Flex system, with a heavy-duty motor, a foot switch with variable-speed control, double-ball-bearing handpiece, plus various collets and wrenches.

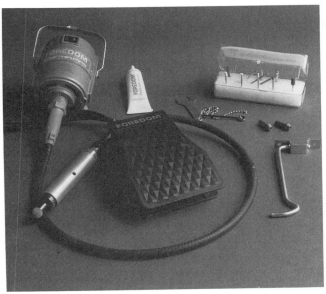

The Foredom woodcarving system, with a ⅛-HP hang-up motor unit, FCT-1 foot control, ball-bearing handpiece with wrench and lock pin, plus accessories.

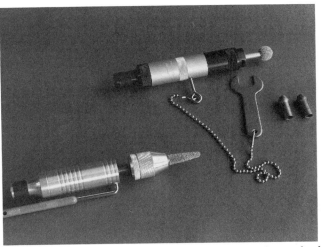

(Top) Wood Carvers Supply rotary handpiece, with standard collets ³⁄₃₂, ⅛, and ¼ inch, and with changing wrench. The design is such that you can get really close into the workpiece. (Bottom) with the quick-change handpiece accepting bit shaft sizes up to ¼-inch diameter, the design allows for fast changeover of tools.

Rotary Flexible-Shaft Carver

As with the flexible-shaft reciprocating carvers, the rotary system can be recognized by being comprised of three or four separate components—a boxed and contained motor unit, a flexible-shaft snaking out from the motor, a push-fit handpiece on the end of the shaft, and a foot pedal and/or a manual switch on the control box.

Although the flexible-shaft system is both larger and more powerful than the handheld carver—with a great many more handpieces and chuck options—it is also less compact. Once again, you have to make a choice between a dedicated handheld system—only reciprocation or only rotary—and a system that allows you to tackle larger projects at a greater speed. One of the pleasures of using a flexible-shaft system is that you have a huge number of handpiece options.

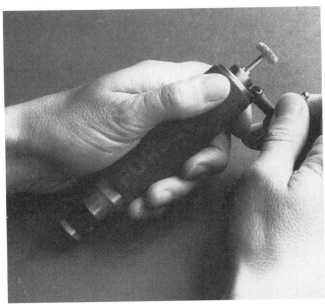

A Jacob's handpiece with a chuck key accepts a broad range of bit types and sizes. Note the stay-cool, antislip handpiece sheath—a great idea!

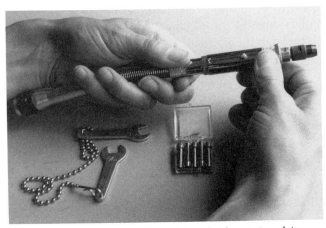

The Foredom 8AD handpiece with a duplex spring drive connection that provides extra flexibility allows you to get right up close to the workpiece. It's really good for delicate, difficult-to-reach close-up work. Note the sleeve guard that slides over the chuck.

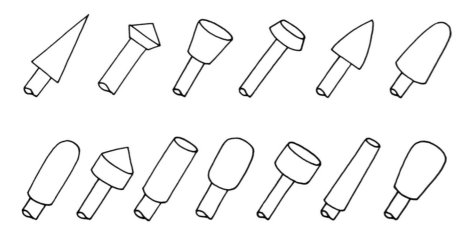

Rotary bit CONE shapes—cone, cone cap, inverted cone, square cone, tree-point cone, and tree-radius cone.

Rotary bit CYLINDER shapes—ball-nosed cylinder, cone-cap cylinder, cylinder, round cylinder, short cylinder, tapered cylinder, and tapered ball-nosed cylinder.

Rotary Carving Tool Bits

Rotary carving is an abrading process of shaping the wood with all manner of fast-turning burrs, cutters, and points. As there are literally hundreds of bits to choose from—some called by fancy trade names that give little or no clue as to their shape and function—so, throughout the book, we tend to group them all under the generic term "tool bits" or simply "bits."

When we describe such and such a bit as being a "coarse, cylinder ruby," the "coarse" refers to the abrasive grade, the "cylinder" describes the shape of the head, and "ruby" is a description of the bit type.

Since rotary carving is a process of using a graded series of bits—usually starting with large and coarse and finishing with small and fine—it is necessary to have a good range of bits to choose from. For example, in carving the mask, a selection of coarse burrs were used to swiftly clear away the rough, then a selection of steel cutters, and then a selection of diamond points, and so on through the options.

POWER CARVER ACCESSORIES

Study the manufacturer's accessories catalogue. Start by buying a general-purpose kit or set of bits, have a try-out, and then, in light of your experiences order specific bits to suit your particular type and scale of carving.

The following summaries of generic types—running from coarse to fine—will give you some idea of the options.

Structured-Tooth Tungsten Carbide Bits

Structured-tooth tungsten carbide bits—sometimes called burrs and cutters, and colored gold or silver—are available in both a fine and standard tooth grade. They have shaped stainless-steel heads—balls, cylinders, tapers, flames, trees, and wheels—that are covered with hundreds of fast-cutting needle-sharp teeth, and they are mounted on either ⅛-inch or ¼-inch-diameter shanks.

The stay-sharp teeth are permanently bonded to the steel core in such a way that they stay cool and resist

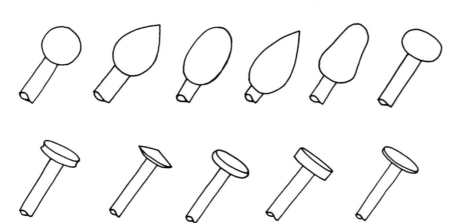

Rotary bit ROUND shapes—ball, bud, egg, flame, pear, and oval.

Rotary bit WHEEL shapes—hollow-edge wheel, knife-edge wheel, round-edge wheel, square-edge wheel, and wheel.

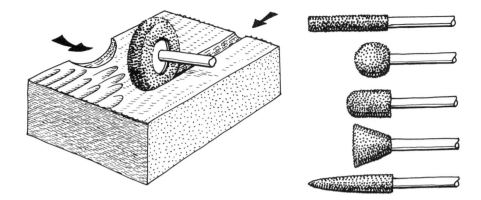

Structured-tooth tungsten carbide burrs are ideal for roughing out and for "combing" the surface to a finish. They come in many shapes and sizes, with shank diameters of ⅛ inch to ¼ inch.

clogging. That said, if the teeth do become clogged, then the debris can easily be burnt away without doing damage.

The burr is really good for the primary roughing-out stages, when you want to remove the wood fast. The stroking, scouring action results in a surface that looks as if it were rough combed. Note that although burrs remove waste at great speed, they do have a tendency to grab at the wood. They need to be used with care and caution.

Carbide Cutter Bits

Carbide cutter bits—sometimes called burrs—are available in both standard and crosscut versions. With all manner of head shapes and sizes to choose from—some as big as your index finger and others as small as a pin head—and being mounted on shanks that range from ³⁄₃₂-inch- through to ⅛-inch- and ¼-inch-diameter, carbide bits are the ideal tool for carving both hard and soft woods to a smooth finish. Carbide cutters leave a finish that looks much as if it has been worked with a knife or gouge.

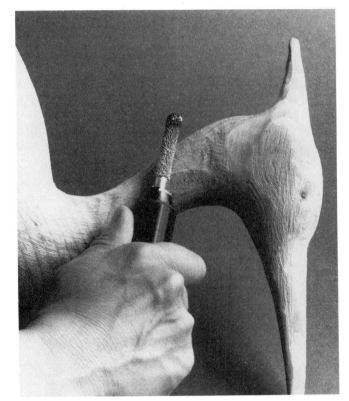

The structured-tooth tungsten carbide cylinder burr being used to comb and shape a surface.

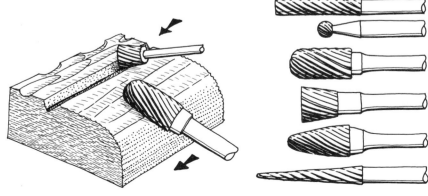

Carbide cutter bits are ideal for light to heavy roughing and modelling—they can be used to incise details, and to bring the work to a good gouge-like finish. Shank sizes range from ⅛-inch to ¼-inch diameter.

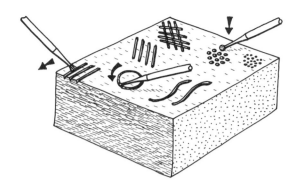

Vanadium-steel cutter bits—shanks range from ³⁄₃₂-inch to ⅛-inch to ¼-inch diameter. The pinhead size are good for delicate surface texturing and fine engraving.

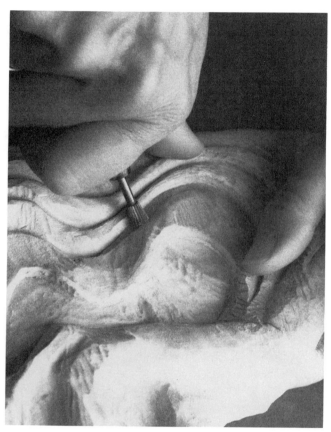

Use the rotary handpiece and the vanadium-steel inverted cone bit to cut V-section trenches and grooves.

Vanadium-Steel Cutter Bits

Vanadium-steel cutter bits—also called points and burrs—are available in a large range of head shapes, sizes, and shank diameters. With some cutters being as big as a cherry, whereas others are no bigger than a pin head, vanadium-steel bits are the ideal tool for cutting grooves, dips, and hollows, and V-section slots, as well as for engraving and modelling. I think of these cutters as being a general-purpose tool, the tool that I use to bring the roughed-out carving to order.

Depending upon the shape of the head, and the type of wood, these cutters are able to leave a crisp tooled finish—like a knife or gouge cut. Vanadium-steel cutters are relatively inexpensive compared to other cutters—less than half the price of, say, carbide cutters.

Ruby Carver Bits

Ruby carver bits—also called ruby carvers, and ruby points—are variously shaped heads that are coated with crushed ruby particles. Made in various grades, these bits cut the wood away at a good speed, while at the same time they leave a relatively smooth finish. These bits are extremely long-lasting, and will, so it is claimed, outlast conventional steel cutters many times over. They are good for taking the wood to completion.

Note that it is also possible to purchase sanding drum bands that are coated with ruby—one band will outlast dozens of ordinary sanders.

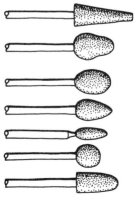

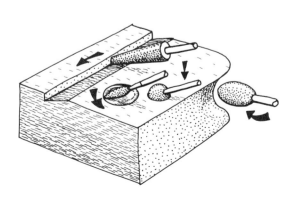

Ruby carver points/bits come in many shapes and sizes and are the ideal tool for fine shaping and smoothing. The various head shapes mean that you can "touch carve" to a swift finish.

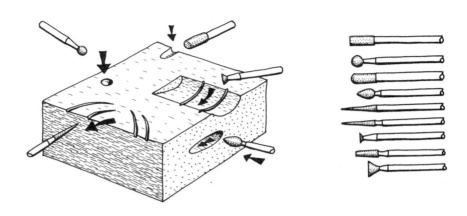

Diamond points/bits come in many shapes and sizes and are the ideal tool for light modelling and very fine detailing. If you enjoy engraving delicate surface decoration or you want to carve miniatures, then a full range of diamond points in shank diameters of $\frac{3}{32}$ and $\frac{1}{8}$ inch are just what you need.

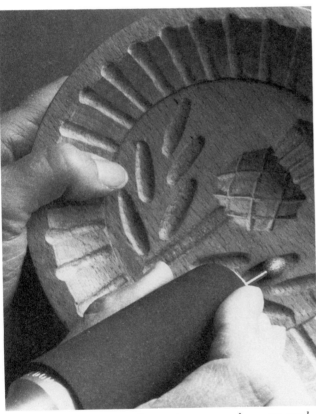

Ruby carver points—in fine and coarse grades—are good for light shaping and detailing. They are easy to control, they remove waste efficiently, and they leave a relatively smooth finish.

Diamond Carving Bits

Diamond carving bits—also called points and engravers—are no more or less than shaped metal heads that are bonded with crushed diamonds. It is claimed that a diamond bit will outlast the best grade of carbide bit—the hardest metal—by up to 1500 times! Of course these bits are expensive, and they only come in small sizes, but they are wonderfully efficient for fine detailing and finishing.

If you enjoy working on a small scale, for example, on duck decoys, fish, or birds, and you are looking for bits to carve details in miniature, then a full set of diamond bits will serve you well. They are much cheaper by the set!

Aluminum Oxide Bits

Although aluminum oxide bits—also called mounted points and oxide points—are primarily designed and used for shaping steel and iron; they can also be used to good effect for detailing hard wood. For example, if you want to engrave a really hard and brittle exotic wood, then you might use an oxide point. The oxide bits come in two grades—red for medium to fine work, and white for a super-fine finish.

Red oxide bits are really good for getting into the small, awkward-to-reach areas that need sanding and polishing! I also used oxide bits to bring my gouge blades to a swift, sharp finish.

Aluminum oxide points are good for cutting super-fine details, polishing, and honing gouge bevels. If you want to engrave very hard and brittle exotic woods such as ebony, then oxide points are the ideal tool.

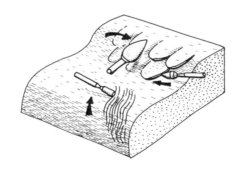

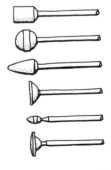

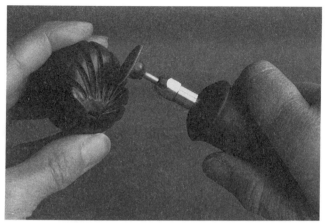

A sanding disc is a good tool for shaping and cleaning delicate grooves.

Sanding Drums, Discs, Flap Wheels, and Bobins

Sanding drums, discs, flap wheels, and bobins—also called abrasive points and tools—come in many shapes, forms, and grades. There are small drums on mandrels, flat discs that stick to rubber pads, long cylinders that slide sleeve-like over points, rubber caps, and so on. Some abrasive points are covered in crushed ruby; others are covered in aluminum oxide, and yet others are coated in carbide. There are many, many different forms. The only thing all these bits have in common is that they are designed to be used at the finishing stage—in much the same way as traditionally a carver might use sandpaper or glasspaper. I favor using small bobin caps for fine details and flap wheels for large smooth areas such as inside bowls.

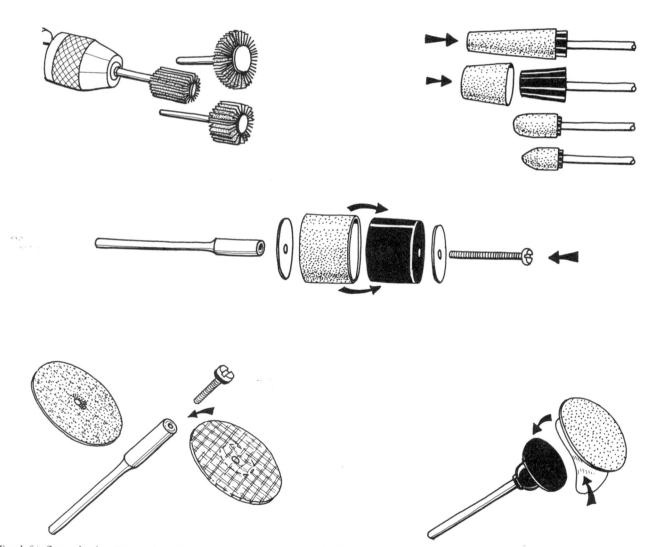

(Top left) flap wheels. (Top right) abrasive sleeves and caps. (Middle) sanding drum and mandrel—ready to be put together. (Bottom left) mandrel and heavy-duty cutter and sanding discs. (Bottom right) rubber disc mandrel with self-adhesive sanding disc. (Note that most screw-type mandrels only work in forward rotation.

Keeping Up with New Accessories

Power carving is a growing craft, so much so that manufacturers are continually coming up with new and exciting extras and accessories. This is not to say that you need to keep buying accessories, only that, since power carving is a dynamic craft and carvers are ever on the lookout for new ideas and materials, it is possible to upgrade your tool kit.

Just looking through the recent catalogues I have at hand, I see that there are, for instance, new quick-change headpieces, diamond cutter discs, smaller bits designed specifically for decoy duck carvers, extra-long sanding drums, carbide burrs three to four inches across, mandrels, arbors and chucks designed to take all manner of cutting, sanding, and polishing discs, a new carving system, and a new dust-collecting system.

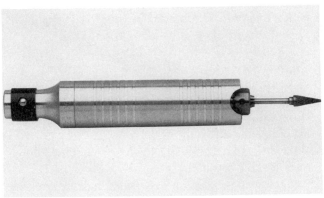

The Foredom 30 quick-change Jacob's chuck—a beautifully designed handpiece.

The Delta band saw model 28-180 is a great machine for light to medium work. If you have limited workshop space and want a band saw that sits on a bench, then this is a choice machine.

BAND SAW

If you have in mind to do a lot of power carving, then it's a good idea to get yourself a medium-size band saw. For example, if you want to cut a large blank out of slab wood or you want to cut out a complicated decoy duck profile, then a band saw is the answer. You could use a bow saw or maybe a combination of flat saw, drawknife, and gouge to achieve the same end; but a band saw takes the sweat out of the precarving preparation.

Our particular, rather modest machine is easily able to slice through 4-inch-thick wood. It's just a matter of setting the table to the required angle, adjusting the various guides, and pushing the wood through the saw.

Being mindful that, as with all machinery, a band saw is potentially dangerous, it's always a good idea to run through a safety check list prior to switching on the power. For your own safety, read the instruction manual, learn the applications, and generally be aware of the machine's qualities, limitations, and hazards.

Band Saw Safety Checklist
- If you are at all worried about the machine, then seek help and advice.
- Wear eye protection such as goggles.
- Make sure that your hair/cuffs/jewelry are tied back out of harm's way.
- Make sure that the upper blade arm and guard are well adjusted.
- Make sure that the blade is correctly tensioned.
- Always keep your fingers away from the front of the blade.
- Hold the workpiece down fair and square on the cutting table.
- Never allow someone else to turn on the machine for you.
- Feed the workpiece at an easy pace into the blade.
- Never leave the machine switched on.
- Never leave children alone in the workshop.

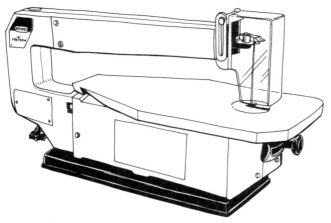

The Draper 16-inch scroll saw is the ideal machine for cutting anything from thin plywood to plank wood up to about 1¾ inches thick. It takes both super-fine and heavy-duty blades. If you want to make relatively small carvings, then this is a good machine.

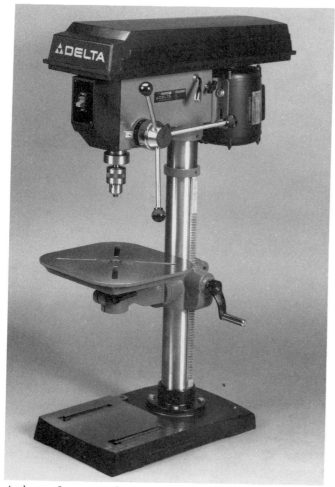

At last, after years of wanting one, we have gotten ourselves a Delta bench drill press. It doesn't wobble or make odd noises; it just gets on with the job of boring out holes. It's a beautiful machine!

SCROLL SAW

A scroll saw is the perfect machine for sawing thin section wood—wood as thin as a veneer to planks up to about 1¾ inches thick. With a flat worktable and a saw blade that jigs up and down, a scroll saw is wonderfully safe and easy to use. Our particular machine—fitted with various blades—is well able to fret out projects ranging from large circles in thick wood to intricate puzzle profiles in thin plywood. And as for safety, our local school allows children as young as seven years old to work on the machine with the minimum of supervision.

If you have had enough of using a hand coping saw, but don't as yet feel the need to buy a band saw—and if you prefer working on small projects in thin wood—then I would say that a scroll saw is the answer.

Note that most suppliers are more than happy to let you have a tryout on a machine—or even let you have a machine on approval. Or perhaps your local school will show you around its woodworking rooms.

Scroll Saw Safety Checklist
• Make sure that you are familiar with the workings of the machine.
• Make sure that your hair/cuffs/jewelry are tied back out of harm's way.
• Make sure that the blade teeth are pointing down towards the worktable.
• Feed the workpiece at an easy pace, making sure that the blade is aligned properly before starting the next cut.
• Never leave the machine switched on.
• Never leave small children alone with the machine.
• Make sure the blade is correctly tensioned.

BENCH DRILL PRESS

Although a bench drill press is one of those machines that most of us take for granted—it's something like a power drill, only bigger—it is also one of the most useful pieces of equipment. You might think that a drill press can only be used for boring holes, but it is quite versatile. It can be used for lowering waste, for hollowing out deeply carved bowls and containers, for running small router bits, for roughing out contours and profiles, and so on. My particular machine might seem unnecessarily large and cumbersome, but its very weight and stability are qualities that make it so useful. A fairly substantial drill press is well worth a place in the power carver's workshop. If you enjoy power carving, and if you want to get seriously into the craft, then you will find many uses for a drill press.

Note that in many instances a large drill press is a better buy than a small machine. I've asked around, and it seems that the larger machines are preferred, resulting in more sales, and so consequently the low price. Demand has brought the price down.

Bench Drill Press Safety Checklist
- Make sure that you are familiar with the machine.
- Wear eye protection such as goggles.
- Make sure that your hair/cuffs/jewelry are tied back out of harm's way.
- Make sure that the guard is down.
- Use a clamp if the hole to be drilled is much larger than ½ inch in diameter.
- Work at the recommended speed.
- Be sure to remove the chuck key before switch-on.
- Adjust the depth stop so that the drill bit doesn't run through to the table.
- Never leave children alone with the drill.

Drill Bits
As with the carving bits, there are many types of drill bits to choose from. There are standard bits, spoon bits, multispur bits, flat bits, spade bits, and all the rest. Over the years I've tried them all. That said, in the context of power carving, I favor using Forstner bits in a drill press.

My Forstner bits bore straight down through awkward side and end grain, through hard knots, through the toughest wood without a wobble, whine, or complaint. They produce a beautiful clean-sided, flat-bottomed hole. Better still, they can be used to bore out overlapping holes.

RESPIRATOR

To a greater or lesser degree, wood dust is dangerous to our health. If you breath in large amounts of wood dust—any more than two milligrams per cubic meter of workshop space—then there is a chance that it can contribute to a range of irritations and ailments.

If you want to enjoy your power carving, all you need do is wear either a pair of goggles and a dust mask or, better still, a battery-powered respirator. The particular battery-powered respirator we use is totally self-contained. It has an all-over-face visor, and a dust filter. Air is drawn in through the filter and passed down over the face; no more dust in the nose and eyes, no more steamed-up glasses, no more sweat and dust on the brow. The respirator keeps me cool and clean.

Note that if you only expect to do a small amount of power carving, then you can buy a small dust-collecting system that draws the air past your work. Such systems claim to collect over 90 percent of the dust and debris.

The perfect partnership—a bench drill press and a set of high-quality Forstner bits! If you are looking to bore out clean-sided, smooth-bottomed holes, then Forstner drill bits are the answer.

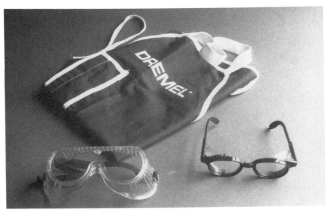

If you are going to do power carving, then you need a good stout coverall and a pair of goggles.

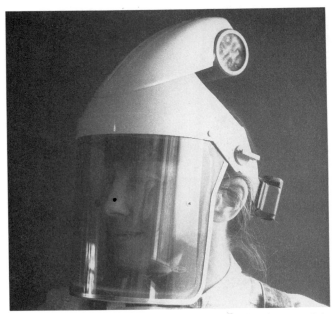

A perfect alternative to a pair of goggles and a dust mask is a respirator. Air is sucked in through the filter, and then distributed around the face; Gill is cool and comfortable.

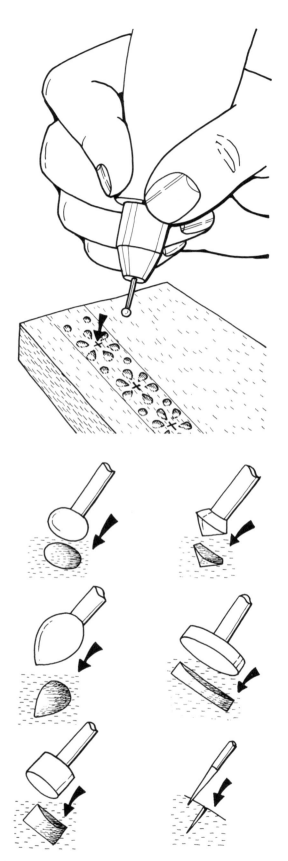

Touch carving—hold the tool as you might grip a pencil and touch the point down on the surface of the wood. Let the shape of the point/bit make its own characteristic mark.

POWER CARVING TECHNIQUES

As with traditional knife, gouge, and chisel carving, power tool woodcarving is no more or less than a technique of shaping wood. It is a process of removing—cutting away, shaping, patterning, and lowering wood—and then bringing the resultant surfaces to what you consider is a good finish. Traditional carvers and power carvers both want the same ends—it is only the means that differs.

This being so, the best way of describing the various power carving techniques is to make comparisons with traditional carving techniques, and then to note the differences.

Touch Carving

Touch carving is a technique of using a rotary tool to cut away a surface, and/or to create small designs and motifs. Whereas the traditional carver would have been stabbing and cutting in order to "pickle out the waste" and cut in small designs, so a power carver will be removing the waste with a burr and making marks with a gentle touching action. Both carvers will finish up with carvings, the only differences being that the power carver will be able to take a more direct route, and he won't have to worry too much about grain and knots.

Incised Carving

In the context of traditional woodcarving, incised carving is a technique of using a knife, gouge, or chisel to variously decorate the surface of wood with V-section lines, patterns, and motifs. The V-section lines are in themselves the sum total of the design.

Power carvers can create incised carvings with the minimum of effort and expertise. A shaped bit is fitted in the rotary handpiece—it might be anything from a "ball" to "inverted cone"—and then shallow grooves, trenches, and lines are drawn across the surface of the wood. The shape of the tool bit—whether sharp edged or round—will determine the section of the trench or groove. For example, a ball-shaped bit will cut a part-circle groove, and a knife-edge wheel will cut a sharp-sided trench. You can of course use a reciprocating carver and a V-gouge to decorate a surface with V-cuts.

High and Low Relief Carving

Relief carving is, in many ways, a logical follow-on from incised carving. That is to say, once the various grooves and trenches have been worked on the surface of the wood—as in incised work—the relief carver then goes on to cut away and lower areas so that selected details are left standing proud or, you might say, standing in low or high relief. And of course once the waste areas have

Use the reciprocating tool and the V-section blade to achieve incised-vee cuts.

The rotary handpiece fitted with a wheel cutter bit is really good for cutting slots and for setting in/edging a design motif. If the tool kicks back, grasp the handpiece firmly and use the thumb and fingers of the other hand to guide and track the point over the surface of the carving.

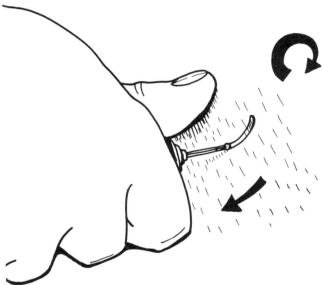

Incised carving—(top) hold the tool in a pencil grip and pivot the finger on the work. To cut in the other direction, switch the motor into reverse, and pivot in the other direction. (Bottom) if your system doesn't have a reverse option, then pivot on your thumb.

been lowered, the proud areas of the design can be variously patterned, shaped, modelled, undercut, and detailed.

Whereas a traditional carver might trench out with chisels, lower the waste ground with special-shaped tools, and then go on to use more chisels and gouges to achieve the modelling, the power carver might well use a rotary wheel saw bit to trench out, a router or drill to lower the ground, and then one or other of the rotary or reciprocating tools to achieve the fine modelling.

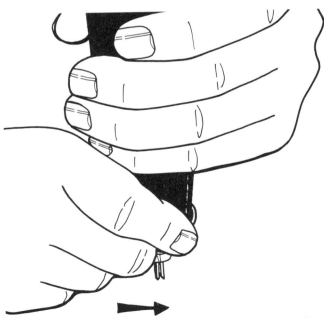

Hold and grasp the router in both hands—one hand guiding the tip, and the other holding the tool steady.

I consider applied work a shortcut answer to high-relief carving. In this instance, the horse is fretted out, mounted on the textured ground, and then carved.

Built-up work refers to a carving that is made from separate pieces of wood that have been laminated together. In this case, Project 15 the duck decoy, is made up from three pieces of wood—two for the body, and single piece for the neck and head.

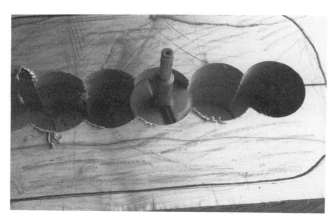

If I want to remove a lot of waste fast—from inside a bowl or whatever—then I use the bench drill press and the biggest possible Forstner bit.

The power carver is by far the faster when it come to lowering the ground, since the various rotary options do the task at speed.

Another form of relief carving is to cut out the motif as a separate image—as in Project 10, the running horse—and then mount it onto a tool-textured ground.

Carving in the Round and Built-up Work
Although the term "in the round" is used to describe carvings that are meant to be seen from most angles—for example, a freestanding figure, a duck decoy, or maybe a small box—and "built-up" is used to describe carvings that are put together from a number of different component parts, they are, more often than not, techniques that go hand in hand. For example, Project 15, the duck decoy, or Project 14, the mask, might well be built up—glued, screwed, pegged, bolted—and then carved in the round.

Of all its woodcarving applications, this is where power tool woodcarving comes into its own. Whereas the traditional carver might use a bow saw to painstakingly saw out profiles, a hand drill to bore out waste areas, and then a huge selection of gouges and chisels to shape and model the carving, the power carver can use a band saw to swiftly cut out the profiles, the drill press with a router or Forstner bit to swiftly lower the waste, a reciprocating carver to cut away the waste, and finally one or other of the rotary bits to detail the surface.

DEVELOPING A STRATEGY OF WORK

I'm always being asked . . . What is the best way to proceed? And of course the question is a tricky one, because there are as many ways of working as there are carvers. So, the following order of work isn't necessarily the best way to proceed, but rather it's the way that works for me!

I usually start by making sketches. This done, I make drawings to size and take tracings. If needed—as with a sculpture—I make a full-size Plasticine maquette and make more drawings of the various views. Next, I have a look at the project and make decisions as to what wood and equipment to use. Do I need to search out some more wood or a piece with a more attractive grain? What tools do I use? Do I need to use a special clamp or vise? If I decide that I can't manage such and such a procedure because my band saw isn't big enough or whatever, then I either have to use another tool/machine, or I have to modify the project.

When I have decided how and what with, I slice the wood down to size on the band saw—maybe gluing and

Always try to use the run of the grain—the patterns and shape—to good effect. For example, see how I have used a knot for the eye and the shape of the grain at the sides to suggest wings.

laminating the blocks together. Then I use the band saw and/or the drill press to clear away as much of the waste wood as possible. This done, I redraw the imagery onto the wood, and then I use the reciprocating carver to chop away as much waste as possible and to rough out the basic shape and form. This is the stage that I most enjoy! If it's a large sculpture, I might first make stop-cuts with the chisel, and then use the gouge to slice at an angle into the stop-cuts. Or then again, if it's a large, shallow bowl, I can more or less use the gouge to take the

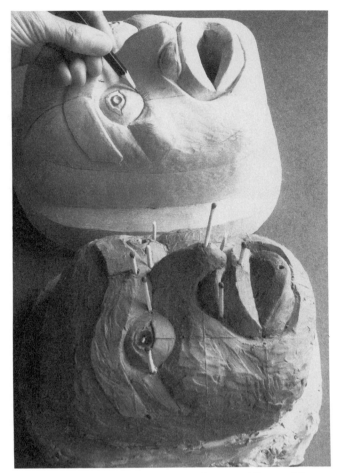

If I'm going to carve a complex in-the-round form—like Project 14, the mask—then I start by making a full-size Plasticine maquette. I use matchstick markers, and dividers to step off the various measurements.

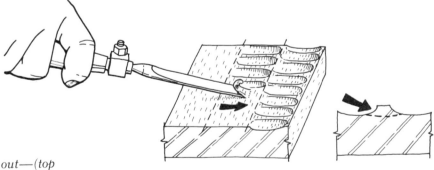

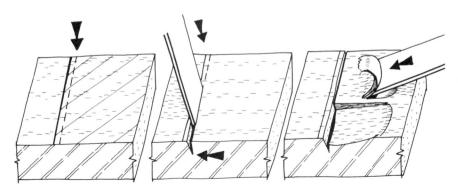

Removing waste and roughing out—(top left) use the gouge to remove scoops of waste, working across the run of the grain—(top right) having scooped away the waste in one direction, then reangle the tool to cut away the remaining peaks of waste—(bottom, left to right) to remove the waste from stepped areas, first mark out the areas of waste that need to be cut away, then use the straight chisel to sink stop-cuts; then slice at a low angle into the stop-cuts so that the waste wood falls away.

I use the reciprocating carver fitted with the large U-section gouge to scoop out the waste from shallow bowls and from the surface of large sculptures.

If the project is difficult to hold—too small, or too big—then use a vise to grip and support your workpiece. This particular vise has soft sleeves over the jaws and a ball-and-socket system that allows the workpiece to be presented at the best angle.

project to completion. I work through the reciprocating options using whatever blade and technique that best fits the task at hand. And of course, every time I remove wood, I have to keep reworking the drawn guide lines.

When I have taken the roughing out as far as I can, then I go to the rotary carver, fit an appropriate handpiece and tool bit, and start the procedure of pulling the surface together. Once again, the type of project will dictate the type of handpiece, the choice of tool, and the angle and method of approach. And so I continue . . . working through the bit options until I have what I consider is a fair piece of work. Next, I work through the sanders—from coarse to fine—paint or stain the project, and then finish up by waxing and polishing.

Finally, I show the carving to my friends and wait for the applause—or not!

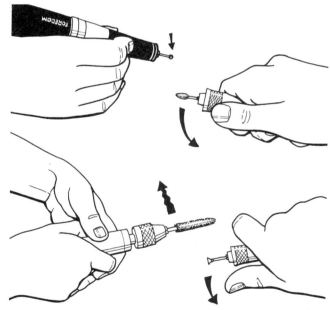

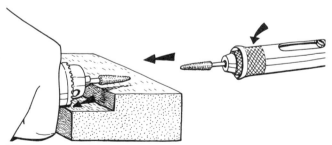

It's important that you select and use a handpiece that relates to the job at hand. If, for example, you need to get in closer and the chuck is in the way—as in this illustration—then use a handpiece with a narrower/longer chuck reach and/or one with a chuck guard.

Holding the rotary tool—(top left) the pencil grip is used for fine detailing and careful modelling—(top right) the single-handed grasp is used for light shaping and modelling—(bottom left) the two-handed grip is used for light to heavy roughing out—(bottom right) the thumb paring grip is used for careful surface work.

Projects

1
Decorating a Found Box with Incised Carving

Primary techniques—router and touch carving

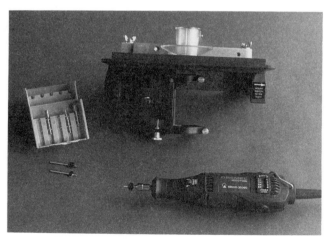

1-1   Project picture. A cigar box—with router and incised touch-carved decoration.

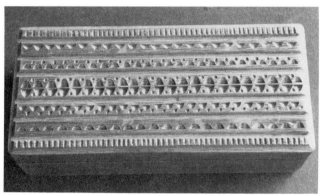

1-2   The Dremel Moto-Tool wood carver 395/396 is shown with the router/shaper attachment (231) and cutter bits. It plugs into 120/220 volt mains, the cutting bits can be changed in moments, and a variable-speed finger switch gives you full control. This project uses the small cylinder, small ball, inverted cone, and high-speed inverted cone cutters. We also use this system in part to carve an Icelandic knot roundel in Project 6 and to carve a miniature lidded box and decorate it with a shell motif in Project 17.

When I was a kid, I used to love making patterns! You know the sort of thing—basic repeat zigzags with lots of dots, dashes, and little geometrical shapes. Give me a large sheet of paper and a pack of colored pencils, and I was as happy as happy can be. I had this system . . . I would divide the paper into small squares—like a chess board—and then I would set to, using the grid as a framework guide for the pattern.

I still enjoy pattern making, only now I decorate wood rather than paper. I search around for a suitable surface to decorate—usually a box—then I divide the surface into a grid and use the power carving tools to block in the design with a series of repeated, incised touch-carved designs.

Estimated Working Time
1–2 hours

Materials
For this project you need a small, nicely made wooden box (see 1–1). It could be a cigar box, a pencil box, a sewing box, or whatever. It makes no difference, as long as it is well built, made from a firm-grained wood, and made up from panels that are at least ¼ inch thick. My chosen box was probably made in the 1950s and measures 7¼ inches long, 3½ inches wide, 2¼ inches high. The panels are about ¼ inch thick, and are, as far as I can tell, made from a soft, easily worked wood like Japanese oak.

Tools and Equipment
• power carving system with router/shaper attachment and cutter bits (see 1–2)
• workbench
• pencil and ruler
• one sheet of workout paper
• pack of graded sandpapers
• wax polish and a brush

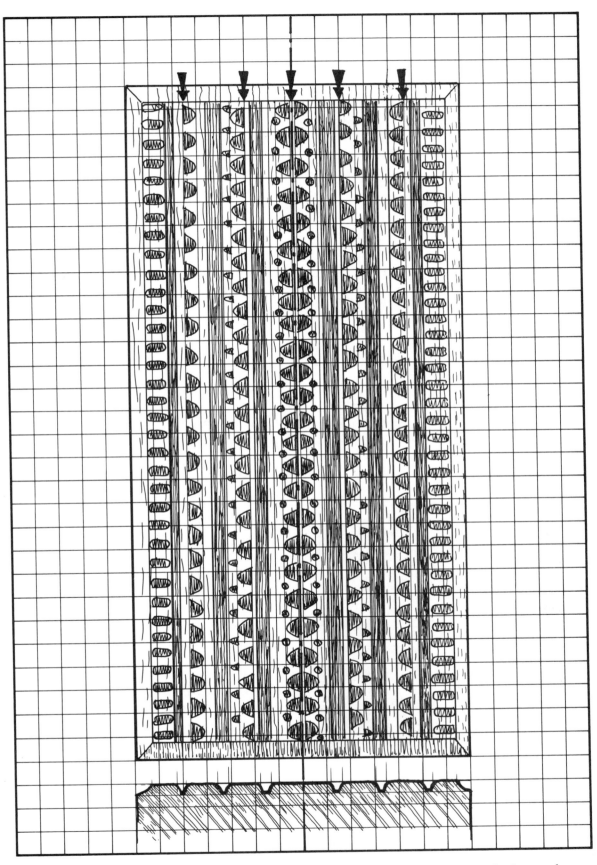

1-3 Working drawing. At a scale of four grid squares to one inch, the box is about 7¼ inches long and 3½ inches wide. Note the way that all the touch-carved details use the routed grooves as guide lines.

DESIGN, STRUCTURE, AND TECHNIQUE CONSIDERATIONS

When you have found yourself a suitable box, and generally gathered together all your tools and materials, take a look at the working drawing (see 1–3) and see how, at a scale of four grid squares to one inch, the pattern completely fills the 7¼-inch × 3½-inch top of the lid. Note how the guide grid is made up by cutting six router grooves—in the direction of the grain—along the length of the lid. The design is pretty basic in that it is centered symmetrically on the middle strip. That is to say, there are seven high-relief strips, and the whole design is mirror-imaged along a midline, with the simplest pattern at the side edges.

Of course, if you have a bigger box or you want to cover all the surfaces with pattern or whatever, then all you do is stay with the overall approach, but modify the project to fit.

SETTING OUT THE DESIGN AND MAKING TRIAL CUTS

When you have settled on a box to decorate, draw the lid out to full size on the workout paper, and then use the pencil and ruler to set out just how you want the various

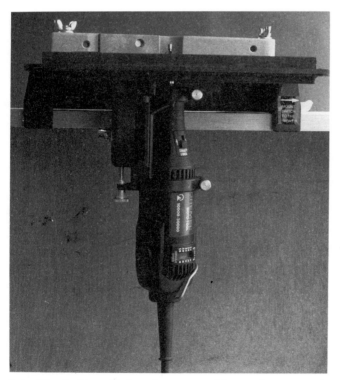

1-4 Fit the Moto-Tool to the router table attachment, and secure the whole works to the edge of the workbench.

touch-carved cuts to be placed. It's worth a mention at this point that, in the context of this book, I liken the marks made by the small rotary cutters as being very much like the marks made by a small knife. A knife cuts out little slivers, whereas the rotary cutter tool abrades the wood; but the end result is much the same. The term "touch carved" describes the process of making primary marks—like chip carving or incised carving. The marks are made simply by touching down the cutter on the wood. If you are a raw beginner to routing, you might well need to have a practice run before you start work on your chosen box.

Power Carving Tip
In the context of this project there are two types of router/shaper cutter—plain and piloted. The plain are used for cutting grooves and mouldings, whereas the piloted are used for cutting edges. In use, the "pilot" part of the bit acts as a guide or stop against which the workpiece is pushed or run.

When you have drawn out a suitable grid, pencil-press transfer the lines to a piece of scrap wood; then have a tryout with the Moto-Tool and the router shaper. First of all, fit the piloted cove bit in the Moto-Tool and the tool in the router table as described by the manufacturer (see 1–4). Check that you have read all the pre-switch-on warnings and then to work.

Try, first, to rout along the side of the wood to cut a decorative hollow-curve edge. All you do is adjust the router table fence so that it is slightly behind the piloted bit and there is only just enough room for the cut to be made (see 1–5, left)—and then switch on and pass the wood from right to left past the cutter. Although the procedure needs a bit of getting used to, once you have the hang of it, then it's possible to achieve a beautifully smooth cut.

Power Carving Tip
If you want to cut all four sides of your tryout wood— just as you might when you come to work the box lid— then rout the end-grain edges first (see 1–5, bottom right); then the side edges. If you do it the other way around, there's a chance that the spinning tool will spit off the grain as the wood exits at the end of its pass.

Continue running lengths of scrap wood past the cutter until you are able to achieve a smooth, confident cut. When you are happy with using the piloted cutter, then fit the beading router bit in the Moto-Tool and have a tryout cutting a curve-shouldered V-groove. The procedure is much the same as already described, except that this time you set the fence back from the bit to give

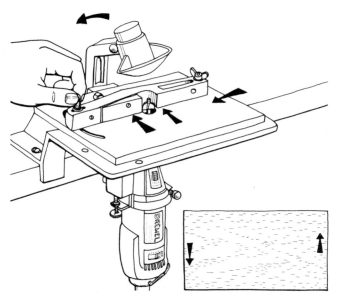

1-5   (Left) Adjust the router table fence so that it is slightly behind the piloted bit. (Bottom right) Start by routing the end grain edges/ends.

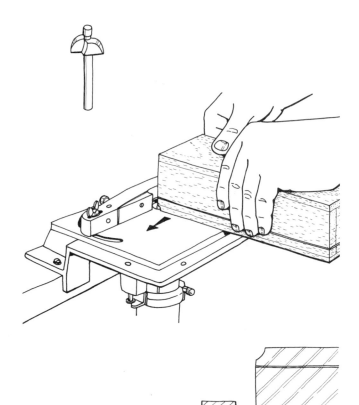

1-6   (Top left) The piloted cove bit. (Top right) Starting with the end grain edges, run the box from right to left past the cutter, all the while making sure that the top of the piloted bit is hard up against the side of the workpiece. (Bottom) When you have run the cove decoration around all four sides/edges of the box lid, then repeat the procedure on the bottom of the box.

you the required position of cut. For example, if you want the groove to run ½ inch in from the side of the wood, then you set the fence ½ inch back from the middle of the bit. When you come to make the cut, all you do is to run the wood along the fence and past the bit. The depth of the cut is controlled by loosening off the wing nut on the underside of the table and adjusting the screw so that the cutter bit pokes up more or less through the hole in the table. And, of course, the higher the cutter bit, the deeper the groove.

If you are at all nervous or unhappy with the procedures, then sit down and relax. Have a good long read through the instructions as supplied with the Moto-Tool and the router table. Note all the warnings and the tips, and then keep making trial cuts until you feel confident that you have it right.

ROUTING THE BOX EDGES AND THE GROOVES

You have fitted the router table to the workbench and played around with the various bits until you are clear in your own mind as to the function of the tool. Then comes the fun task of actually working on your box for real.

Fit the piloted cove bit in the Moto-Tool and the tool to the table, and then to work. With the fence set out of the way, turn on the tool to high speed. Then, starting with the end-grain ends of the lid, run the box from right to left past the cutter (see 1–6, top right).

Power Carving Tip

Be warned . . . if you change the rate of feed—meaning you pause, go slower, or speed up—the cut might well be wobbly and irregular.

When you have routed the end edges of the box lid, repeat the procedure with the side edges. If you have a close-up look at the project photograph (1–1), you will see that I was so taken up and pleased with the results that I decided to shape the bottom edges of the box in like manner (see 1–6, bottom).

Having shaped the edges of the lid, refer to your initial working drawings; use the pencil and ruler to transfer all the guide lines through to the top of the lid. If you have another look at the working drawings you will see that I decided to position the groove centers about ½ inch apart.

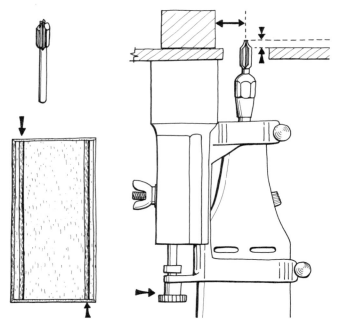

1-7　(Top left) The beading bit. (Right) Set the fence ½ inch back from the center of the bit, and adjust the height of the bit to cut a ⅛-inch groove. (Bottom left) Having passed the box past the cutter—one side of the box and then the other—the lid should be set out with two grooves.

If you want to stay with my general design, then fit the beading bit in the router, set the fence ½ inch back from the center of the bit, and adjust the height of the bit so that the groove is going to be ⅛ inch deep (see 1–7, right). When you have set everything up just so, tighten all the nuts and screws, switch on the power, turn the Moto-Tool up to high speed, and make a trial cut with a length of scrap wood.

When you have achieved a good trial cut, turn the box upside down, and run it along the fence and past the cutter. Run one side edge along the fence, then turn the box around and repeat the procedure with the other side edge. If you now turn the box over, you should have two grooves, one each side of the lid and set about ½ inch in from the edge (see 1–7, left). If you want to have another groove set ½ inch away from the first, then set the router fence back so that it is one inch behind the center of the router bit, and repeat the pass. And, of course, if you want another groove, set the fence back another ½ inch and so on. If you look at the working drawings, you will see that by the time I had cut three grooves on each side of the box lid midline, I was left with a central raised area a little under ¾ inch wide.

Finally, when you are happy with the placing and depth of the grooves, take a sheet of fine-grade sandpaper and give the lid a swift rubdown to remove all the burrs and wisps of wood.

TOUCH-CARVING THE DESIGN

By the time you have shaped the edges of the lid and worked the ⅛-inch-deep routed grooves, you will be left with a number of high-relief tracks on which the carved design is to be set. If you want to stay with my design, then take a pencil and ruler, and draw in a midline down the middle-of-box track and lines that are about ¹⁄₁₆ inch in from the edges of the tracks. Note the arrows on the working drawing (refer to 1–3). The idea is that these lines are an additional grid or guide when you come to touch carving.

With router table packed out of the way, and with the medium-size inverted cone cutter fitted in the Moto-Tool, have a tryout on a piece of scrap wood, just so you can get the hang of the tool. The procedure is simple enough; you just switch the tool on to high speed, and then touch the spinning cutter down on the wood.

Power Carving Tip

If the wood looks to be burnt, then, depending upon the type of wood being worked, you might have to adjust the speed of the tool and/or the rate of cut. The "rate of cut" refers to the contact time between the wood and the spinning bit. Then again, if you are working with a light-colored wood and you like the burnt "pyrography" effect, you could aim for a small amount of burn.

The lower the angle at which you hold the tool, and the longer it is held, the deeper and broader the mark (see 1–8, top left). For my part, I enjoy using the inverted cone cutter, because the resultant mark looks to be much the same as the cut made with a traditional U-section carving gouge. And of course, a line of such marks, all set side by side, results in a very attractive curved zigzag border.

If you look at the working drawings, you will see that by touching the inverted cone down a little to one side of the midline to make a line of side-by-side marks, and then turning the box around and repeating the line of marks on the other side of the midline, it is possible to achieve a design that has a thin line of wood in high relief (see 1–8, top right). Continue, using the small cylinder cutter to make the side-by-side grooves on the outer track, using the little ball head cutter to make all the dots (see 1–8, bottom), and so on.

Although the technique is easy enough, the trick is knowing when to stop. If you don't make enough touch marks, the design looks empty; if you make too many, the design looks crowded, and there is a danger that the wood left in high relief will be so fragile that the short grain "bridges" between cuts will be so weak that they will break away.

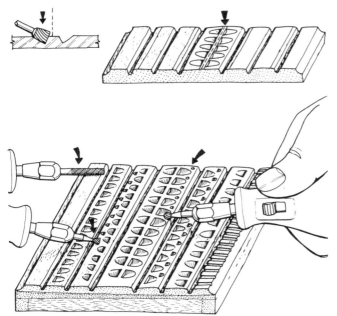

1-8 (Top left) The lower the angle at which you hold the Moto-Tool and the longer it is held in position, the deeper and broader the mark. (Top right) By making repeated cuts—on both sides of the midline—it is possible to achieve a design with a thin band of high-relief wood. (Bottom) Use the small cylinder, the ball, and the small inverted cone cutters to complete the design.

Power Carving Tip

I usually figure that with a design of this type and character, I will try to achieve a fifty-fifty balance between the cuts—meaning between the lowered wood and the wood left in high relief.

FINISHING

When you have achieved what you consider is a nicely balanced design, then brush the box down to remove all the debris. Stand well back, and try to see the total workpiece with fresh eyes. Ask yourself whether you could make another line of touch cuts—could you perhaps fill in with a line of smaller dots? Could the cuts be deeper? Be super-critical.

Power Carving Tip

I sometimes find that by the end of a carving session, I am so weary that I can't really assess my progress. If this is the case, then put the workpiece out of sight for a day or so, and come back to it with fresh eyes.

When you decide that the carving is finished, first swiftly sand the carved areas with a fine-grade sandpaper to remove rough edges, and then fit the small sanding

1-9 Finally, use the sanding disc to bring the carving to a crisp, clean finish.

disc in the Moto-Tool and tidy up the channels (see 1–9). Finally, brush away the dust, give the whole box a generous coat of wax polish, and burnish it to a dull-sheen finish. Then set the box on the coffee table, and watch people's eyes and hands when they pick it up.

HINTS, TIPS, AND AFTERTHOUGHTS

- If you are a beginner to routing, be sure to read the directions. Don't do what I did the first time around—try to run the wood the wrong way past the cutter! Feed the workpiece from right to left.
- Touch carving is ideal for beginners in that with the minimum of effort and expertise it is possible to achieve quite complex designs and motifs.
- If your chosen box has hinges or clasps that are going to get in the way of the fence or the pilot bit, then remove them all at the start of the project.
- If, like mine, your box has been varnished, then it's best to rub it down before you start carving. If you leave the rubbing down until after the box has been carved, you risk blurring the cuts.
- When you are fitting a cutter, always be sure to switch off the power—or better still, unplug the tool from the power.
- My chosen box was a bit tricky in that the grain was rather rugged and open. In light of my experience, I would have searched around for a box made of bland, smooth-grained wood such as lime or sycamore.

2

Carving and Painting a Found Container

Primary techniques—incised touch carving

2-1   *Project picture. The lidded pot, incised and touch carved.*

Estimated Working Time
2–3 hours

Materials
You need a small, inexpensive, ready-made, hand-sized, plain wooden article or container that looks as if it needs decorating. We have gone for a small wooden, lathe-turned, lidded pot (see 2–1) that we picked up in a thrift shop—I think it comes from India—but this is not to say that you can't decorate a salt pot, or a small frame, or whatever takes your fancy. Apart from the size—best if it's small—the only other requirement is that the item be made of a close-grained, pale wood.

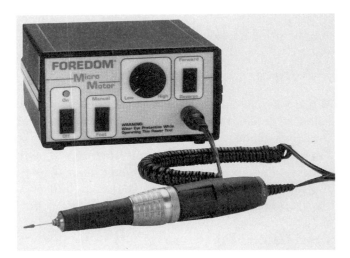

2-2   *The Foredom Micro Motor rotary carving system (kit No. 1035/1045), with the comfortable handpiece. The high-quality system provides variable speeds with both a dial and a foot pedal. All switches are located on a single control panel, and the motor runs both forward and reverse with a 115/220-224 volt option. Tools can be fitted swiftly into the rotary quick-release collet (⅛ inch or ³⁄₃₂ inch). We also use this system for carving a treen butter stamp in Project 11.*

I've always had a thing about pattern! No sooner do I see a plain wooden item in a shop or flea market than I have this overwhelming urge to start covering the item with carved designs. The perfect solution to my obsessive craving for pattern is the technique we introduced in Project One called incised touch carving. We fit diamond points in a rotary handpiece and switch the handpiece on to high speed. Then we touch the point down on the surface to make our marks. There's no need to follow up with sandpaper, because the touch-carved marks are finished the first time around. If you want to introduce color, color-stain the item before carving so that the points reveal the pale wood or leave the natural wood of the item, but finish up by blocking in the depressions with paint, as in this project, to create a dark pattern on a light ground (see 2–1).

Tools and Equipment

- power carving system (see 2–2)
- set of ³⁄₃₂-inch-diameter shank diamond-mounted points (see 2–3)
- pencil and ruler
- one sheet each of tracing and workout paper
- roll of masking tape
- ball of Plasticine
- small quantity of acrylic paint in a color to suit—we have chosen brown
- small fine-point paintbrush
- sheet of fine-grade sandpaper
- respirator or mask and goggles
- wax polish and a brush

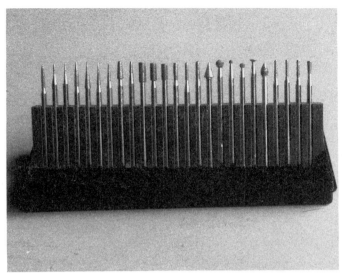

2-3   A set of ³⁄₃₂-inch-diameter shank diamond-mounted points needed for this project. These are a Wood Carvers Supply accessory.

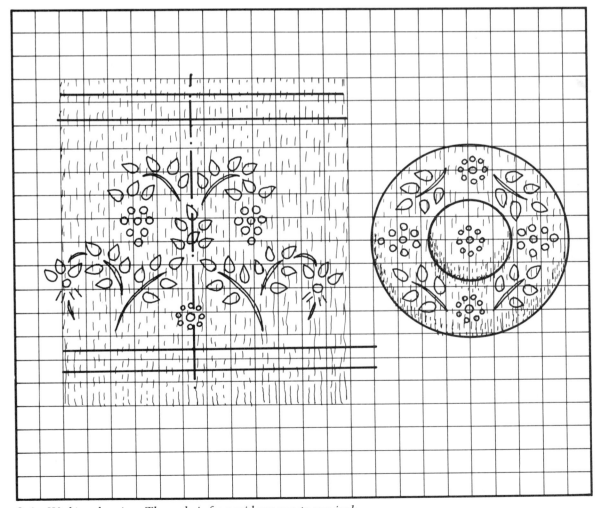

2-4   Working drawing. The scale is four grid squares to one inch.

DESIGN, STRUCTURE, AND TECHNIQUE CONSIDERATIONS

When you have gathered your tools and materials, have a look again at the project picture (refer to 2–1) and the working drawing (see 2–4). See how we have decorated the little lidded pot that measures four inches high and two inches in diameter. See how, at a scale of four grid squares to one inch, the pattern design of stylized leaves, grapes, and flowers is comprised of matching two-inch-high motifs that wrap around the sides of the pot—a little repeat design is set around the lid. Note the way we use the three existing dark-burn lines and the lid juncture line as a guide or framework for the motifs.

Of course, as you will almost certainly be decorating a completely different form, you will also have to modify the design to fit. For example, you might have to increase the number of motif repeats to decorate a much larger cylinder, or you might want to set the motifs around a picture frame, or then again, you might want to run the design over the inside/outside edge of a large fruit dish or whatever. Find your item to decorate first, and then take it from there.

Power Carving Tip

If you want to go for an easy-to-carve option, then choose a relatively small item that is free from knobs, catches, and such. Since the tool is best held and used at a low, flat angle, any additions and projections would be a hindrance.

SETTING OUT THE DESIGN

Give your small wooden item a swift rubdown with the finest-grade sandpaper to remove any wax and grime. This done, consider how you want the design to fit the surface areas. Draw your pot/box up to full size and make a tracing-paper pattern of the surfaces that need to be decorated—the lid and the sides.

Take the Plasticine and roll it out flat like pastry; cut it to the size of your patterns. Next, have a tryout with your diamond points—with the rotary tool turned off—and see what sort of marks they make when they are pressed firmly side-down into the Plasticine (see 2–5, bottom right). Spend time grouping the marks until you have what you consider is a sound arrangement. We have gone for grapes, leaves, and flowers, but this is not to say that you can't have a geometrical design or an abstract grouping or whatever appeals to you.

When you know just how the resultant marks are going to be set in relation to each other and to the item to be decorated, then carefully draw the design out to fit the tracing paper. Every now and again throughout the design process, take the tracing paper design and wrap it around the workpiece to check on how the envisaged patterns and motifs relate to the shape and form. For example, with our little pot, although we wanted the wraparound design to encompass the cylinder without a break, we also wanted to achieve a "wave" balance between space and pattern. We had to try several arrangements to achieve the balance and fit we wanted.

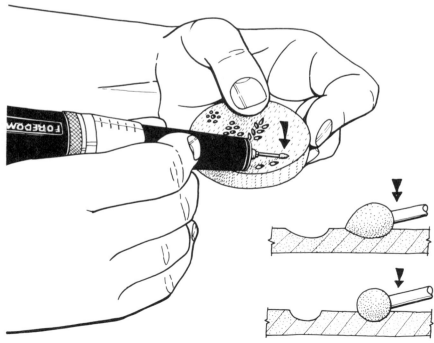

2-5 (Bottom right) Work out the design by pressing the diamond points into the Plasticine. (Left) Have a tryout on a scrap of wood. Never press hard-down on the points, but rather always let the tool do the work. Hold the point steady, make a number count, and remove the point when the cut is complete.

After completing the paper pattern, roll out a slab of Plasticine—the same size as the tracing paper—then select diamond-mounted points to match up with the envisaged forms.

Play around with both the pattern and the selection of tools until you have a well-thought-out design. Bear in mind along the way that, depending on the shape of your workpiece, you will only be able to view a small part of the total design at any one time.

Power Carving Tip

Since it is much more difficult to carve in the direction of the grain, at the design stage plan out the forms so that they run either across or at an angle to the grain. For example, the grain of our little pot runs from top to bottom; so we set the stems and stalks in sweeping diagonal curves rather than straight up and down.

When you have planned out all the how's and what with's, wrap the tracing paper pattern around/over the workpiece, secure it with tabs of masking tape, and then pencil-press transfer the imagery to the wood.

Finally, remove the tracing paper, and redraw the imagery so that every mark is clear and positive.

FIRST CUTS

Before you start carving for real, take a small scrap of wood, of a similar type and texture to the workpiece, and have a tryout with your chosen tools and points. Experiment with various handholds, angles of approach, and speeds.

We found that a positive, down-hold-and-off way of working (see 2–5, left) was much better than a tentative touch-and-look approach. If you make the mistake of fussing around with the tool repeatedly making contact, then the marks are going to look blurred and indecisive.

Power Carving Tip

If you make a slow, steady count while the point is in contact with the wood, then you will know how long it takes to achieve a good cut. You will be able to adjust the contact time accordingly as well as produce a consistent desired mark over and over.

CARVING THE STEMS

To cut the stalk and stem strokes—the little dashes that link the petals and the berries—fit the fine-cone point in the handpiece and set to work with a steady down-on-and-off stroking action.

If you find that the point follows the direction of the grain, and in so doing makes a jagged or stepped cut, then set the motor running "forward" (see 2–6, bottom), grasp the handpiece—so that it is at a very low angle to the wood being carved—and, using one finger as a guide, pivot and turn the tool towards your body. You should be able to achieve a smooth-curved stroke. If you find that the point vibrates intensely, burns, or simply fails to make a mark, then try a flatter angle of approach, and/or change the speed of the rotary tool. To make a cut that curves in the other direction, all you do is turn the workpiece "upside down" and work in the same way as just described.

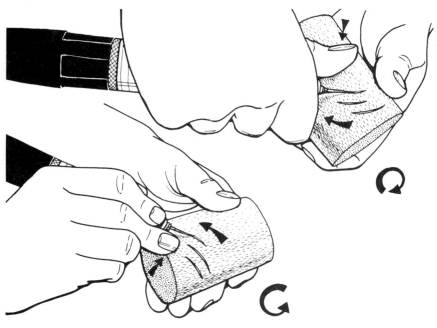

2-6   (Bottom) Hold the tool at a low angle to the surface of the wood—so that it is over the drawn line—and pivot the tool on your fingers and towards your body. (Top) Switch the rotation to reverse and pivot the tool with your thumb—swing the back of the handpiece around towards your body.

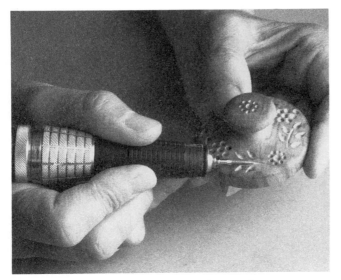

2-7 *Use the fine-cone point to cut the stem lines.*

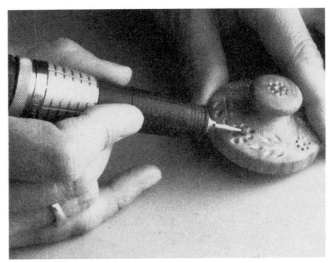

2-8 *Use the large-ball point to carve the flower centers and the grapes.*

If for some reason or other you are unable to work in the way described above, then switch the motor rotation to "reverse" and pivot the tool on your thumb so as to swing the back of the handpiece around towards your body (see 2–6, top). Aim to make a feathered line or little trench that runs into the wood from shallow to deep and back out to shallow (see 2–7).

CARVING THE FLOWERS, GRAPES, AND LEAVES

Fit the large-ball point and cut each flower center and each individual berry with a single positive touch of the point (see 2–8). Don't fuss around; just set the point down on the wood—until the required cut has been made—and then lift it off, all in a single, clean action. Use the small-ball point to carve the flower petals (see 2–9), and the bud point to carve the leaves (see 2–10).

Power Carving Tip
Keep one eye on your tracing-paper pattern; then you will be able to see at a glance whether or not all the elements are well placed.

Continue setting in all the individual cuts that go to make up the total design. If you work in the order we've presented—stems, flowers, grapes, and leaves—you will be able to arrange the leaves in such a way that they use the space to best advantage. For example, if, after you have carved the stems, flowers, and grapes, the design still looks a bit gappy or off balance, then all you do is fill in with a few more leaves. Finally, check the carving to make sure that it is nicely balanced and "pulled together" (see 2–11).

PAINTING AND FINISHING

When you have what you consider is a crisply worked carving, brush away all the debris, wipe it over with a damp cloth, and move to the dust-free area that you have set aside for painting. Take the fine-point brush and your chosen color; mix the paint to a nonrunny consistency. Then very carefully set to work blocking in all the little cuts that go to make up the motifs. Once the paint is good and dry, take a scrap of fine-grade sandpaper and gently rub the surface of the workpiece down in the direction of the grain to cut back unwanted paint.

Finally, after giving the carving a generous coat of wax polish, burnish it to a dull sheen finish. Now you can wrap it up and present it to your nearest and dearest—or is the carving just too beautiful to give away?

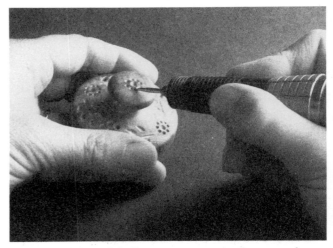

2-9 *Use the small-ball point to carve the flower petals.*

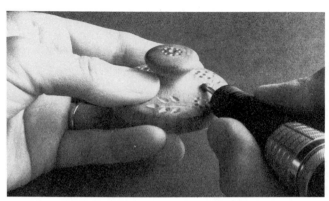

2-10 *Use the bud point to carve the leaves.*

HINTS, TIPS, AND AFTERTHOUGHTS

- Since the Micro Motor system has both a dial and a foot control, you can maximize carving concentration by setting the tool to a preset speed. If you would rather go swiftly up and down the speed range, you can use the foot control.
- The Wood Carver Supply diamond points can be used without wood "snatch," making for a very swift and efficient cut—a cut so smooth that it doesn't need any extra finishing. A good option for the beginner!
- With a project of this size and type, the choice of wood is all-important. The wood must cut smooth, be close-grained, and be pale in color.

2-11 *Check the design over, and make sure that all the elements are crisply carved.*

3

Carving an American Folk Art Rooster

Primary techniques—gouge carving

3-1 *Project picture. A rooster carved in the American folk art tradition, worked in lime.*

In the hard, down-to-earth world of the early American settlers and pioneers, their very life depended on being able to predict the next spell of good or bad weather—when to plant or harvest, whether or not to build a bigger barn or keep more stock, and so on. A shift in wind direction gave a fairly reliable indication that a change of weather was in store.

The weather vanes or "wind flags" were usually made from wood; cut with a bow saw from a plank or a riven slab; then swiftly shaped and textured with a knife and gouge. Finally painted with bright colors, the vanes could clearly be seen at a distance when silhouetted against the sky. The early Americans favored bold forms such as horses, Indians, fish, and perhaps the most popular image of all—a form that symbolized fertility, Christianity, and luck—the rooster (see 3–1).

Estimated Working Time
8–10 hours

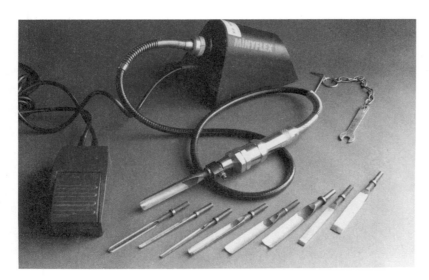

3-2 *The Hegner Moviluty Minyflex wood carving system is shown set up for the reciprocating option. (The system is also capable of rotary cutting action.) The system includes the wall/bench-mounted 150-240 volt motor unit, a heavy-duty foot pedal, flexible shaft, spanner, and selection of gouges. Changing gouges can take a few moments, but that is balanced by the smooth and efficient cutting action. The blade only starts to move when it is in contact with the workpiece, so it is safe and easy to control. We also use this system to carve a duck decoy in Project 15 and to carve the cigar-store figure of "Captain Jinks" in Project 16.*

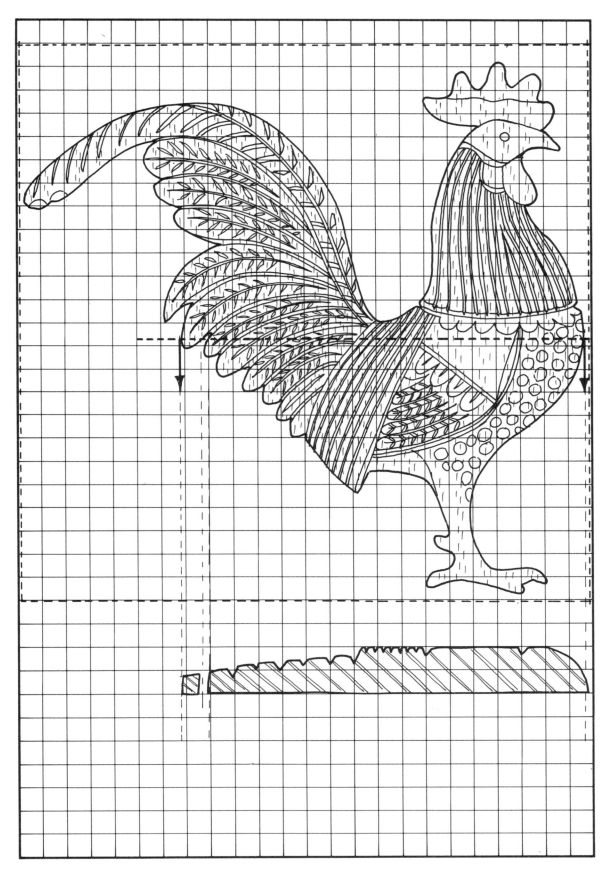

3-3 *Working drawing. At a scale of two grid squares to one inch, the rooster stands about 10 inches wide and 12 inches high. Note the relatively slender cross section and the direction of the grain.*

Materials

You need a one-inch-thick piece of soft, easy-to-carve straight-grained wood of about 12 inches by 12 inches—what better than a nice piece of lime or jelutong? The important thing—no matter what your choice—is that the wood must be free of knots, ragged twisted grain, sappy areas, stains, and all the other "nasties" that can spoil a woodcarving. Ideally you need a white wood that cuts smooth—a wood with a minimum of texture and color. Our choice is lime—also called linden or basswood.

Tools and Equipment

- power carving system including gouge/chisel set (see 3–2)
- workbench with a vise
- large clamp or holdfast
- pencil and ruler
- one sheet each of tracing and workout paper
- scroll saw
- chip-carving knife
- pack of graded sandpapers
- gas blowtorch
- wax polish and a brush

DESIGN, STRUCTURE, AND TECHNIQUE CONSIDERATIONS

When you have gathered your tools and materials, take a look at the working drawing (see 3–3). Notice how, at a grid scale of two grid squares to one inch, the rooster measures about 10 inches wide and about 12 inches high.

The imagery is basic and stylized, with all the marks left by the tools being direct and uncomplicated. Study the details and consider how the profile has first been rounded to give a stylized form, and then incised and tooled to give the effect of plumage.

To minimize the number of weak short-grain areas, the profile has been carefully placed and cut so that the grain runs from head to foot. Finally, the finished carving has been scorched with a blowtorch and then waxed to give it an old, weathered, much-handled look.

SETTING OUT THE DESIGN AND FIRST CUTS

When you have a good clear picture in your mind's eye of just how you want the rooster to be—size, type of wood, and so on—draw the design at full size and make a clear tracing. This done, take your slab of wood and check it over for possible problems. Avoid wood that looks in any way to be knotty, stained, marred by wane, or, worst of all, split.

Set the tracing on the wood, and arrange it to limit the number of fragile short-grained areas. Fix the tracing in place with tabs of masking tape, and carefully pencil-press transfer the traced profile lines through to the wood. Don't bother about the secondary details at this stage, just make sure that the outline is clear (see 3–4, left).

When you have achieved a good clean outline, remove the tracing, take the wood to the scroll saw, and set to work fretting out the design (see 3–4, right). Run the wood through the machine at a steady, easy pace, all the while being ready to change the angle of approach so

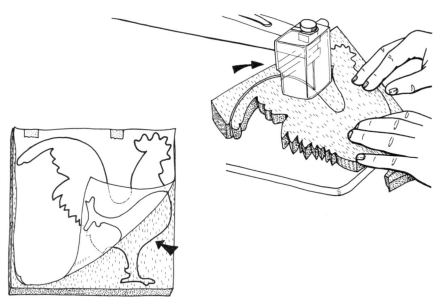

3-4 *(Left) Use tabs of masking tape to hold the tracing secure, and pencil-press transfer the traced lines to the wood. (Right) Present the blade with the line of next cut, and run the cut a little to the waste side of the drawn line.*

that the blade is presented with the line of best cut. Try to place the line of cut a little to the waste side of the drawn line.

Power Carving Tip
If you twist and/or force the scroll saw blade at the tight turns—around the head and the feet—then there is a chance that you will split the wood at the fragile, short-grained areas.

WORKING THE ROOSTER FORM

Once you have fretted out the basic profile, then comes the very exciting task of using the power tool to carve the overall rounded and stylized rooster. Fit the reciprocating shaft and handpiece to the power carver motor unit, tighten up, and then fit a large shallow-curve U-gouge in the handpiece (see 3–5).

Power Carving Tip
If you are new to this tool, it might be best at this stage to have a tryout on a piece of scrap wood.

It's all pretty straightforward—when the power is on and you touch the cutting edge of the gouge to the wood and exert a small amount of forward pressure, the blade starts to vibrate back and forth. It's a little bit of a surprise at first just how easy it is to smoothly scoop out the wood, but you will soon get the hang of it.

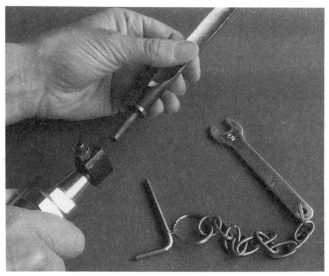

3-5   *Fit the large shallow-curve U-gouge in the handpiece, and tighten the allen screw and lock-nut.*

When you have played around with the tool and tried out the various blades, then take the rooster cutout. Working from center to side and holding the tool at a low, flat angle, set to work rounding off the sharp edges (see 3–6, top). You can hold the wood in your hand or place it flat on the bench. You do have to watch out that the blade doesn't slip off the edge of the wood at the end of a cut and do damage. Don't try to remove all the waste in one great thrust—it's much better to go for lots

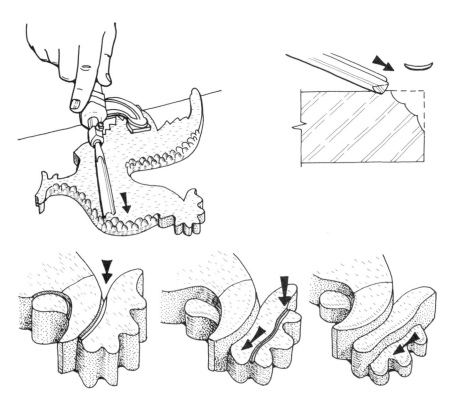

3-6   *(Top) Working from side to center— and holding the tool at a low flat angle— use a series of small strokes to remove the waste and to create the rounded form. (Bottom, left-to-right) Modelling the head and comb. Outline the head with a V-trench stop-cut, lower the comb and under the beak divide the comb and lower the crown. Note the direction of the cut.*

of small strokes. Be careful not to run the blade into end grain. If you find that the rotation slows down—the motor starts to complain—then turn off the motor, and resharpen the blade. If that doesn't work, change to a smaller gouge blade and try a lighter stroke. Continue working backwards and forwards over the workpiece, all the while rounding off the sharp corners and working towards a nicely considered rooster shape. Round over the top of the tail, the back, and the breast. Lower the area around the leg; step and lower the comb and the fleshy area under the beak, and so on (see 3–6, bottom).

When you have taken the shape as far as you want it to go, put down your tools and stand back for a good look at your work. Be super-critical. Bearing in mind that you are aiming for a simple, naive form, ask yourself—is the head right? Has the breast got a full self-confident curve? Is the tail right? Has the tail got a proud sweep?

Finally, when you have achieved a nicely worked form—one with plenty of small scooped tool marks—then take a sheet of fine-grade sandpaper and give the workpiece a swift rubdown to remove the rough edges and jags.

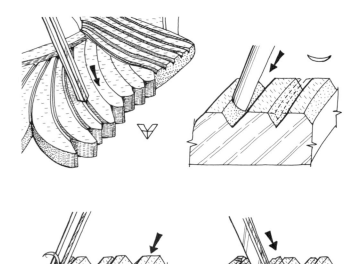

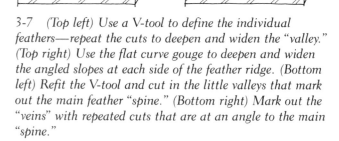

3-7 (Top left) Use a V-tool to define the individual feathers—repeat the cuts to deepen and widen the "valley." (Top right) Use the flat curve gouge to deepen and widen the angled slopes at each side of the feather ridge. (Bottom left) Refit the V-tool and cut in the little valleys that mark out the main feather "spine." (Bottom right) Mark out the "veins" with repeated cuts that are at an angle to the main "spine."

Power Carving Tip
Don't overdo the sanding to the extent that the shapes are blurred; just settle for a swift rubdown until the wood feels smooth to the touch.

MODELLING AND INCISING THE DESIGN

Once you have brought the rooster to a good smooth shape and finish, take the tracing and pencil-press transfer the imagery to the surface of the wood. This isn't easy because the surface is curved rather than flat. The best way is to transfer the imagery one piece at a time—each time removing the tracing and fixing it in place with tabs of masking tape.

After comparing the drawn lines on the wood with the lines on the tracing, spend time with a soft pencil pulling the design together and perhaps modifying it here and there so that the details fit the wood.

The next stage is a bit tricky, so go at it slowly. Fit the V-section parting tool in the reciprocating handpiece, turn on the power, and have a tryout on a piece of scrap wood. Note how, although it is very easy to run V-sections in straight and gentle curves both with and across the grain, it is very difficult to cut tight curves.

Once you have explored the tool's qualities, use the V-tool to cut in all the primary incised lines that go to make up the design. Concentrate in the first instance on the deep valleys—the lines that mark out the individual feathers that go to make up the tail and wings. This is easy enough, as long as you cut, wherever possible, from center to side—that is, from the middle of the rooster out towards the side edges (see 3–7, top left). Working in this way, you will find that the tool will stop cutting as soon as it runs off the edge of the wood.

Continue, reworking the cuts deeper and deeper, until the center of each feather stands proud like a ridge with the wood falling away at each side into the between-feather valley. After all the primary cuts have been marked out with the V-tool, fit the small flat-curve gouge or the small chisel, and continue working the angled slopes at each side of the feather ridges (see 3–7, top right). If, when you are cutting up the side of such-and-such a feather, you find that the blade cuts rough, then change the direction of cut. Make the line around the base of the rooster's neck—the line that marks out the bottom of the fringed collar—a good ¼ inch deep.

Having deepened all the between-feather lines so that each feather stands out as a ridge, then switch off the tool to refit the V-tool in the handpiece. Cut in all the secondary incised lines—the veins of the feathers (see 3–7, bottom right and left). Also be sure that you cut in all of the fine lines that mark out the collar or ruff.

FINISHING

Once you have worked all the small incised lines, and when you are happy with the overall effect, refit the medium U-section gouge and set to work texturing the collar, breast, and leg areas. Don't overwork the wood; just settle for a line of well-placed scoops around the bottom edge of the collar and on the wing. Use the large shallow-curved U-section gouge to texture a scattering of dappled cuts across the breast and leg (see 3–8, top). This done, put the power tools to one side; take up the chip carving knife, and work over the carving, tidying up all the "loose ends" (see 3–8, bottom). Cut in the eye, cut in an extra bit of texturing on the feathers, and so on.

Take the finished carving away from the workshop—away from all the sawdust and shavings—and set it down flat in the yard. If you haven't used a blowtorch before, then now is the time to have a tryout. Take a piece of tool marked and textured scrap wood, set it down on a safe surface—I prefer a concrete slab—light the torch, and give the wood a swift once-over with the flame. Aim first to remove the small rough areas and debris and then to darken selected areas.

When you have learned to control the torch, then run the flame over the rooster. Darken the top of the feathers, the tooling at the breast, and anything else that takes your fancy. If needed, now is a good time to refit the V-tool and crisp-up cuts that look blurred (see 3–9).

Finally, go over the whole workpiece with fine-grade sandpaper in the direction of the grain. Give it a generous coat of wax polish, and buff it to a high-shine finish. The rooster is now finished and ready to be mounted on the wall.

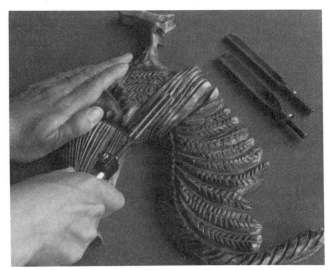

3-9   Refit the V-tool in the handpiece, and clean up any cuts that look to be blurred or fuzzy.

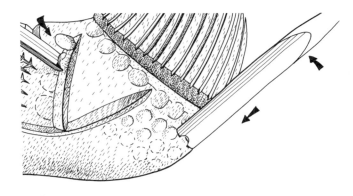

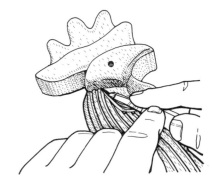

3-8   (Top) Use the medium-curved V-section gouge to texture the collar and the wing, and the large shallow curved U-section gouge to make the dappled cuts across the breast and leg. (Bottom) Use the chip-carving knife and small, controlled strokes to tidy up the imagery.

HINTS, TIPS, AND AFTERTHOUGHTS

- At about 12 inches high, our rooster is worked at half size—just perfect for a display piece. If you decide to make the rooster for an actual weather vane, double the thickness of the wood and go for a bird about 24-inches high. Be prepared to reinforce weak short-grained areas with brass or copper straps.
- If you want to display the rooster out in the garden, then leave off the polish, and give it several generous all-over coats of clear varnish instead.
- If you want to go for a smaller, more detailed and fancy image, then you might consider using the Hegners rotary shaft and handpiece rather than the reciprocating ones.
- If the wood cuts rough or ragged, then your wood is damp or ill chosen or the blade needs resharpening.
- When you are resharpening the V-tool, be very careful that you don't wear through the vertex—the point of the V.
- If you work in such a way that the shaft is tightly kinked or bent, you will find that the handpiece will heat up. Arrange yourself so that the shaft bends in an easy curve between the motor and the handpiece.

4

Carving a "Sunflower" Panel in the American Colonial Tradition

Primary techniques—gouge and touch carving

4-1   Project picture. The Sunflower panel, gouge and touch carved.

Introduced into Holland from the East sometime in the early sixteenth century, tulips soon became so popular that they sparked off a phenomenon that is now known as "tulipmania"—wild and fervent financial speculation around the development of rare and exotic tulip varieties. Within the space of a hundred years, the decorative motif of the tulip spread from Holland to

Germany, and then to England and America, where, especially during the Arts and Crafts Movement of the late nineteenth century, it linked up with the sunflower.

Known variously as strapwork, Jacobean flowers, and low-relief ribbon-work flowers, the sunflower and tulip carvings are characterized by being flat-faced, sharp-edged, smooth-lined, and symmetrical. The flower image is minimally modelled and raised up as a flat plateau on a sunken ground. The lowered ground is usually cut away to a depth of between ⅛ inch and ¼ inch, with both the motif in relief and the ground looking, to our eyes, to be almost mechanically carved.

The flowers became so abstracted and conventionalized that in many instances they became barely recognizable. In the design for this project, you will see that not only have the two flowers been reduced to a single rather curious hybrid (see 4–1) with the central motif still more or less sunflower-shaped, but the "tulips" have become simple leaf-like forms that spring out at each side of the main stem.

Estimated Working Time
3–4 hours

Materials
For this project you need a "found" panel of easy-to-carve wood about seven inches wide and 10 inches long. This size allows for the 4½-inch by 7¼-inch image to be set within the center of the panel so that there is an all-around border of uncarved ground—like a picture frame.

We chose to set the sunflower motif (see 4–2) on a small cupboard door, but this is not to say that you couldn't just as well go for, say, the side of a chest, a set of kitchen cupboard doors, the top of a small box, a front door panel, or whatever.

4-2 Working drawing—the scale is four grid squares to one inch. Note the symetrical arrangement, and the way the two side tulips have become so stylized that they look more like leaves.

Tools and Equipment

- power carving system including gouges (see 4–3)
- set of ruby carver points
- small ⅛-inch-diameter router cutter
- workbench with a vise
- table, pillar, or bench drill press
- bench holdfast or hold-down clamp
- pencil, ruler, and compass
- one sheet each of tracing and workout paper
- pack of graded sandpapers
- small quantity of wax polish
- polishing cloth
- goggles and a mask, or a respirator

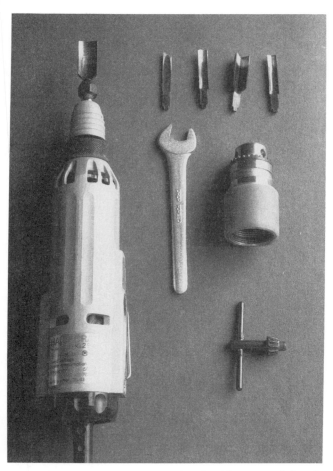

4-3 *The Tokyo Automach Handcraft self-contained, hand-held carving system is shown fitted with the reciprocating headpiece—the quick-change rotary option is alongside. The unit accepts 100/120/220/240 volts. Note the selection of gouge blades. The Handcraft wood carving system supplied by Woodcraft Supply Corp. USA is efficient, lightweight, and quiet as well as user-friendly. We also use this system to carve a gilt ribbon bow in the French tradition in Project 8, to carve a water dipper ladle in the American pioneer tradition in Project 12, and to carve a mask in the American Northwest Indian tradition in Project 14.*

It doesn't matter too much on your choice of wood, as long as it's easy to carve, straight-grained, and free from knots and splits. Make sure that you remove any catches, hinges, or whatever from your found item.

DESIGN, STRUCTURE, AND TECHNIQUE CONSIDERATIONS

When you have sorted out your tools, selected your wood, and generally prepared yourself for the task at hand, have a good long look at the working drawing (see 4–2). See how, at a grid scale of four squares to one inch, the actual carved part of the panel measures about 4½ inches by 7¼ inches. Note how the stylized flower is symmetrically placed within the area to be carved and how the ground around the flower is cut away and lowered so that the flower is left standing in relief. The sunflower head has been set out with a compass and divided up geometrically. Consider the way each sunflower petal is drawn to show that it is scoop-carved and angled towards the center of the flower; between each petal there is a small ridge of wood that runs around the entire motif.

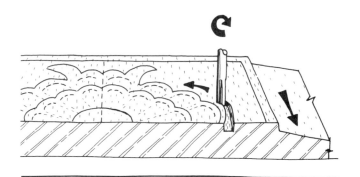

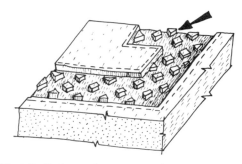

4-4 *(Top) Pull the workpiece towards you to cut a trench in a counterclockwise direction around the design. Try to cut a little to the waste side of the drawn line. (Bottom) Subdivide the waste with a series of criss-cross trenches, and then clear the islands.*

This way of carving not only leaves each petal with a strong stepped outer edge—easy to carve and hard-wearing—but it also gives the illusion that the petal circles are set behind each other and that the whole flower has been carved and worked in greater depth and detail that it actually has. The edge of the "plateau" has been sharply stepped, and the lowered ground textured to add to the illusion of depth.

Finally, note how the design has been organized in such a way that there is always plenty of room in and around the motif—in the tight areas of the lowered ground—for the easy movement of tools.

SETTING OUT THE DESIGN AND ROUTING OUT THE GROUND

After you have drawn the design at full size and made a clean line tracing, align the tracing on your chosen panel and fix it in place with tabs of masking tape. Use a hard pencil to press-transfer the traced lines to the face of the wood. Since it's important that the design be crisply set out, spend time with a pencil, ruler, and compass making sure that the image is aligned with the midline and square with the frame.

Design Transfer Tip
Since the design is symmetrical, you can speed up the drawing and tracing time by only drawing out and tracing one-half of the design; then reverse the tracing to complete the full image.

Having pencil-pressed the profile to the wood, remove the tracing paper, and then very carefully go over the outline and shade in the ground area that needs to be lowered and cut away. Try all the while to ensure that the various curves and angles that go to make up the design are kept as crisp and as sharp as possible.

Move to the drill press and fit the ⅛-inch-diameter cylinder router bit in the chuck. Be very careful to pay full attention to the job at hand, and be mindful to hold on tight to the workpiece. Switch on the power, and wind the drill table up so that the live router bit runs down into the wood to a depth of about ⅛ inch.

After making the initial cut, grasp the panel firmly in both hands, and move it around on the drill table so that the router bit runs to the waste side of the drawn line. Cut a trench right around the design. Although you can move the workpiece in any direction, it is best if it is pulled towards you so that the line-to-follow is on the left side of the spinning bit and so that the trench is cut in counterclockwise direction around the motif (see 4–4, top).

Power Carving Tip
If you have any doubts as to which direction to cut or how to position the waste in relation to the router bit, then draw a circle on a piece of scrap wood and have a tryout.

It's all pretty straightforward as long as you follow a few simple rules of thumb:

- Wear a mask and goggles or a respirator.
- Don't wear dangling and trailing clothes that might get caught up in the drill.
- Make sure that you hold the workpiece with a firm, positive two-handed grip.
- Don't let your attention wander.
- Make sure that you stay about ¹⁄₁₆ inch to the waste side of the drawn line.
- Don't try to rush or force the pace.
- Let the router work at its own pace.

After cutting the trench in a counterclockwise direction around the motif, start to clear the shaded-in waste area. The best procedure is to subdivide the waste with a series of criss-crossed trenches, and then to clear each of the islands (see 4–4, bottom). As each island is cleared, move the workpiece hither and thither so that the router leaves the ground looking smooth-bottomed (see 4–5).

4-5 *The workpiece after the "drill" routing is complete.*

Once you have used the router bit to clear the waste—as near to the edge of the design as you dare—then secure the workpiece to the bench, fit the router in the rotary tool, and carefully cut to the drawn line. Make sure that you hold and control the tool with both hands (see 4–6).

Finally, when you have cleared the waste ground—by which time you will have gained confidence and worked out the best method of cut—have a rerun so as to cut right up to the drawn line. Change over to the small flame ruby point, and work systematically over the lowered ground, dot-texturing the surface. Aim for a random effect that ever so slightly concentrates the dots at edges and angles (see 4–7).

USING THE RECIPROCATING GOUGES TO MODEL THE PETALS

With the routing complete, take the power carver and screw on the reciprocating head; fit the broad U-section gouge. Being mindful that there is no going back if you make a mess-up, tentatively set to work carving each of the scooped petal shapes. With the workpiece held with a clamp flat on the workbench, set the blade vertically on the curved edge of the inner petal ring. Set out the image with stop-cuts that run straight down into the wood to a depth of about 1⁄16 inch (see 4–8). When you have worked right around the circle of petals, then set the blade down at a low angle on the shaded edge of the outer ring of petals so that the blade is facing towards the center of the flower; run an angled slicing cut into the stop-cuts to remove a single small curl of waste (see 4–9).

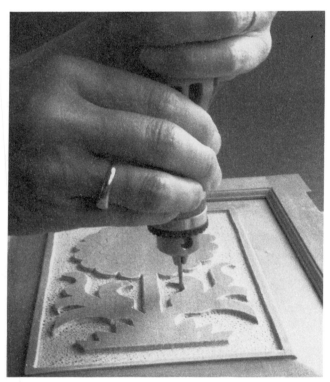

4-6 Having fitted the router bit in the Automach—the rotary headpiece—use both hands to run the tool as close as possible to the drawn line.

4-8 Define the shape by making straight down-into-the-wood stop-cuts. Chop to a depth of about 1⁄16 inch.

4-7 After fitting the ruby flame point in the chuck, systematically dot-texture the lowered ground.

4-9 Work around and around the flower, shaping the petals by running low-angled cuts into the stop-cuts.

Continue running a series of scooping cuts down the length of the petals towards the stop-cut to model the little concave trough details that make the characteristic petal forms. When you have scooped out one petal, just go to the next, and the next, and so on. And of course, if along the way you need to deepen or tidy up the stop-cuts or change to a small gouge, then no problem; you do just that!

Once you have scooped out and modelled the outer ring of petals, you repeat the procedure by making stop-cuts around the circle at the center of the flower (see 4–10, top) and then scooping and modelling the inner circle of petals (see 4–10, bottom, left and right). It's all very straightforward as long as you don't overrun the stop-cut and damage the area that needs to be left in high relief and don't cut the scooped petal area so wide that it intrudes on the small between-petal ridge that needs to be left in high relief.

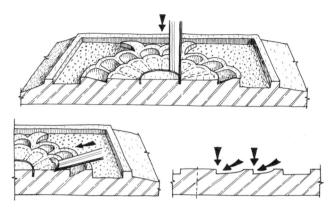

4-10   (Top) Make stop-cuts around the circle at the center of the flower. (Bottom) Scoop out the inner circle of petals—remove the waste little by little until the required shape is achieved.

USING THE ROTARY CARVER TO MODEL THE DETAILS AND TO TEXTURE THE GROUND

When you have taken the gouge carving as far as it needs to go, change to the rotary head, and fit the small cylinder ruby carver point. With the workpiece held flat on the bench with the holdfast, switch on the power, grasp the power carver in both hands, and carefully work around the relief area to bring the vertical face to a crisp, clean finish (see 4–11, left). Run the ruby point along the straight edges and around all the concave and convex curves that go to make up the design. Run the point as far as you can into the sharp angles, and then back off. This done, take a sharp-point knife and go over the entire carving, cutting in all the tight angles that couldn't be reached with the point.

Change to the small flame ruby point, and tidy up the scooped petals by redefining the edges and curves (see 4–11, right). Don't try to remove all the gouge marks; just crisp up the dishing so that each scoop comes to a clean-edged finish.

Finally, go over the whole carving with fine-grade sandpaper, clean away the dust and debris, give all surfaces a generous coat of wax polish, and burnish to a dull-sheen finish.

Power Carving Tip
If you want to achieve an "old" effect with a strong dark-light contrast between the raised motif and the lowered areas, you can use an "antique" polish to darken the lowered ground and all the little nooks and crannies.

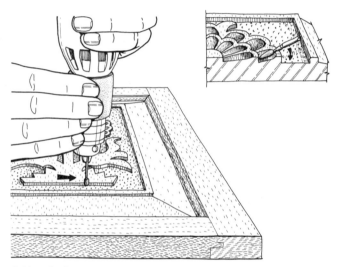

4-11   (Left) Use the small ruby cylinder bit to bring all the vertical planes—I call them "cliffs"—to a crisp, clean finish. (Right) Tidy up the scooped petals with the small flame ruby point/bit.

HINTS, TIPS, AND AFTERTHOUGHTS

- It's most important that your gouges are razor sharp. This being the case, stop every five minutes or so, fit the little aluminum oxide grinding cylinder in the rotary head, and swiftly bring the bevel of the gouge blade to a keen edge.
- Be very careful, when you are scooping out the petals, that you don't overrun the stop-cut and do damage to the wood that needs to be left in relief.
- When you are carving the petals, be ready—keeping in mind that grain conditions will change as you move around the circle—to change your angle of approach for the best cut.

5

Carving a Shortbread Mould with a Thistle Motif

Primary techniques—turning, and stroke and touch carving

5-1 *Project picture. The shortbread mould—turned on the lathe, and then stroke and touch carved.*

The traditional country cottage kitchen was a treasury of turned, carved, and decorated woodwork. Depending on the country, there were carved wares that related to specific ways of preparing food and to favored forms of woodcarved decoration. For example, in Sweden there were beautiful chip-carved boards, in Poland there were deeply carved and whittled cheese moulds, in England there were pastry rollers with very delicate imagery, in Germany there were springerle boards with pictures of animals, and in Scotland there were shortbread moulds that used national symbols.

From a woodcarver's viewpoint, the moulds are particularly exciting in that the designs are, by necessity, naive, bold, and swiftly and crisply worked. With short-bread moulds, in particular, the usage or function is the primary factor that shapes the design (see 5–1). A damp, soft mix is pressed into the mould, and then turned out on a baking tray. The resultant motif on the cooked shortbread needs to be boldly standing proud so that the

mould has to be carved in relief with the actual motif being hollow-carved and generally uncomplicated (see 5–2). If the mould is too deep, or if the motif is too fancy, then the shortbread mix won't leave the mould and the whole thing is a mess-up.

Materials
You need a 1¾-inch-thick slab of hard, smooth, dense-grained, easy-to-carve, easy-to-turn wood about 6½ inches by 6½ inches square. Bearing in mind that the wood must be completely safe and nontoxic—yew is poisonous, a dark wood might bleed a sticky staining resin, some woods leech a tainting smell—select a hardwood such as lime, plum, apple, or beech. If you have any doubts, ask the advice of a specialist wood supplier.

Tools and Equipment
- power carving system with no-slip handpiece (see 5–3 and 5–4)
- set of tungsten carbide burrs (see 5–5)
- sets of six coarse and ten fine ruby carvers
- lathe with a 6-inch-diameter faceplate
- set of woodturning tools
- pair of calipers
- pair of dividers
- pencil, ruler, and compass
- small saw like a tenon or bead ("joiner's fancy" or "gent's")
- three ¾-inch-long countersunk screws to fit the faceplate
- screwdriver to fit the screws
- large ball of Plasticine big enough to test out the mould
- one sheet each of tracing and workout paper
- roll of masking tape
- brush
- vegetable oil—such as walnut oil—and a soft cloth

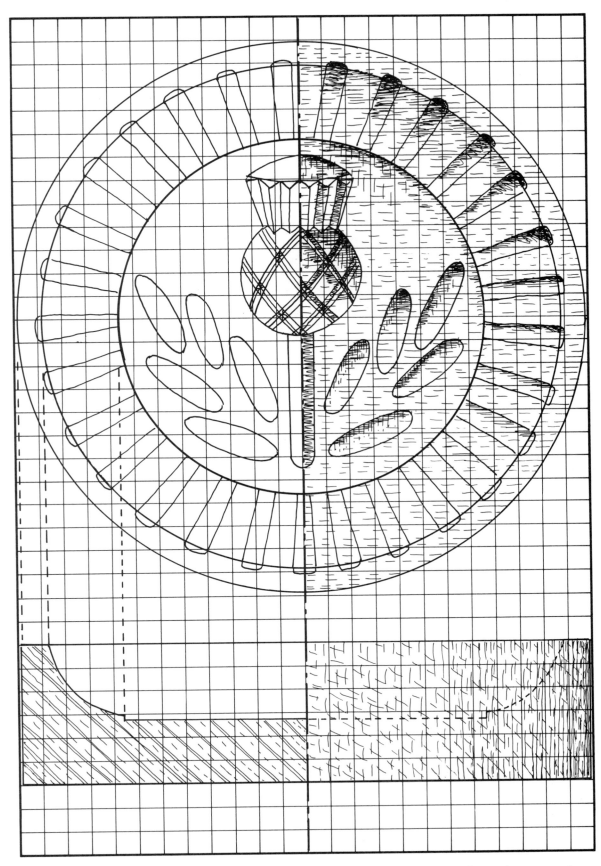

5-2 *Working drawing. At a scale of four grid squares to one inch, the mould is 6 inches in diameter and 1½ inches thick. Note the depth of the dish and the thickness of the side wall/rim.*

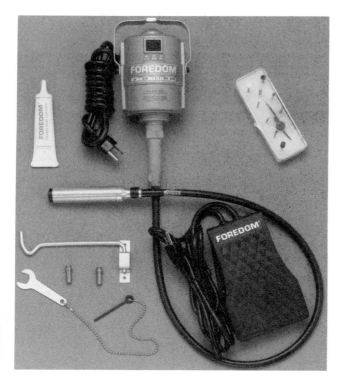

5-3 *The SR Series Foredom Electric woodcarving kit No. 5240 is shown with drive shaft, handpiece, heavy-duty foot pedal, ¼-, ⅛-, and 3/32-inch collets, spanner, and tools. The ⅛ HP motor runs forward and reverse at either 110-13 or 220-240 volts. The reverse rotation is particularly good if you are a left-handed carver. Note that we used the Jacob's chuck handpiece shown in 5-4 rather than the one shown here. We also use this system to carve a mirror frame in the European primitive tradition in Project 7.*

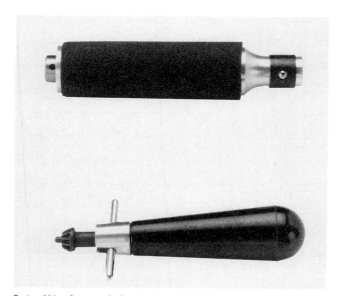

5-4 *We also used the G-30 Jacob's chuck handpiece with no-slip rubberized grip and chuck key rather than the one shown in 5-3. The Jacob's handpiece allows for the quick-change of tools. It is so comfortable and easy to use that we choose it for a wide selection of tools.*

Estimated Working Time
4–6 hours

DESIGN, STRUCTURE, AND TECHNIQUE CONSIDERATIONS

When you have gathered your tools and materials, take a look at the working drawing (see 5–2). See how, at a grid scale of four squares to one inch, the mould measures 6 inches in diameter and 1½ inches thick. Note the ¼-inch-wide rim, the central sunken area at a little over 3¾ inches in diameter, and the way the flat-based sunken area curves down from the rim to a depth of ⅞ inch. Consider how the border and the stylized thistle motif—the national emblem of Scotland—is swiftly worked from a few primary cuts. The border design is made up of a series of fluted grooves that follow the curve down into the sunken area. The motif is made up of a central fluted groove for the stem, ten fluted scoops for the foliage, a sunken half-sphere for the body of the flower, and a scooped-and-grooved area for the seed head.

Finally, consider how the resultant shortbread biscuit will be round in plan view, shallow-domed in cross section, and topped off with the thistle in proud relief.

5-5 *A selection of ruby carvers and two carbide burrs needed for this project.*

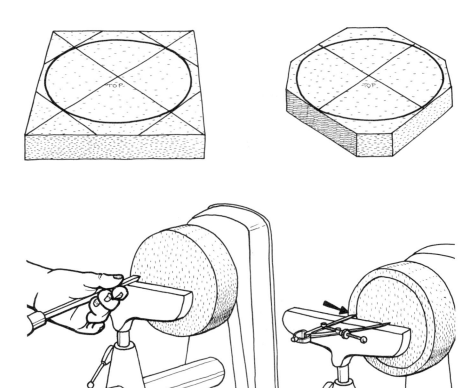

5-6 *(Top left) Having established the center of each square face by drawing diagonals, draw out a 6-inch-diameter circle. (Top right) Saw away the bulk of the waste. (Bottom left) Turn the wood down to a smooth-faced clean-edged disc/blank. (Bottom right) Set the dividers to a radius of 2¾ inches, and scribe out a 5½-inch-diameter circle.*

TURNING THE DISC

When you are clear as to how the project needs to be worked, take the 6½-inch by 6½-inch-square slab of wood, and pencil-mark the two square faces—one top and the other bottom. Establish the center of each face by drawing crossed diagonals. Fix the compass/dividers to a radius of three inches, and set each square face out with a six-inch-diameter circle (see 5–6, top left). This done, use the saw to swiftly cut away the bulk of the waste (see 5–6, top right).

Center the roughed-out blank of wood on the faceplate, and screw it firmly in place so that the top face— the best side—is uppermost. Once you are sure that the wood is secure, screw the faceplate on the lathe, and bring the T-rest up over the bed of the lathe so that you can approach the blank of wood face-on. Make sure you have the tools you need and take safety precautions— eye protection, no dangling hair or clothes. Switch on the power and use the tool of your choice to turn the face of the wood down to a smooth, level finish. This done, move the rest so that you can approach the wood edge-on, and turn the wood down to a disc. Don't worry too much about the center face of the wood, because this is going to be cut away; rather, concentrate your efforts on making sure that the edge and the rim are smooth and level (see 5–6, bottom left).

When you have achieved a clean-cut, smooth-edged 6-inch-diameter disc, take the dividers and set out the two inner circles that make up the design of the mould. Scribe the circles out one within another: one circle with a radius of 2¾ inches for the 5½-inch-diameter edge-of-rim line (see 5–6, bottom right), and one circle with a radius of about 1⅞ inch for the line that marks out the diameter of the lowered area.

When you are sure that all is correct and as described—study the cross section (refer to 5–2, bottom)—take the parting tool and sink a ¾-inch-deep pilot slot to the waste side of the inner circle line. Next, take the tool of your choice—I used a round-nosed gouge and a skew chisel—and turn the area within the pilot slot circle down to a smooth-based depth of a little over ¾ inch.

Take the round-nosed gouge, and turn away the sharp corner of wood between the inner lowered area and the marked-out inner rim line. Lower the waste little by little, until you have a sweeping concave quarter-circle curve that runs from the rim line down into the lowered area. If all is well, the curve should have a radius of about ¾ inch. Give the whole disc a swift rubdown with fine-grade sandpaper, and take it off the lathe. Finally, rub the back of the disc down to a smooth finish.

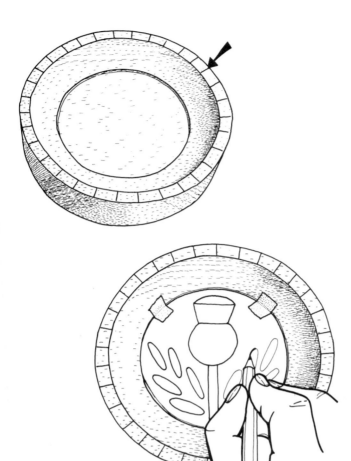

CARVING THE FLOWER HEAD

Move to a comfortable corner of the workshop, hang and fit the power carver motor unit, outfit yourself with goggles and dust mask, and then settle down to have a tryout on a piece of scrap wood. Generally play around with the various combinations and permutations of speed, motor direction, tool, wood type, and direction of cut until you are reasonably confident that you know what you are doing.

Power Carving Tip
Although the Foredom unit we used is so smooth running that it is possible to sit down and do the carving on your lap, it is always wise to wear a thick apron—just in case the tool slips.

When you have familiarized yourself with the power carving unit, and when you know how the various tools behave, then fit the tungsten carbide round-edge wheel in the Jacobs handpiece (see 5–8). Set to work carving the main part of the motif—the thistle seed head. Working with a delicate stroking action, variously, draw the wheel towards you, and run it both across and with the grain. Proceed little by little until you have carved a dished half-sphere shape that is about ¼ inch deep (see 5–9, top left). Next, concentrate your efforts on the top of the seed head or crown. Once again, work with a delicate stroking action until the motif has been lowered to a depth of about 3/16 inch.

After clearing the bulk of the waste with the round-edged wheel burr, change to the cylinder burr, and

5-7 (Top) Step off the guide marks around the rim to start and finish on the same mark. (Bottom) Use a hard pencil to press-transfer the traced image to the wood.

SETTING OUT THE DESIGN

When you have achieved the basic turned blank, set the dividers to ½ inch, and then carefully step off around the edge of the rim, marking out the "spokes" that make up the outer wheel-like design. Depending on the size of your blank, you might have to adjust the step-off size to a little over ½ inch so that you start and finish on the same mark (see 5–7, top).

Draw the thistle design at full size, make a tracing, and then cut the tracing down to a circle that fits into the lowered part of the turned blank. Position the tracing within the blank so that the grain runs from side to side and so that the midline is running through the stem of the thistle. Hold it in place with tabs of masking tape, and use a hard pencil to press-transfer the traced imagery to the wood (see 5–7, bottom).

Design Transfer Tip
Use a soft pencil for tracing and a hard pencil for press-transferring.

5-8 Set the carbide burr in the chuck, and tighten with the key.

further carve out the shape of the crown. You will see as you are carving that you will have to chop and change about with the direction of cut and the angle of approach. For example, if you are to achieve the nice crisp cut at top of the crown, you will have to first approach it in one direction and then from another (see 5–9, top right).

When you have worked the main part of the flower head with the burr, use the coarse and fine ruby cutters to bring the flower head to a good finish. We used the coarse tapered-cylinder ruby for the crown area and then the coarse tree-radius ruby for the main part of the flower. Finally, to finish, we used the fine pear ruby on the crown area and fine egg ruby for the main part of the flower.

DETAILING THE FLOWER HEAD

Before you do anything else, have a close-up look at the project photograph and the working drawing (refer to 5–1 and 5–2). See how the flower head—the round shape and the seed head—have been detailed with a pattern of fine V-cut lines. The concave half-sphere has

six lines—three on each side—that cross each other diagonally to make a diamond-shaped grid, whereas the seed head has five lines running from top to bottom to create a ridged texture.

After drawing in the position of the lines, fit the coarse tapered-cylinder ruby in the handpiece. Work each V-trench with two strokes or cuts—run along one side of the V to achieve one angled slope or plane, and then turn the workpiece around and work the other side (see 5–9, middle left). When you have roughed out the V-trenches with the coarse ruby, then fit the fine flame ruby, and rework the trenches until they are smooth and clean-cut (see 5–9, bottom).

CARVING THE STEM AND LEAVES

When you have drawn in the position of the stem and the leaves, first use the coarse tree-radius cone ruby to clear the bulk of the waste (see 5–10, top) and to rough out the shape. Then follow through with fine pear ruby and/or the ball to clean up and bring the surface of the wood to a good finish (see 5–10, bottom). The procedure is much the same as already described. All you do is fit the tool in the handpiece, and then clear the waste with a delicate stroking action. Don't press too hard, don't run the tool at too low a speed, and don't be in too much of a hurry to get the job done.

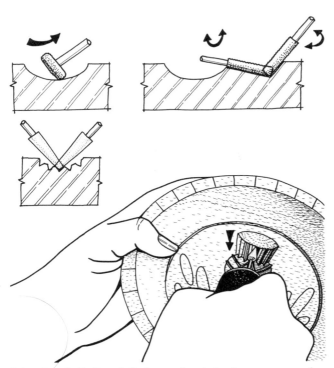

5-9 (Top left) Carefully lower the circle that goes to make up the main part of the thistle until you have a dished half-sphere at about ¼ inch deep. (Top right) When you come to carve the crown, approach it from top and bottom to achieve the angled slopes. (Middle left) Cut the V-trenches first from one side and then from the other. (Bottom) Use the flame ruby to work the cuts to a smooth finish.

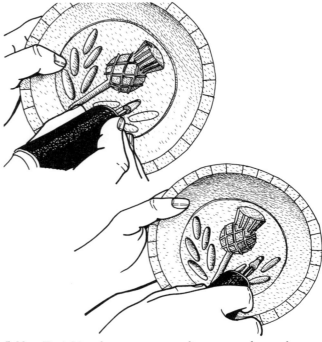

5-10 (Top) Use the coarse tree-radius-cone ruby to clear the bulk of the waste. (Bottom) Use the fine pear ruby to bring the surfaces to a good finish.

5-11 *Hold the mould on edge, and stroke the ruby cutter up-and-out along the flutes.*

CUTTING THE EDGE SPOKE DESIGN AND FINISHING

Having marked out the position of the spokes around the circumference of the mould with compass step-offs and drawn them in with a pencil, use the two pear-shaped ruby carvers—first coarse and then fine—to cut out each of the spokes. Although the procedure is much the same as already described, you do have to watch out when you come to cut in the direction of the grain. I say this, since, as you are working right around the edge of the mould, you will come to cut—sooner or later—in just about every direction of the run of the grain. For example, as you work around the "clock," the grooves from 2 to 4 o'clock, and the grooves from 8 to 10 o'clock will be running with the direction of the grain. Take it nice and easy, all the while being ready for unexpected hard and soft areas of grain.

5-12 *Use the fine ruby carver to bring the cuts to a good smooth finish.*

5-13 *Have a tryout by pressing a ball of warm Plasticine into the mould.*

Power Carving Tip

It's a good idea to keep a selection of off-cuts handy so that you can try out various cuts. Only thing is, if the workpiece is a piece of beech, for instance, then the tryout wood also needs to be beech. From one type of wood to another, the carving characteristics are quite different.

The procedure is straightforward enough—you hold the workpiece in one hand and the tool in the other, all the while being ready to turn both the wood and the tool, so that the tool is presented with the area of the next cut. Stroke the cutter from the central lowered area, up the curved slope, to stop short at the inside edge of the rim (see 5–11). On no account let the tool slip off the outside-edge rim.

After you have variously cleaned up rough edges with a scrap of fine-grade sandpaper and the fine ruby carver points (see 5–12), and when you have generally brought the whole mould to a good finish, brush off the dust and have a tryout with Plasticine to see what sort of image the mould produces (see 5–13). If necessary, trim back and adjust areas accordingly. When you have achieved what you consider is a good mould, then sign and date the back with a pencil. Finally, give the whole workpiece a rubdown with the vegetable oil, and then . . . set it down in the kitchen and wait for the reviews!

HINTS, TIPS, AND AFTERTHOUGHTS

- Don't try this project with a piece of coarse-grained wood like knotty pine or oak. You must use a close-grained wood such as lime, box, sycamore, plum, apple, or beech.
- If you like the idea of the project, but are not so keen on the thistle motif, then you can make up your own coat-of-arms or family symbol. If you decide to go for initials or dates, then don't forget to carve them in reverse.
- If you haven't got a lathe, then there are specialist suppliers who deal in ready-turned blanks. Or you could broaden the project somewhat, and carve your blank.
- Make sure that you hang the motor unit up and position yourself so that the sheath runs in a smooth, easy curve.

6

Carving an Icelandic Knot Roundel

Primary techniques—drill, router, and touch carving

6-1 Project picture. A characteristic Icelandic "knot" motif—drill, router, and touch/stroke carved.

In the context of traditional Icelandic woodcarving, the interlaced or "magic" knot design was used for objects that needed supernatural protection. The design was carved onto food and clothes boxes, on bed ends and cradles, on bread boards and cutting boards, and on just about anything that might be susceptible to ill fortune.

One of the oldest and most beautiful of all the entwined magic knot forms is that made of two or three ribbon-like loops that are interwoven and contained within a circle (see 6–1). In the eighteenth and nineteenth centuries, the knots became known—in the context of love-token woodcarvings—as "true love" knots, the analogy being that, like the knot, love has no ending. .

Estimated Working Time
6–10 hours

Materials
You need a one-inch-thick, 9½-inch-diameter lathe-turned roundel or disc of prepared easy-to-carve wood. We have gone for a piece of lime (linden/basswood), but you could just as well choose, say, a piece of jelutong or holly or just about any light-colored wood that is smooth-grained and free from knots, splits, and stains. I specify "light-colored," because the wood is going to be textured with a poker pen, and therefore, by necessity, it must be pale enough to set off the dark "burn" to best effect (see 6–2). A hard white wood that is free from resins helps reduce the buildup of sticky difficult-to-work tars on the tip of the poker pen.

If you have doubts about what wood to use, then make contact with a specialist wood turner's supplier, and tell him your needs. Specify a prepared and turned "blank," as might be used for carving and/or pyrography.

Tools and Equipment
- power carving system (see 6–3 and 6–4)
- set of bits including ⁹⁄₃₂-inch cutter wheel, ⅛-inch straight router bit, tungsten carbide cone burr
- set of diamond point bits including large ball, large ball-nosed cylinder, large taper cylinder, and fine taper cylinder
- woodburning tool with script point
- workbench with a vise
- bench hold-down or holdfast
- pencil and ruler
- one large sheet each of tracing and workout paper—as big as the wood
- ballpoint pen
- pair of compasses
- roll of masking tape
- bench drill press
- selection of Forstner drill bits at ¼-, ⅜-, and ½-inch diameter
- pack of graded sandpapers and a sanding block
- clear wax polish and a lint-free cloth
- dust mask

6-2 *Working drawing—the scale is four squares to one inch. Note the top-to-bottom midline, the overall balance between the lowered ground and the ribbons, and the almost symmetrical design.*

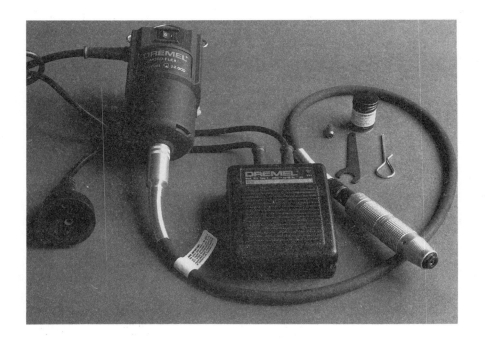

6-3　The Dremel Heavy Duty Flex-Shaft carver kit No. 7360 with a rugged foot control, heavy-duty handpiece, and spanner. Three other Dremel handpieces are available so that you can choose the most satisfying handpiece. The ⅕ HP motor is smooth-running and takes 120 or 220 volts. We also used the Dremel Flex-Shaft tool stand No. 7360 and the Dremel woodburning tool No. 1500.

DESIGN, STRUCTURE, AND TECHNIQUE CONSIDERATIONS

When you have gathered your tools and materials, have a good look at the project picture (see 6–1) and the working drawing (see 6–2). Spend time studying the design. See how the design has been fitted and set within the circle so that there is a nice balance between the ribbon that is left in high relief and the lowered poker-worked ground. These two features—the ribbon and the ground—have been arranged so that they are equal partners.

Note how there are three ribbons in total, with the two near-identical secondary ribbons having branch lines that fork off and run out at the edge of the design.

Put your fingertip on one of the center-of-circle ribbon ends, and trace it through the design. See how it travels alternately over and under itself and the other two ribbons. Study the way that the design is almost—but not quite—symmetrical.

Consider how the total design is arranged so that the grain runs from side to side across the midline. Finally, note how the ground needs to be lowered by no more than about ⅛ inch.

SETTING OUT THE WOOD

When you have a clear understanding of how the design needs to be set out and worked, draw the motif at full size, and make a clear tracing.

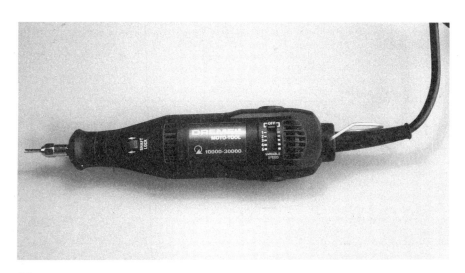

6-4　The Dremel Moto-Tool wood carver No. 395/396 is shown fitted with the straight ⅛-inch router bit. The handheld motor unit uses 120/220 volts and has a variable-speed finger-controlled switch. The Moto-Tool features a quick-change ⅛-inch-diameter collet and a collet wrench. We use this tool for decorating the found box with incised carving in Project 1, and we use it again for carving a miniature lidded box and decorating it with a shell motif in Project 17.

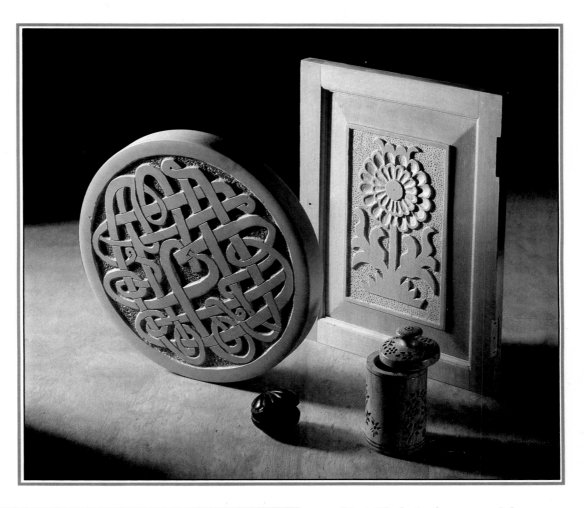

(**Top**) *Clockwise from upper left: Icelandic knot roundel, Project 6; sunflower panel in the American Colonial tradition, Project 4; a carved and painted found container, Project 2; miniature lidded box with a shell motif, Project 17.*

(**Left**) *Mirror frame in the European Primitive tradition, Project 7.*

(Top) *From left to right: a found box decorated with incised carving, Project 1; treen butter stamp, Project 11; shortbread mould carved with a thistle motif, Project 5.*

(Left) *American folk art rooster, Project 3.*

B

(Right) Clockwise from top: running horse plaque in the American weather vane tradition, Project 10; gilt ribbon in the French tradition, Project 8; water dipper ladle in the Pioneer tradition, Project 12; dough bowl in the American folk art tradition, Project 9.

(Left) Duck decoy, Project 15.

(Left) A figure in the African Ashanti tradition, Project 13.

(Above) "Captain Jinks" cigar-store figure, Project 16.

(Right) Mask in the Pacific Northwest Native American tradition, Project 14.

6-5   *Use the drill to clear away the bulk*
of the waste ground.

With the grain running from side to side across the 9½-inch-diameter roundel blank, take a pencil and ruler, and draw a midline that runs at a right angle to the grain. Fix the compass to a radius of fractionally under 4¼ inches, and set the wood out with an inner circle. If all is well, the outer rim should be just a bit wider than ½ inch.

With the inner circle nicely drawn out, align the tracing with the midline, fix it in place with tabs of masking tape, and carefully pencil-press transfer the lines of the design to the wood.

Design Transfer Tip
If you use a ballpoint pen to press the design through to the wood, you will be able to see clearly just where you have been and where you are going. This is vital with a design of this character.

Finally, when you are happy with the way the design has been set out—and when you have reworked the transferred lines until all the curves are smooth and sharp-edged—take a soft pencil and shade in the between-ribbon areas that need to be lowered.

DRILLING OUT THE GROUND

First familiarize yourself with the drill press—how to raise the table bracket, how to adjust the depth stop, and all the safety checks. Then fix the ½-inch Forstner bit in the chuck, and have a tryout on a piece of scrap wood. Adjust the depth stop so that you can sink a ⅛-inch-deep hole. Once you are happy that all is correct, then set to work drilling out the waste ground.

Suggested Order of Work
• Hold the workpiece on the table bracket.
• Wind the table up until the point of the drill is just touching the wood.
• Switch on the power, and sink the first hole in to a depth of ⅛ inch.
• Switch off the power and lower the table.

Continue sinking as many holes as possible—½-inch, then ⅜-inch, and then ¼-inch hole diameters—until you have cleared away the bulk of the waste ground (see 6–5). It's simple enough, as long as you make sure the workpiece is well held down, and that each hole is well placed.

Drill "Routing" Tip
Finally, when you have just about cleared the ground, ask a friend to hold the drill handle down, while you move the workpiece carefully to "rout" out all the little "islands" of waste. Note that using the drill to rout is *only* recommended for tidying up the last few small islands of waste.

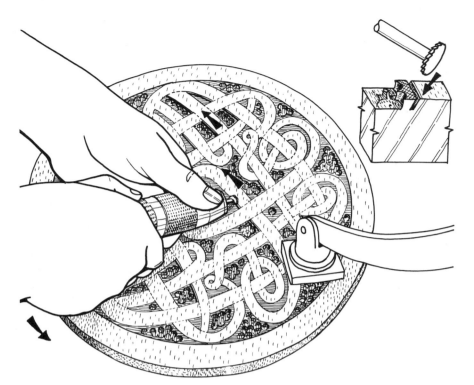

6-6 (Left) Use the high-speed cutter wheel to trench around the design. With the tool held in both hands—one grasping and the other guiding—work with a sweeping pivotal action. Sweep the back of the handpiece around in a smooth arc to avoid having the handpiece vibrate during the cut. (Right) Cut on the waste side of the drawn line.

USING THE FLEX-SHAFT TO SET IN THE DESIGN

When you have cleared away the bulk of the waste ground with the drills, then comes the very satisfying task of defining the edges of the ribbons with the high-speed wheel cutter. This process of defining the drawn lines in readiness to carving out and lowering the waste ground is termed "setting in."

Fit the cutter wheel in the Flex-Shaft handpiece and have a tryout on a piece of scrap wood; draw out a few ribbon shapes and practise cutting smooth curves. I

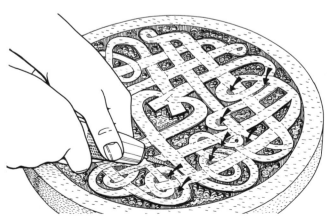

6-7 To prepare for using the router, use the tungsten carbide cone to cut into the small waste areas.

found that the best procedure was to secure the wood with the holdfast, to hold the handpiece with two hands—one grasping and the other guiding—and then to very carefully pivot the tool so that the cutter wheel swings in a natural arc. You will soon discover that by variously moving the workpiece, changing your angle of approach, and adjusting the size of the arc, you will be able to follow a given line.

When you come to cutting the workpiece for real, clamp the wood to the bench and take it nice and slowly (see 6–6). Move both the wood and the tool so that the cutting wheel is presented with the line of next cut, and be careful to cut to the waste side of the drawn line.

Power Carving Tip

If you try, as much as possible, to start and finish at a junction or crossover between two ribbons, then you will be able to minimize the number of jolts and breaks in the curves.

Don't, at this stage, run the little "bridge" lines over the ribbon crossovers. While the Flex-Shaft tool is at hand, fit the tungsten carbide cone in the handpiece, and run pilot holes into the areas of waste that were too small to take the drill bit (see 6–7). Cut the holes to a depth of $\frac{1}{8}$ inch, in readiness for the router.

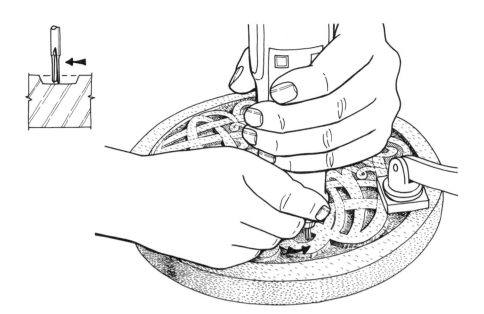

6-8 (Bottom) Fit the ⅛-inch-diameter router straight bit into the Moto-Tool and clamp the workpiece to the bench. (Top left) Work in a counterclockwise direction.

ROUTING OUT THE WASTE GROUND

Start by fitting the ⅛-inch-diameter straight router bit in the Moto-Tool, reading through the manufacturer's instructions and having a tryout on a piece of scrap wood. In use, grasp the tool in one hand with your elbow supported and braced on the work surface—as if you are trying to stab downwards—and then guide the tool with the other hand (see 6–8, bottom).

With the workpiece held securely flat-down on the bench—with a clamp or holdfast—work in a round-and-round counterclockwise direction, all the while aiming to tidy up the bed of the ground to a depth of ⅛ inch (see 6–8, top left). Carefully rout up to the cut line—to the line that you set in with the cutter wheel. It's all pretty straightforward, the only real difficulty being that when you are working in one of the very small between-ribbon areas, you will have to be increasingly careful not to do damage to the edges of the ribbons (see 6–9). Don't split off a short-grained section of ribbon.

6-9 After you have used the router, stand back and consider your progress.

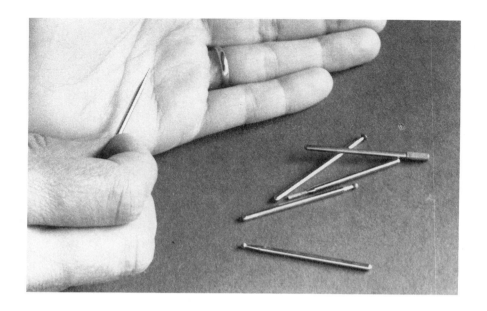

6-10   *The diamond points remove the wood at speed and leave a smooth finish.*

FINISHING WITH THE FLEX-SHAFT TOOL

Go back to using the Flex-Shaft tool, and have a tryout with the diamond points. See how they are easy to control, and they remove the wood speedily and leave a smooth finish (see 6–10). Fit the large ball-nose-cylinder diamond point in the handpiece, and set to work systematically travelling backwards and forwards over the carving, smoothing the lowered ground, carving and defining the ribbon edges, and generally bringing the whole carving to a good finish (see 6–11, top left).

When you have edged the ribbons with the ball-nose point, then change to the large taper cylinder, and further refine and define the ribbon edges by cutting away the broad curve at the plateau edges (see 6–11, top

right). Work the little vertical face between the lowered ground and the ribbons until it looks crisp and sharp. This done, change to the fine taper-cylinder diamond point, and cut in the little "bridge" lines that mark out the crossing or under-and-over details of the ribbons (see 6–11, bottom).

Continue, generally working backwards and forwards over the carving—adjusting and modifying the various curves, corners, and angles—until the ribbon appears to be smooth-flowing in its entirety. If all is well, the total motif should give the illusion that a three-dimensional ribbon has been arranged so that it crosses over and under itself. Keep at it until you are satisfied and everything is crisp.

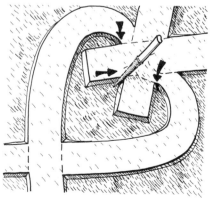

6-11   (Left) Use the large ball-nosed-cylinder diamond point to tidy up the waste ground and to bring the edges of the ribbon to a smooth, clean finish. (Middle) Use the large-taper cylinder to cut back the plateau edges—the edge face of the ribbons. (Right) Use the fine-taper cylinder to cut away the tiny ribbon outlines and to tidy up the crossover lines.

Once you have taken the carving as far as you want it to go, take the sanding block and a sheet of fine-grade sandpaper, and rub down the proud relief areas—the ribbon and the border—to a silky-smooth finish. Work in the direction of the grain, all the while being very careful that you don't do damage to the relatively fragile short-grained ribbon edges that occur on some of the tighter curves.

TEXTURING THE LOWERED GROUND

Clear away all the dust and debris, and clear the work surface in readiness for using the poker tool. Poker-work or pyrography is the technique of burning designs with a heated tool. In the context of this project, poker-work is no more than a way of burning the wood to make it a darker color. Bear in mind that each and every mark counts—there is no going back or rubbing out.

Although there are many forms, the basic pen looks very much like an electric soldering iron. Most tools of this type come with a selection of copper tips. I used the bullet-shaped or "script point" tip. In use, the tool is plugged in, allowed to get hot, and then used like a branding iron. And of course, the longer the hot copper tip is held against the wood, the darker the burn.

When you have had a tryout with the poker, then fit the script point and set to work dotting in the lowered ground. Aim to achieve a swift effect, with all the dots being more or less the same tone and density (see 6–12). Finally, after you have textured the ground, brush on a generous amount of wax polish, and burnish the carving to a high-shine finish. The job is done.

HINTS, TIPS, AND AFTERTHOUGHTS

- Although the high-speed cutter wheel is a swift and efficient cutting tool, its use does require agility and concentration. It is so efficient that we were able to outline the whole design in about twenty minutes.
- If you enjoy using the Moto-Tool as a freehand router, then it might be a good idea to set yourself up with the Dremel Router Attachment No. 230—it's really good for edging, shaping, and grooving.
- If you like working on a small scale, then you can't do better than to get yourself a set of diamond carving points. They are perfect for miniatures—for carving small, sharp, crisp details.
- If you are a raw beginner to using a woodburning poker pen/pyrography pen, then check your tool over, and carefully read the instructions. Never remove screws, wires, or casing panels without first switching off the power and reading the manual.
- BE WARNED—A poker pen is by its very nature potentially dangerous. Never leave it unattended, never fiddle with the wiring when it's switched on, be very careful about fumes, never try to decorate in-flammable plastics, and never wave the tool around when you are giving demonstrations. If you are at all worried about toxic fumes, sparks, or whatever, then wear suitable goggles and/or a mask.
- This carving project is deceivingly tricky in that its success hinges on the design being crisp and clean. Be very careful that you don't split off a short-grained section of ribbon, and try all the while to ensure that the ribbon looks to be a smooth-flowing, three-dimensional wholeness.

6-12   Use the woodburning poker tool to dot-texture the lowered ground.

7

Carving a Mirror Frame in the European Primitive Tradition

7-1   *Project picture. The mirror frame—gouge and touch carved.*

There is a style of early European woodcarving that I think of as being folk primitive. There are all manner of ancient carvings—in churches, on bench ends, chests, and such—that draw their inspiration from pre-Christian scenes, figures, and imagery.

Although, almost certainly, these works are separated from each other by time and culture—from pagan Saxon and/or Scandinavian to primitive Welsh, Cor-

nish, and who knows what—they are all naive, "tribal" renderings of ancient folklore, fables, and myths. To my mind, they all have the same simple, direct, child-like quality.

Estimated Working Time
About four working days

Materials
You need a 1¼-inch-thick slab of easy-to-carve wood—I use lime—at about 24 inches square. This size allows for a small amount of all-round cutting waste.

Although I decided to work the design into a mirror frame (see 7–1 and 7–2), this is not to say that you can't set the carving on a found item, such as the side of a chest, or the back of an old chair, or whatever. No matter what the setting, the wood must be straight-grained, well-seasoned, and free from warps, grain twists, splits, stains, and dead knots.

Tools and Equipment
• power carving system (see 7–3, 7–4, and 7–5)
• set of tungsten carbide burrs
• set of ruby carver points
• workbench
• table, pillar, or bench drill press
• Forstner drill bits at ¼-, ½-, and 1½-inches diameter
• scroll saw
• pair of goggles and a dust mask, or a respirator
• small vacuum cleaner
• bench holdfast or hold-down clamp
• pair of dividers
• pencil and ruler
• one sheet each of tracing and workout paper
• roll of masking tape
• pack of graded sandpapers
• wax polish and a clean cloth

7-2 Working drawing. The scale is four grid squares to
three inches. Note the simple as-it-happens design.

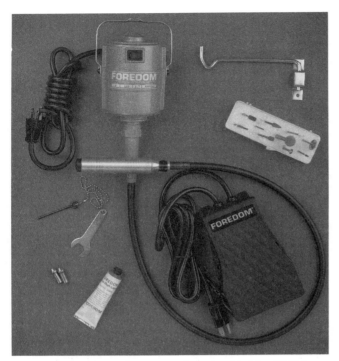

7-3 *The Foredom Electric woodcarving kit No. 5240 is shown with the flexible-shaft motor unit, handpiece, heavy-duty foot pedal, and various tools and accessories. We used this system for carving a shortbread mould with the thistle motif in Project 5.*

DESIGN, STRUCTURE, AND TECHNIQUE CONSIDERATIONS

When you have gathered your tools and materials, have a look at our working drawings (see 7–2). Note how, at a scale of four grid square to three inches, the frame measures about 18 inches wide and 18 inches high, with the opening measuring about 12 inches high and 8½ inches wide at its broadest point.

Apart from deciding at the outset that we wanted the carving to have a straight-line base, a grotesque mask, and a female figure, we tried to let the character of the wood and the naive imagery shape the carving. For example, if you look closely at the project photograph, you will see that we have made features of two knots, and used the easy-to-cut-along-the-grain characteristic of lime to describe the flame-like hair that rises up from the mask. You should let yourself follow your fantasies and the particular character of your wood. You don't need to be literal in using our working drawing.

CUTTING OUT THE BLANK

After you have studied the project picture and the working drawing and made a few swift sketches as to the type of figures and forms that you want to build into the carving, draw the design at full size, and make a clear tracing. This done, press-transfer the design to the wood. Make sure that the profile outline is clear, and shade in the areas that need to be cut away (see 7-6, top left).

Having checked that all is correct, fit the 1½-inch Forstner bit in the drill, and sink four or more pilot holes through the corners of the opening waste (see 7–6, top right). This done, move to the scroll saw and set to work fretting out the basic shape of the frame and the opening. The outside shape is easy enough; you just run the workpiece at an easy pace through the saw and cut away the waste. The opening is a little more tricky in that you have to unhitch the blade.

Scroll Sawing Tip

A smear of furniture wax polish wiped over the scroll saw table reduces wood-to-table friction, and ensures an easy passage.

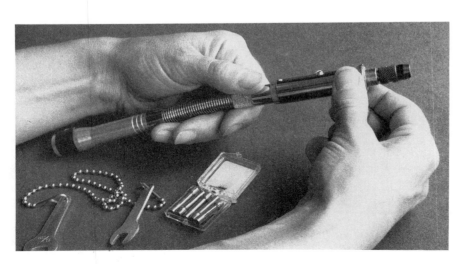

7-4 *The Foredom No. 8AD handpiece. Note the flexible middle section and a sleeve guard that slides over the chuck.*

Cutting the Opening with the Scroll Saw

- Release the tension and unhitch the top end of the scroll saw blade.
- Pass the blade through one or other of the pilot holes.
- Refit the blade and retension.
- Switch on the power and move the workpiece through the saw, so that the line of cut is a little to the waste side of the drawn line, and so that the blade is always presented with the line of next cut (see 7–6, bottom).
- Finally, release the tension and unhitch the blade.

SETTING OUT THE DESIGN AND ROUGHING OUT

When you have used the scroll saw to clear away the bulk of the waste, tape the tracing in place on the workpiece, and transfer all the imagery to the face of the wood. Having studied our drawings and seen how the various details within the design need to be lowered to different depths, shade in and code your design so that you can see at a glance what's going on (see 7–7). For example, if you think that the darkest shading is the deepest at ½ inch and the lightest is more or less the surface wood, then the medium shading can be at ⅜ inch deep, and other shades can mark out the various depths in between. This done, use the ¼-inch and ½-inch-diameter drill bits to lower the most obvious areas

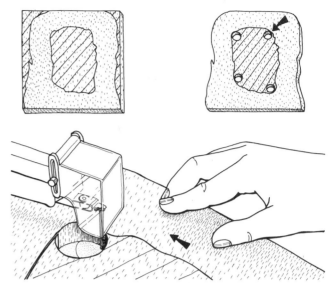

7-6 (Top left) Press-transfer the traced outline to the wood, and shade in the areas of waste. (Top right) Use the 1½-inch-diameter drill bit to clear the four main inside corners of waste. (Bottom) Use the scroll saw to cut out the opening.

of waste—between the top branches, behind the tree nymph's body, and in and around the tree roots.

With the main areas of waste cleared with the drill, set up the power carver. Fit the No. 44 Foredom handpiece to the shaft, clamp the workpiece to the bench,

7-5 Foredom collet set 600—1/32 to 1/8 inch.

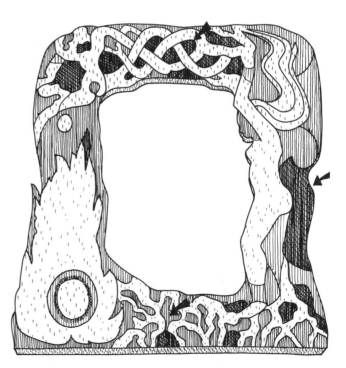

7-7 Press-transfer the basic design to the wood, and shade in and depth-grade the areas that need to be lowered.

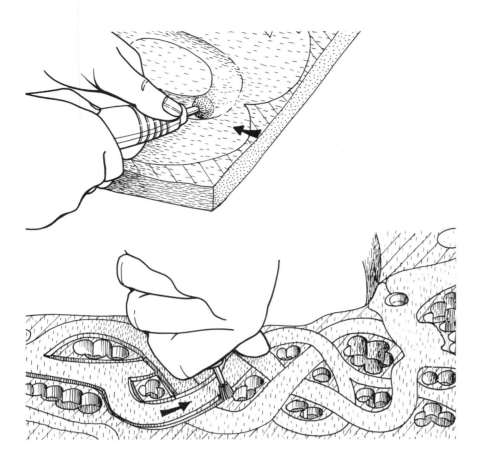

7-8 (Top) Fit the structured carbide ball burr/bit in the handpiece, and carefully lower the area in and around the head. Hold the tool in both hands and remove the waste with a series of stroking passes. (Bottom) Use the vanadium-steel inverted-cone bit to cut V-section trenches around the waste areas to define the shape of the branches and roots.

and be ready with the large carbide burrs. Having fitted the gold-ball burr, start by lowering the "moat" around the flaming head mask (see 7–8, top), the area above the flames, and the deep channel at the back of the figure. Take time to redraw any guide lines that have been cut away.

After using the coarse burrs to clear away the deeper areas of waste, bear in mind that the whole carving process is a continuous one of chopping and changing between the various tool options. Clean up with the vacuum, and redraw the design; then—still working with the large handpiece—fit the vanadium-steel inverted-cone cutter, and start to work the V-trenches that define such details as the branches and roots (see 7–8, bottom).

When you are ready to start working the smaller, more intricate details, fit the flexible Foredom No. 8AD handpiece. With the slender handpiece in place, then comes the pleasuresome task of carving all the small details. Being mindful that you might prefer to use different points, we used the carbide round-edge-wheel burr to lower the face area in front of the nymph's arm and between the branches and roots (see 7–9), as well as the carbide ball-nosed-cylinder burr to undercut the branches and roots (see 7–10). Although the burrs are great, in as much as they hog the waste at speed, they do have a tendency to grab at the wood and run off track. This being so, you do have to use them with care and caution.

Power Carving Tip
For maximum control, and keeping in mind that burrs are a bit wild and "hungry," have the workpiece clamped down on the bench so that you can grasp the handpiece with both hands.

Each time you complete a detail, clear away the dust and debris with the vacuum, prop the workpiece on the bench, stand back, and be super-critical. Ask yourself—could such and such an area be deeper? Are the forms well considered in relation to each other? Are you perhaps overworking a single area? And so on. Take your pencil and redefine the imagery and the next areas to be worked.

Continue to carve, rounding the inner and outer edges of the frame, lowering and shaping the branches and roots so that they appear to pass bridge-like under each other, lowering the nymph's right leg so that it appears to be set farther back in space, lowering the wood at the top of the raised arm so that it runs in a smooth curve through to the branches, and so on (see 7–11).

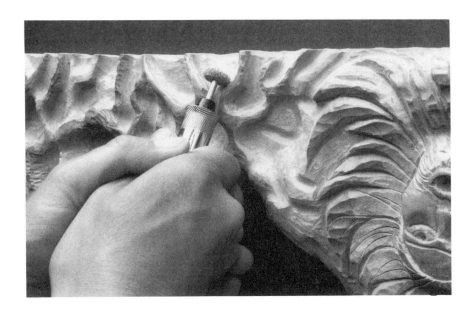

7-9 *Swiftly remove the unwanted wood from between the roots.*

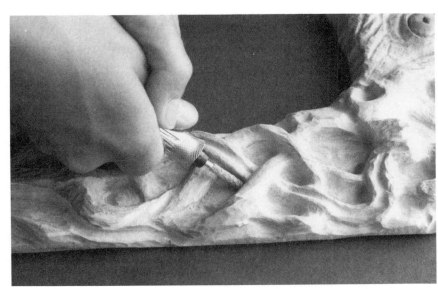

7-10 *Use the structured-tooth ball-nosed-cylinder carbide burr to slightly undercut the branches.*

7-11 *Lower the wood at the top of the raised arm so that it appears to flow naturally into the branches.*

MODELLING THE FORMS WITH THE CUTTERS AND POINTS

After testing out the steel cutters on a piece of scrap wood and adjusting the speed to avoid friction burn, use the cutters to model and carve the details.

Recommended Vanadium-Steel Cutters
- the inverted cone, the cylinder, and the cone cap for the hair/flame and all the other V-section cuts (see 7–12)
- the cone and the drill for the eyes and mouth
- the small ball to carve the inside of the mouth
- the flame for all the undercut areas
- the tree radius for the sloping stepped areas around the figure and around the edges of the head

Once you are pleased with the overall effect left by the steel cutters, then comes the very rewarding stage of using the ruby points to bring the whole carving to a good finish.

Recommended Ruby Points
- the small ball for inside the mouth
- the large ball for inside the edges of the roots and branches
- the tapered ball-nosed cylinder for around the figure
- the egg for around the head and in the various grooves around the roots and branches
- the small bud for the eyes

Continue, choosing and using the ruby point that best fits the task at hand.

FINISHING

After you have used the ruby points to generally bring the whole surface of the carving to a smooth finish, it's time to add all the small details of line and texture that go to complete the design. This procedure is not so much like carving as it is drawing with a pencil. The workpiece can be held and supported with one hand, while you hold and manipulate the tool with the other.

Recommended Fine Points
- the fine-grade flame ruby carver to dapple and texture the tree trunks, the branches, and the areas where the nymph's arms and legs run into the tree (see 7–13)
- the inverted-cone white aluminum oxide abrasive point to texture the hair
- the red aluminum oxide tree point for small, difficult-to-get-to areas

Use the fine points much as you might use a pen or pencil. For example—in the context of the nymph's hair—stroke the point, following the flow of the form. In so doing, further describe the form by drawing in the texture as a series of ripples (see 7–14).

When you have used the full range of tools—from large and coarse to small and fine—then stroke the whole carving over with a sheet of fine-grade sandpaper—in the direction of the grain. Lay on a generous coat of wax polish with a brush, and buff the whole works down to a dull-sheen finish.

Finally, get a mirror tile that is slightly larger than the opening, secure it with clips, fit a hanging wire, and the job is done.

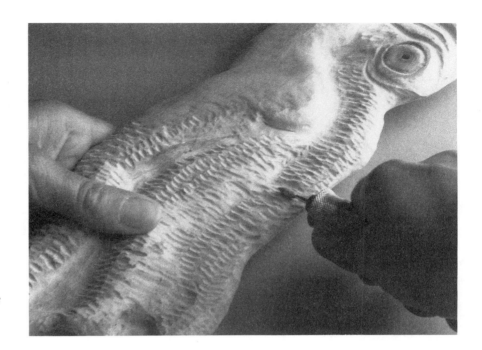

7-13 *Use the fine-flame ruby point to dapple and texture the work—touch-carve by holding the point down against the wood.*

HINTS, TIPS, AND AFTERTHOUGHTS

- With a project of this size and type, the choice of wood is all-important. The wood must cut smooth and be close grained.
- This is one of those projects that allows you to follow your "feelings." Use our design as a guide, and then you can bring your own thoughts and fancies into play as the carving takes shape.
- In many ways, this project is deceptively difficult, in that you can't suddenly become primitive and work in a naive style. My advice is to keep it basic and bold, and try as far as possible to let the carving take you over. If you feel that the design is moving away from being primitive, carry on carving; let your own style and personality take over, and leave the "Where did I go wrong?" inquiries to another day.
- Be careful not to blur the carving by over-sanding.

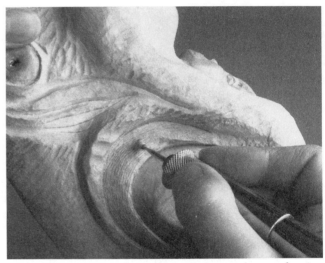

7-14 *Carve the hair by stroking the inverted-cone abrasive point in the direction of the grain.*

8

Carving a Gilt Ribbon Bow in the French Tradition

Primary techniques—gouge and burr carving

8-1 Project picture. The gilt bow—gouge and stroke carved.

"Carved in the French tradition" evokes for me King Louis XVI, Madame de Pompadour, the Sun King, Marie-Antoinette, and all the gloriously carved and gilded bows, ribbons, swags, masks, and knots that decorate the furniture of the Baroque, Rococo, and Revival periods. The gilt bow motif was especially popular among eighteenth-century designers such as Robert Adams and Thomas Hepplewhite. Many decorators and woodworkers today may well view gilded carvings as being vulgar and garish, but I think there is something really beautiful and sumptuous about the gilded carvings of those periods. Decorating our home with a splash or two of gold—a little unrestrained period elegance—might lighten up our lives and do us some good.

Estimated Working Time
5–10 hours

Materials
You need a one-inch-thick slab of easy-to-carve wood about 10 inches long and 4 inches wide, with the grain running along the length (see 8–1 and 8–2). Although the surface of the wood is going to be blanked out with gold paint—wood color and grain pattern aren't impor-

tant—bear in mind that the bow is quite a complex form and the wood must be completely free from structural weaknesses like sappy edges, knots, and splits.

I used lime (linden/basswood), but you may use any easy-to-carve wood like, say, jelutong or holly.

You also need a ⅛-inch-thick piece of best-quality plywood at the same size as your chosen piece of wood.

Tools and Equipment
- power carving system (see 8–3)
- set of ⅛-inch-diameter shank tungsten carbide burrs including a long tree cone, a long cylinder, and a ball head
- set of ⅛-inch-diameter shank high-speed carbide cutters including a long tree cone, a long cylinder, and a ball head
- set of ³⁄₃₂-inch-diameter shank ruby carver points/bits, fine grade, in types small, ball, and flame
- workbench with a vise
- scroll saw
- table, pillar, or bench drill press
- ¼-inch-diameter Forstner bit
- small saw
- pencil and ruler
- one sheet each of tracing and workout paper—slightly bigger than the workpiece
- bottle of white PVA wood glue
- couple of G-clamps
- block of Plasticine
- stick modelling tools
- graded sandpapers
- two small pots of acrylic paint in matt white and yellow-gold
- small quantity of clear high-shine boat varnish
- small soft-haired paintbrush
- dust mask or respirator

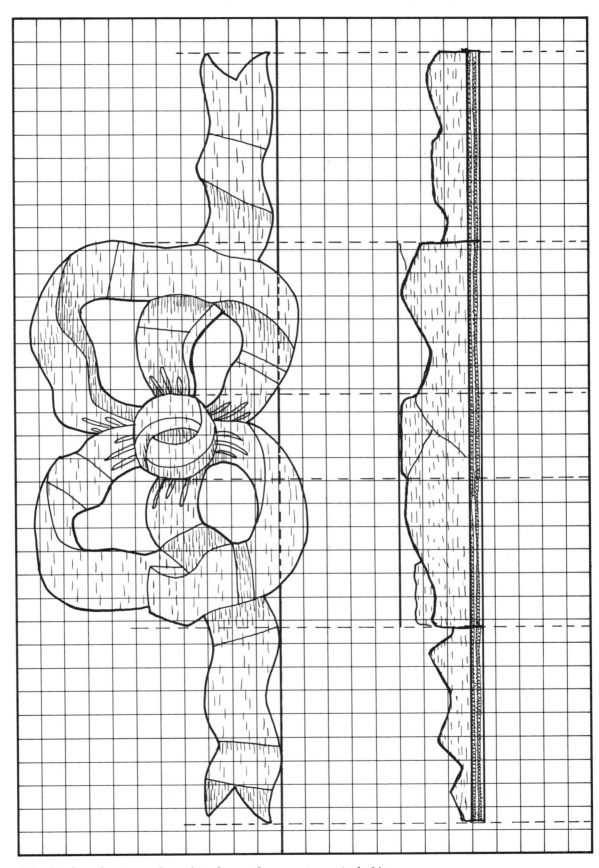

8-2 Working drawing—the scale is four grid squares to one inch. Note
that the cross section shows the ⅛-inch plywood backboard.

DESIGN, STRUCTURE, AND TECHNIQUE CONSIDERATIONS

When you have gathered your tools and materials, take a look at the working drawing (see 8–2). See how, at a scale of four grid squares to one inch, the gilt bow measures about 8½ inches long and 3 inches wide, with an average ribbon width of ¾ inch. Note how the lime wood has been laminated to the ⅛-inch plywood to minimize the chance of the ribbon splitting across the relatively weak areas of short grain. Look at the cross section and see how, in essence, the carving is no more or less than a stylized interpretation of a bow, with the bow image being seen front- or flat-front-on.

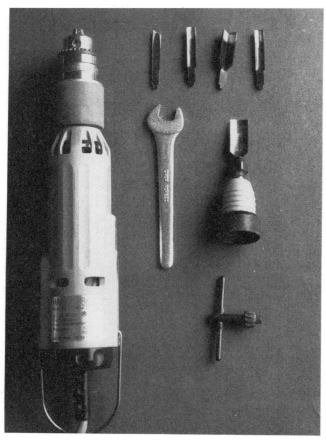

8-3   *The Tokyo Automach Handcraft woodcarving system is shown with the two options—the rotary head with the Jacob's chuck, and the reciprocating head. The unit accepts 100/120/220/240 volts, and it includes a set of five gouge blades. The Handcraft wood carving system supplied by Woodcraft Supply Corp. USA is compact, self-contained, and easy to use. We also use this system to carve a sunflower panel in the American Colonial tradition in Project 4, to carve a water dipper ladle in the American pioneer tradition in Project 12, and to carve a mask in the American Northwest Indian tradition in Project 14.*

Finally, consider how, although we have designed and scaled the bow to fit an existing mirror—with the bottom back edge of the bow being rabbeted so that the ribbon ends sit flat—this is not to say that you can't make it a little bit larger or change the flow emphasis so that it fits your own existing frame.

GLUING UP, MAKING A MAQUETTE, AND SETTING OUT

When you have studied the project picture and the working drawing so that you have a clear understanding of how the project needs to be made and put together, smear a generous amount of PVA glue on both mating surfaces—the lime wood and the plywood. Press the two components together to remove air bubbles and excess glue, and clamp up and leave for 24 hours. While the glue is setting, draw the bow design at full size, and make a couple of identical tracings.

Roll the Plasticine out flat on the workboard so that it's the same size and thickness as your piece of wood. Take one of the two tracings and—after using scissors to cut around the profile—use a sharp-point pencil to indent and line the image in the surface of the soft Plasticine.

With the ribbon bow clearly set out, take a modelling tool and set to work sculpting the shape of the bow. It's all simple enough as long as you appreciate that all you are trying to do is create the illusion that the ribbon realistically twists, turns, ripples, and runs bridge-like over and under itself. Start by cutting out the overall shape, and then lower the primary details—like the two ribbon ends that run from the side to the middle.

Continue adding and taking away—a little bit here and there—until you have achieved a convincing form.

Bow Design Tip
If you want to individualize the bow in some way or other—with initials, a date, or a family motto—then now is the time to do just that.

Finally, when you are happy with the maquette, take the other tracing, and carefully press-transfer the imagery to the top face of your laminated workpiece.

FRETTING AND DRILLING THE BLANK

Once you have made the maquette, pinned up your drawings so that they are clearly within view, and set the wood out with the bow profile, move to the drill press. When you have checked that the drill is in good working order, set a piece of scrap wood under the workpiece, and run a ¼-inch-diameter hole through each of the four enclosed "windows." It's all pretty straightforward as long as you take it at a steady pace, all the while making sure that the drill is well centered within the window of waste (see 8–4, left and top).

Drilling Tip

If, when the bit enters and exits, you run the drill at too high a speed and/or apply too much pressure, then there is a chance that you might tear the surface wood.

Once you have bored out the four pilot holes, move to the scroll saw; fit and tension a fine-toothed blade, and generally make sure that the machine is in good order. The procedures are easy enough as long as you go at it nice and easy. Start by running the work through the saw to swiftly clear away the waste to within ¼ inch of the drawn line (see 8–4, bottom). This done, run the work through the saw at a very relaxed pace, cutting a little to the waste side of the drawn line.

Suggestions for Scroll Sawing

- Make sure that the blade is sharp and well tensioned.
- Don't force the pace to the extent that the blade tears and rips the back face of the plywood.
- Keep the wood moving so that the blade is always ready in advance for the line of next cut.
- Don't try to make a fast turnaround at tight corners—instead, mark time on the spot until the blade has created a little space for itself, and then change direction.

When you come to fretting out the enclosed windows of waste, the procedure is much the same as already de-

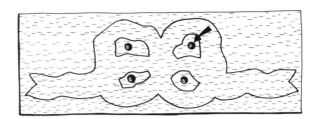

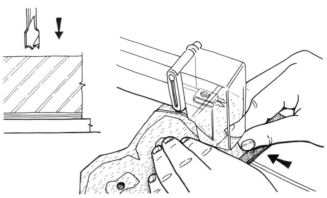

8-4 (Left) Set a piece of scrap wood under the workpiece, and run a ¼-inch-diameter hole through the total wood-plywood thickness. (Top) Drill a centered pilot hole through each of the four "windows" of waste. (Bottom) swiftly clear the waste away to within ¼ inch of the drawn line.

scribed, the only difference being that you have to unhitch the blade. The working order is to release the tension and unhitch the blade, pass the blade through a pilot hole, refit and retension, fret out the waste as described, release the tension, and unhitch the blade—then on to the next hole. Finally, use the small saw to cut the rabbet along the back bottom edge of the bow (see 8–5).

8-5 (Top) The bow at the scroll saw stage. (Bottom) Use a small handsaw to cut the rebate along the underside of the bottom edge.

USING THE RECIPROCATING OPTION— FIRST CUTS

When you have cleared away the bulk of the waste with the drill and saw, then comes the good fun of making the initial carved cuts. When I am making the first few starter cuts, I experience the excitement and challenge perhaps especially because I know that these cuts are going to set the scene for all that follows.

Fit the small U-section gouge in the reciprocating head, tighten up, and then to work. Shade in the four main areas that need to be lowered (see 8–6, top), then run the blade across or at an angle to the run of the grain, and lower the one-inch thickness of lime wood by about ½ inch. With one eye on the Plasticine maquette and the other on the wood, start to remove the waste with a rapid series of shallow cuts. Don't be tempted to chop away the waste in only one or two deep thrusts— make a rapid series of low-angle cuts to remove the wood as fine slivers. Working in this way, not only are you less likely to do damage to the wood, but, more to the point, the little-by-little process will enable you to spend time finding out about the wood, the tool, and your skills.

Initial Cutting Tip

If you are a beginner, then it's a good idea to think of this initial stage as being a gradual lead-in to the project, a time when you can really begin to come to grips with the design, the wood, and the tools.

After you have lowered the two ribbon ends by about ½ inch—and the two little "under-bridge" lengths that run from the side ribbons through to the central knot—then stop awhile. Shade in all the secondary areas that need to be roughed out and lowered (see 8–6, bottom). Grade the shading from dark to light so that the "dark" marks out areas of deep cut and "light" marks out all the little peaks that are halfway between the deep cuts and the surface high relief.

Keeping in mind that the whole object of the exercise is to try and create the illusion of a flowing, undulating ribbon, set to work carving out the primary dips and hollows (see 8–7). It doesn't matter too much if you modify the forms here and there, or even if you make a bit of a mess-up and change the depths of the cuts

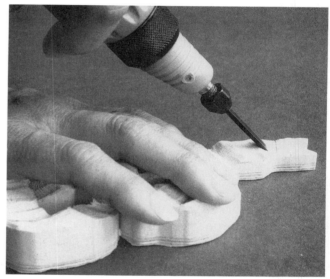

8-7   *Use the gouge to carve the primary dips and hollows.*

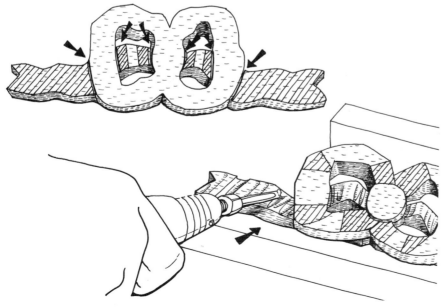

8-6   *(Top) Shade in the four main areas that need to be lowered—leave clean, stepped edges at the ribbon crossover points. (Bottom) Shade in the areas of secondary waste, and further reduce the wood.*

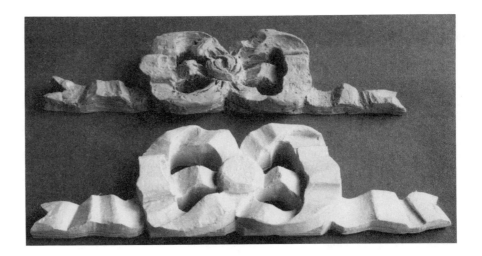

8-8 (Top) The Plasticine maquette. (Bottom) The roughed-out bow.

somewhat, as long as you see to it that you don't cut any closer to the plywood backing sheet than about ⅛ inch.

Continue roughing out the broad lines of the various valleys and peaks, and generally getting closer to the envisaged form, until you reach a point where you need to gear down to a smaller rotary tool. Before you change to a rotary headpiece, use the gouge of your choice to tidy up the rabbet at the bottom edge of the bow. Finally, set the carving alongside the maquette and check your progress (see 8–8).

USING THE ROTARY OPTION— MODELLING THE FORMS

Change over to the rotary option and fit the long tree-point tungsten carbide burr. If you are new to carving, now is the time to have a tryout on some scrap wood.

Power Carving Tip

Since burrs are able to "eat" the wood at an amazing, superfast pace, it's always a good idea to check the tool out on a scrap of wood—the same type as the workpiece—before you start carving.

When you fully appreciate just how fast a burr is able to hog the wood, and when you have decided how best to hold the tool, then start modelling the workpiece in earnest.

With the tool primarily held and angled so that the length of the burr is set across the width of the ribbon, run the tool backwards and forwards over the ribbon to bring the gouged surface to a combed finish (see 8–9). If you come across a difficult-to-work area—a dip or curve that is just too tight for the tree point to handle—then change over to one of the other burrs. Carving the ribbon twists at top and bottom and the center of the

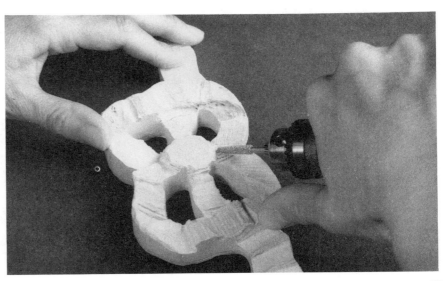

8-9 Use the tungsten carbide tree-point burr to bring the gouged surface to a combed finish.

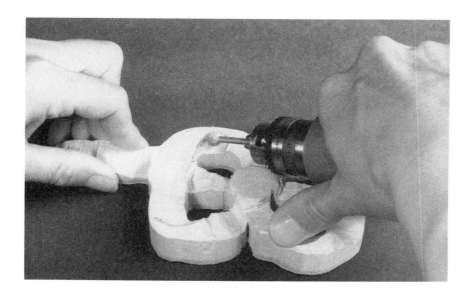

8-10 *Use the small-ball burr to carve the ribbon twists—all the little dips and hollows.*

knot, I found that the best tool was the small ball burr (see 8–10). Work through the range of burrs until the shape is roughed out (see 8–11).

Continue working through the sequence of tools/points—the burrs, the high-speed cutters, and finally the ruby points—all the while bringing the surface of the wood to a more defined finish. If at any point along the way you decide that a particular detail really needs modifying, then all you do is go back to using one of the earlier tools like the gouge or burr.

Power Carving Tip
If you are aiming for a smooth finish, you will need to run through the tool types in sequence—gouges, burrs, high-speed cutters, and ruby points—each time a modification is made.

Use the full selection of ruby points to tidy up and define the details. I used the small ball to define the center of the knot. The small flame was useful to undercut and round off underside edges of the knot, to cut in the various creases and ripple lines, and to detail the slight undercutting that occurs at the point where one ribbon appears to pass under another (see 8–12). Finally, take a small fold of sandpaper, and rub the wood down in the direction of the grain to clean up the details.

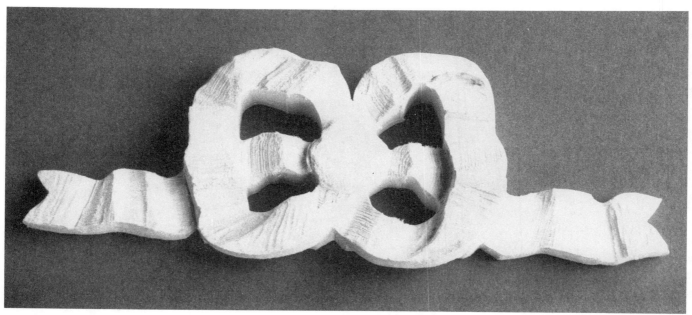

8-11 *The bow after using the tungsten carbide burrs.*

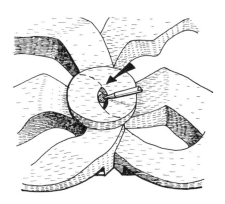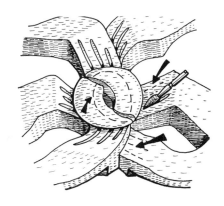

8-12 (Left) Use the small-ball ruby point to define the middle area of the knot. (Middle) Use the small-flame ruby point to undercut and round off the edges of the central knot. (Right) Cut in all the small creases and details.

PAINTING AND FINISHING

With the carving finished, clear away all the debris, and move to the clean dust-free area that you have set aside for painting. Start by giving the whole workpiece a generous coat of matt white acrylic paint. Work it into all the edges and faces, and then put the workpiece to one side to dry. When the paint is completely dry, give the white-painted surface a swift rubdown with the finest sandpaper to remove all the grain hairs and all of the nibs.

Sanding Tip
The more trouble you take with the white paint and the rubbing down with sandpaper, the better the finish. For the best results the wood needs to be sanded down to a smooth finish at each stage—before the white painting, after the white paint has dried, after the gold painting, and so on.

After waiting for the white paint to dry and harden, lay on two coats of gold paint. Finally, when the gold paint is dry, give the whole workpiece a couple of coats of clear varnish. The bow is ready to be fitted in place—over a mirror, or maybe on the bedboard, or over the front door, or . . .

HINTS, TIPS, AND AFTERTHOUGHTS

- This is a beautifully flexible project, in that the bows can be designed and carved to suit your own particular whims and fancies. If you want to make the bow bigger, or with ripples, or as a rosette, or have a series of bows with streamers, or whatever, then all you need to do is stay with the overall working methods, but change the design details to suit.
- If you like the idea of the gold bows, but want to go for something really special and authentic, you could apply gold leaf rather than gold paint.
- The whole idea of backing the lime with plywood is so that you can work at speed without worrying about the wood splitting. If you are prepared to be more picky about your choice of wood, and if you are happy to work at a much slower speed, then you could leave out the plywood.
- When you come to painting and finishing, the simple rule of thumb is the thinner the layers—the white undercoat, the gold paint, and the varnish—and the more effort you put into rubbing down with fine-grade sandpaper between coats, then the smoother the finish.
- When you are using the reciprocating option, you might well need to use clamps or screw-blocks to hold the workpiece down on the bench.

9

Carving a Dough Bowl in the American Folk Art Tradition

Primary techniques—gouge carving

9-1   Project picture. The dough bowl—gouge carved.

Not so long ago, carved wooden dough bowls were a common sight in kitchens (see 9–1). Such bowls were important on several counts. First of all, as bread-

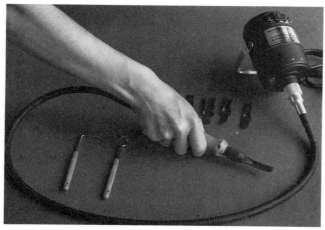

9-2   The Wood Carvers Supply ABCD Mastercarver No. 797030 is shown with the reciprocating handpiece, a selection of gouges, and two wrenches. The ¼ HP 115-volt unit runs in both forward and reverse rotation. This feature is especially useful for left-handed carvers. This project only uses the reciprocating option with the five gouge blades. The system is efficient, smooth-running, and uncomplicated. We also use this system to carve a figure in the African Ashanti tradition in Project 13.

making was a daily chore, they were used for mixing and kneading. Once the dough had been kneaded, it was left in the bowl and set in a warm corner of the kitchen to rise. I can clearly remember my Welsh grandmother in her dark old kitchen—a vast stone sink on which she sharpened her knives, a huge dresser covering one wall, a gigantic iron stove with a big iron kettle on the simmer, and her at the table with a bowl in her lap rolling out a huge flap of dough.

Dough bowls have been much-treasured possessions, particularly since they were traditionally carved by prospective husbands as love tokens—like love spoons and chests—and eventually passed down through the family.

Materials
You need a two-inch-thick slab of hard, smooth, dense-grained wood at about 12 inches long and 8 inches wide, with the grain running along the length. Select an uncomplicated wood such as birch, cherry, maple, poplar, sycamore, or walnut, with the outer tree rings or pith/bark face being at the bottom of the bowl.

Tools and Equipment
• power carving system including gouge set (see 9–2)
• workbench with a vise
• band saw
• table, pillar, or bench drill press
• selection of Forstner bits
• clamp or bench holdfast
• pencil and ruler
• large black pencil or wax crayon
• one sheet each of tracing and workout paper—slightly bigger than the workpiece
• roll of masking tape
• pack of graded sandpapers
• dab of butter and a clean cloth

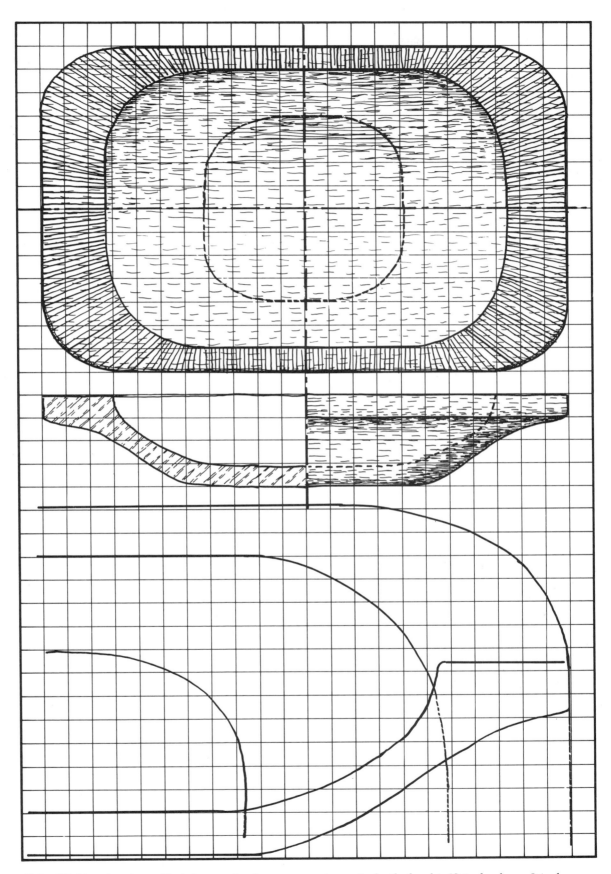

9-3 *Working drawings. (Top) At a scale of two squares to one inch, the bowl is 12 inches long, 8 inches wide, and 2 inches thick. (Bottom) Quarter detail at a scale of four squares to one inch.*

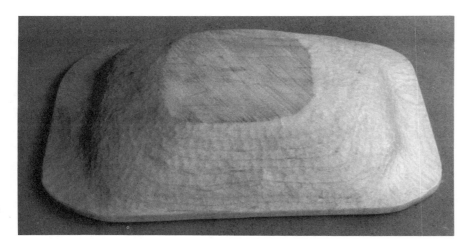

9-4   *Underside and bottom of the bowl.*

Estimated Working Time
10–12 hours

Wood Selection Tip
If you are going to use the bowl in the kitchen, then it's most important that you avoid toxic woods like yew. If you have any doubts at all, then ask the advice of a specialist wood supplier.

When you are choosing your wood, look for a piece that is free from end splits, knots, sappy edges, and warps. Give the wood a good looking over; spike it with your fingernail or a small penknife to search out soft areas. Give it a good sniff to make sure that it is sweet-smelling.

DESIGN, STRUCTURE, AND TECHNIQUE CONSIDERATIONS

When you have gathered your tools and materials, take a look at the working drawings (see 9–3). See how our finished bowl measures 11 inches long, seven inches wide, and a fraction under two inches from the base line to the top of the rim. Note how, in plan view, the side is ½ inch wide, while the end rim is 1¼ inches wide. The extra width of wood at the ends not only makes for extra "body" at what is a somewhat short-grained and fragile part of the structure, it also serves as a handle.

Have a close-up look at the side view profile and the cross section; notice that the shape and form are a direct result of bowl usage, tool function, and the woodcarver choosing to clear away the waste in the most efficient way possible. For example, the outside has been swiftly cleared with the deep U-section gouge and left in the tool-textured state (see 9–4). The inside hollow has been swiftly cleared with the small gouge and then further finished with a smaller shallower gouge before being rubbed down with graded sandpapers. Because

the bowl is used for food and so is repeatedly washed, the wood is actually finished with a blob of butter to seal the grain.

SETTING OUT THE DESIGN

After you have studied the project picture and the working drawing, and when you have a clear understanding as to the order of work, draw the views at full size—the plan, the side and end views, and the section—and finalize the shape of the various curves.

Draw midlines from end to end and side to side around your slab of wood. Take a tracing from your working drawing, and then pencil-press transfer the plan and base views to the wood. If all is well, you should have drawn out a total of seven round-cornered rectangles. There are three on the top face of the wood—one at 11 inches long and seven inches wide for the outside-rim profile, one at nine inches long and six inches wide for the inside-rim profile, and one at 4¼ inches long and four inches wide for the inside-bottom-of-bowl. Last, there is a single small rectangle on the bottom of the wood at 4¼ inches long and four inches wide for the base of the bowl (see 9–5).

USING THE BAND SAW TO ROUGH OUT THE PROFILE

Once you have drawn the imagery out on the wood and checked that all is correct, then comes the exciting but slightly tricky task of using the band saw to cut away the bulk of the waste.

Band Saw Tip
I say "tricky" not because this is a difficult procedure—it's not—but rather because it is potentially very dan-

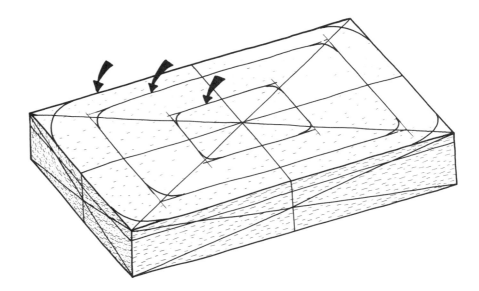

9-5 *Draw in the end-to-end and side-to-side midlines, and the plan view with a total of three round-cornered rectangles—the outside profile, the inside-rim profile, and the bottom-of-bowl profile.*

gerous. It's a good idea to familiarize yourself with the machine and to check that it's in good working order. Make sure the saw blade is correctly fitted; see to it that the on/off switch is working; make certain that the upper blade guide is correctly adjusted; and make sure you yourself are ready.

When you are happy that is all correct, run the workpiece through the machine, and cut out the primary outside-rim form. Don't rush; don't force the wood through; just take it nice and easy, cutting a little to the waste side of the drawn line.

DRILLING OUT THE INSIDE-BOWL WASTE

Having cut the bowl to shape, have a look at the working drawing again—at the cross section—and see how, at an inside-bowl depth of 1½ inches, the base thickness is

½ inch. Check out the drill to make sure that it's in good order, and then go to work.

With the two-inch-diameter Forstner bit securely fitted, and with the depth-stop set to 1½ inches, clamp the bowl slab top-side-up on the worktable. This done, bore out four holes to sink the central area of waste—the inside bottom of bowl down to a depth of 1½ inches. Place the four holes so that the circumference more or less establishes the corners of the sunken area. While the drill is at hand, remove a skim of waste from the whole inside-bowl area (see 9–6).

Drilling Tip
If you only have a one-inch-diameter Forstner bit, then no problem; all you do is modify the procedure and clear the waste by drilling sixteen or so holes. The good thing about a Forstner bit is that as long as the point can be set on wood to be drilled, you can overlap holes.

9-6 *Use the Forstner drills to clear away the bulk of the inside-bowl waste.*

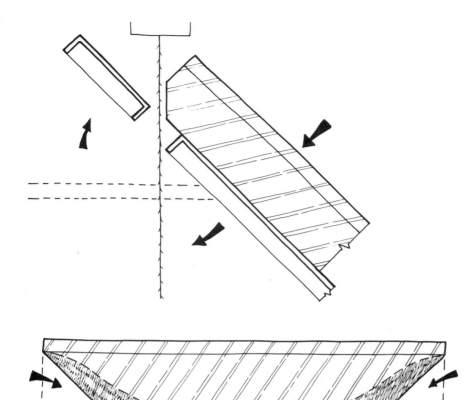

9-7   (Top) With the band-saw table set
to an angle of 45 degrees, repeatedly run
the workpiece through the saw to cut away
as much waste as safety allows. (Bottom)
Shade in the area of waste that needs to
be cleared with the reciprocating gouge.

ROUGHING OUT THE PROFILE ON THE BAND SAW

Once you have established the depth of the inside of the bowl and cleared away the bulk of the inside-bowl waste, then move back to the band saw and set to work clearing away the outside-bowl waste. Tilt the table to an angle of 45 degrees, and tighten up the tilting lock. This done, take a pencil and ruler and run a line ½ inch down from the rim of the bowl—a line that runs right around the two-inch-wide edge of the slab.

With the wood positioned face-up on the worktable, set to work trimming away slivers of waste. Look at the working drawing, and you will see that from the line of the side edge the outside face of the bowl is sharply undercut and angled so that it runs down to the 4¼-inch by four-inch base.

Band Saw Tip

Being very, very careful that your fingers are always well away from the blade, and having the upper blade guide as low as possible, repeatedly run the slab through the saw to pare slivers of waste from what will be the underside rim of the bowl (see 9–7, top). Don't be tempted to try to remove the waste in one great slice; settle for making repeated passes until you reach the outside-rim line.

Continue to turn, push, and slice—turn, push, and slice—turning, maneuvering, and slicing away the waste to cut more or less in a straight line from the outside rim to the base line.

CARVING THE OUTSIDE

After you have removed the bulk of the outside waste with the band saw—and have noted carefully just how much more waste needs to be cut away (see 9–7, bottom)—then move to the bench and position and clamp the workpiece rim-side-down. Fit the quick-change reciprocating handpiece to the shaft; then fit the broad gouge and begin to work (see 9–8). The procedure is beautifully simple; all you do is gouge-carve from the base line down to the rim line until you have achieved what you consider is a good, smooth curve.

Continue working around the curved-corner base, establishing the line of the base and cutting down to the rim line. And, of course, once you have cleaned up one area, turn the bowl around a few degrees and set to work on another side (see 9–9). With the bowl in the upside-down position, it's a simple process of trying to achieve a smooth, curved slope.

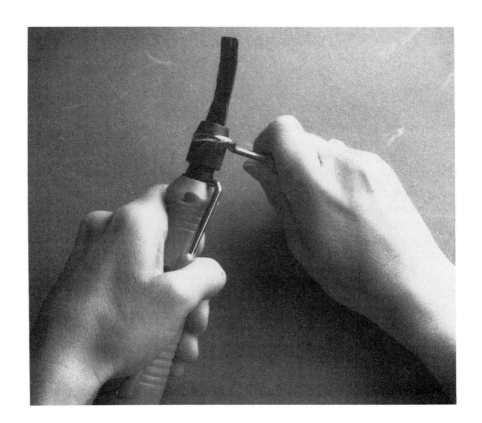

9-8 *Fit the broad gouge in the hand-piece, and tighten up with the wrenches.*

Power Carving Suggestions
- Don't try to remove too much wood at a single stroke.
- Keep the gouge blades sharp.
- Don't overwork any single area in isolation.
- Stand back from your work and assess your progress.
- Don't run the tool towards your body.
- Keep repositioning the workpiece so that you are always presented with the best angle of cut, and be aware of the grain direction.

9-9 *Work the underside of the bowl to a nicely tooled finish.*

CARVING THE INSIDE

Once you have achieved a fair outside profile, then turn the workpiece over so that it is rim-side-up, and set work clearing out the waste. In many ways the procedure is much the same as carving the outside. The only real difference is that, although you also work so that the tool is pointing from side to center, you actually start at the center and back up until you reach the line of the rim (see 9–10, top). That is, you chop away the waste from around the drilled holes and then retreat towards the rim line, removing the waste as you go.

After clearing away the bulk of the waste, tidy up by carving from the inside edge of the rim down-and-in towards the bottom of the bowl. Again, don't try to scoop the wood out in great chunks, but rather remove the waste by taking out lots of small, shallow cuts.

Every now and again along the way, test the thickness of the bowl walls with your thumb and fingers. Much will depend on the use to which the bowl is going to be put, but aim for an average thickness of about ½ inch; that is, about ½ inch thick at the top of the rim and at the side of the base, and then maybe slightly thinner at the center of the base and halfway up the sides.

Power Carving Tip

If you decide that the inside curve of the bowl is just about right, but feel that the walls of the bowl are still a bit thick and heavy, then all you do is flip the bowl over. With the outside uppermost, remove a little more wood from the outside face.

When you are happy with the inside of the bowl, fit the smaller bent gouge in the handpiece. Work backwards and forwards over the inside surface, all the while reducing the size of the tool-mark ripples and aiming for a good, smooth surface (see 9–10, bottom).

CARVING THE RIM AND FINISHING

Once you are happy with both the outside and inside faces of the bowl, fit the smallest, narrowest gouge in the handpiece. Set to work cutting the decorative finish along the rim. Don't fuss around; do no more than run a line of side-by-side cuts around the rim that appear to radiate out from the center towards the outside edge of the rim. Don't go too deep—just enough to make a confident mark (see 9–11).

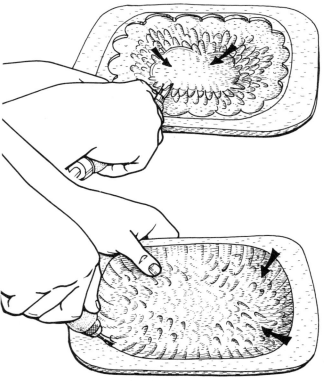

9-10 (Top) Start clearing the wood from the center and work backwards to the rim line. (Bottom) Use the smaller gouge to rework the inside of the bowl, all the while reducing the size of the tool marks.

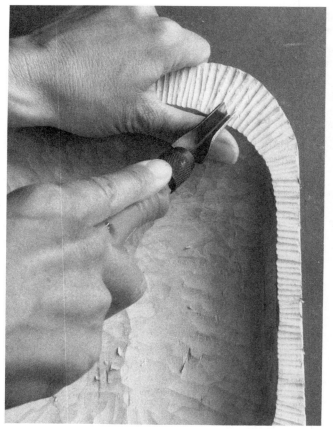

9-11 Use the V-tool to cut the decorative finish on the rim.

92

9-12   *The bowl is ready to sand smooth.*

After working the inside to a good tooled finish, the outside to a delicately scalloped tooled finish, and the rim to a rippled furrow finish, stand back and take time to have a critical look at the total bowl (see 9–12). When you have what you consider is a fair bowl, take a sheet of fine-grade sandpaper and rub down the edge of the bowl until it's smooth to the touch. Don't overwork the edge or blur the marks left by the tool; just remove splinters and rough or sharp edges. Next, sand down the inside of the bowl to a really good, smooth finish (see 9–13).

Finally, having levelled, dated and signed the base— and taken the bowl as far as you want it to go—wipe the bowl out with a blob of butter and a dribble of milk over all surfaces. Let it soak in, and then burnish the bowl to a dull-sheen finish.

Finishing Tip

Traditionally the bowls were variously sealed by being wiped with fat or walnut oil boiled in milk, and so on. If you are going to use the bowl in the kitchen, then just be sure to use a nontoxic vegetable finish.

HINTS, TIPS, AND AFTERTHOUGHTS

- Since this bowl is a traditional form, variations of which can be found all over the world—Sweden, America, Britain, France, and elsewhere—it is, by its very nature, a swift and direct piece to carve.
- Don't try this project with a second-best piece of wood. If the wood looks in any way to be split or knotty, then put it to one side and look for another piece. There's nothing worse than getting to the half-way stage and having to throw the piece away because of splits, loose knots, or whatever.
- When you are fitting a gouge in the handpiece, be sure to clench the chuck up with the two wrench tools—not so tight that you strip the thread, but just tight enough to stop the blade moving in its slotted housing.
- If by chance you discover a small cavity when the carving is underway—or the wood starts to develop small splits—then either accept them as being within the spirit of the dish or make do with a filler mixture of glue and sawdust.
- If you are in a hurry, then you can use a large flap-wheel sander to rub down the inside of the bowl.

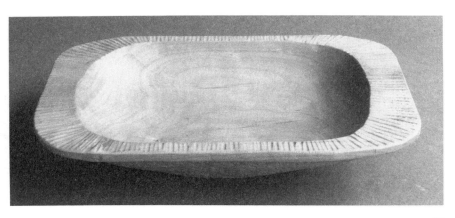

9-13   *Sand the inside of the bowl to a good, smooth finish.*

10

Carving a Running Horse in the American "Weather Vane" Tradition

Primary techniques—gouge and touch carving

10-1   Project picture. The horse—gouge and touch carved.

If we were able to go back in time to an early American small town or village—and discount such obvious changes as the lack of power lines, cars, and highway signs—we just might be struck by how almost all the important buildings were bristling with weather vanes. If early paintings and illustrations are anything to go by, the Colonial Americans favored a few basic designs— arrows, Indians, roosters, fish, and horses—whereas after Independence, the fashion shifted slightly so as to include soldiers, Liberty figures, and eventually steam locomotives.

In the context of woodcarving, it's interesting to note that even in the mid-nineteenth century, when commercial mass-produced metal weather vanes were all the fashion, woodcarving was still a primary part of the design and manufacture process. It was the task of the woodcarver to make the initial pattern or "master" from which a single iron mould was cast, and from which all the other vanes were made.

Our horse plaque carving (see 10–1 and 10–2) draws its inspiration from the carved wooden master that was created for the now famous Black Hawk weather vane— made in New York circa 1870.

Estimated Working Time
10–14 hours

Materials
You need a slab of prepared ⅞-inch-thick wood 8½ inches wide and about 26 inches long, with the grain running along the length. Although we chose to use a piece of old salvaged mahogany—because the grain was uncomplicated, and because we were looking for a natural dark-brown horse-like color—we could just as well have used a light-colored wood such as lime, jelutong, or holly. If you do decide to go for a pale wood, then you can either settle for having a light-colored image or stain or paint it. Color apart, the wood must be straight grained.

Tools and Equipment
- power carving system with set of five gouge blades (see 10–3)
- set of diamond points including two ⅛-inch-diameter shank cylinders, one large and one fine taper, and a ³⁄₃₂-inch-diameter shank bud
- ½-inch and ⅜-inch minidrum fine-grit sanders
- set of three ⅛-inch-diameter shank vanadium-steel cutters in flame, inverted cone, and small cylinder shapes
- ³⁄₃₂-diameter shank ruby carver in flame shape
- workbench with a vise
- scroll saw
- set of four G-clamps or a bench holdfast
- pencil and ruler
- one sheet each of tracing and workout paper—slightly bigger than the workpiece
- roll of masking tape and PVA glue
- pack of graded sandpapers
- wax polish and a cloth
- pair of goggles and a dust mask, or a respirator

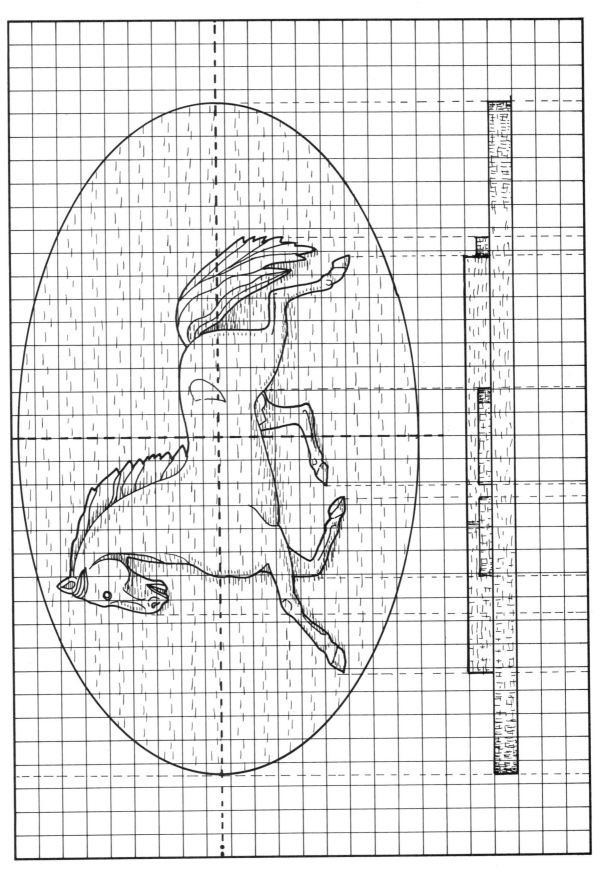

10-2 Working drawing. At a scale of two grid squares to one inch, the plaque measures about 14½ inches long and 8 inches high. Note the direction of the grain and the cross section.

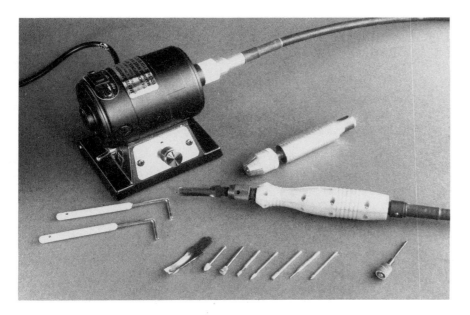

10-3 *The Wood Carvers Supply ABC Portable Mastercarver No. 797042 is shown with rotary and reciprocating carving options—the rotary handpiece, the reciprocating handpiece, a couple of gouges, a selection of points, a sanding drum, and two wrenches. The ¼ HP 115-volt motor runs in both forward and reverse rotation. This feature is especially useful when carving and rounding an edge on a raised profile. The quick-change handpieces are swift and easy to use. The bench unit has a rugged metal base and nonslip rubber feet.*

DESIGN, STRUCTURE, AND TECHNIQUE CONSIDERATIONS

When you have gathered your tools and materials, take a look at the working drawing (see 10–2). See how, at a grid scale of two grid squares to one inch, the oval-shaped plaque is 14½ inches long and about 8½ inches wide, with the horse being about 10 inches long and seven inches high. Note the way in which the traditional procedure of lowering the ground has been updated—the horse profile has been first fretted out and then mounted on the ground. Right from the start the horse is standing in high relief.

Consider how, with the grain running through the horse from nose to tail, the fragile short-grained areas on the legs have been kept to a minimum.

If, when you are choosing your wood, you take along the tracing of the horse, you will be able to see if the horse profile fits the grain. Make sure that the relatively delicate legs are completely free from knots or other defects.

SETTING OUT THE DESIGN AND FRETTING OUT THE PROFILE

After you have studied the design, and perhaps modified the horse profile and/or the oval shape to suit your needs, draw the design at full size. Pencil-press transfer the imagery to your chosen length of wood (see 10–4, top). Make sure that both the oval and the horse are arranged so that they use the wood to best advantage, and so that the grain runs as described.

When you are happy that all is well, move to the scroll saw, and set to work fretting out the two elements. Of course both the horse and the oval need to be cut with equal care, but in many ways the oval will require more attention. I say this because if you make a little slip-up when cutting out the horse, it's not going to show too much, whereas a little kink or wobble with the oval is going to stand out like a sore thumb. This being so, spend that much more time making sure that the oval is as near perfect as possible (see 10–4, bottom).

Suggested Work Order
• Make sure that the scroll saw is in good working order.
• Run the wood swiftly through the saw, and clear away the bulk of the rough.
• Gently feed the wood through the saw so that the blade is oriented correctly inline with each cut and so that the line of cut runs slightly to the waste side of the drawn line.

If at any time along the way, the wood cuts up rough, then either the blade needs changing or you may be forcing the pace and pushing the wood through too fast. And then again, it may be that the wood is damp and/or the blade needs retensioning.

Scroll Saw Tip
If you are new to using a scroll saw, spend as much time as possible prior to working on the project playing around with scrap wood. Test your skills by cutting out coin-sized circles.

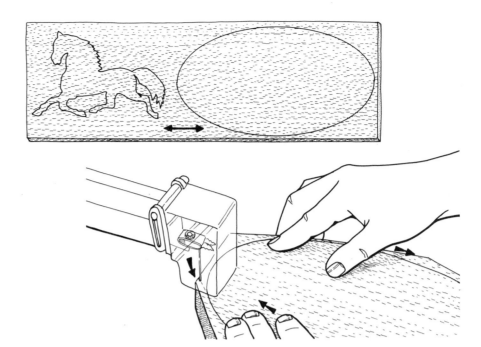

10-4　(Top) Having noted the direction of the grain, transfer the imagery to your chosen length of wood. (Bottom) Guide the wood with both hands, making sure you cut a little to the waste side of the drawn line.

Once you have fretted out both pieces, take the graded sandpapers and rub down the edges of the oval and the back of the horse.

CARVING THE GROUND AND GLUING UP

After cleaning up the horse profile and the background, set the horse down on the oval, and move it around until you feel that it is positioned to best effect. Draw around the horse, shade in the resultant image (see 10–5, top), and then put the horse to one side out of harm's way.

Secure the oval board to the workbench, fit the reciprocating handpiece on the flexible shaft, and check out the machine just to make sure that it is in good, safe order. This done, fit the small U-section gouge, and start carving and texturing the unshaded around-horse area (see 10–5, bottom). We have gone for simple vertical tooling to give the effect of grass. Hold the tool at a low angle, and be very careful not to cut too deep and not to cross into the shaded area. Work systematically across the ground, trying all the while to achieve an even texture.

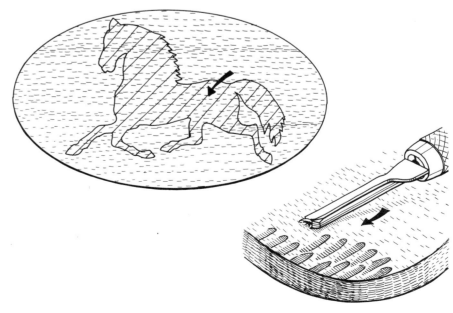

10-5　(Top) Draw around the horse, and shade in the resultant image. (Bottom) Fit the small U-section gouge, and texture the background around the horse. Hold the tool at a low angle, and work systematically across the ground—try to keep the texture even.

10-6 The horse profile has been glued in place on the textured background.

When you have tooled the ground, push a couple of dressmaking pins into the middle of the shaded area and clip off the heads, leaving two points standing proud by about one-eighth of an inch. Next, smear PVA glue on both the shaded ground and the back of the horse, and press the horse in place. Wipe away excess glue and clamp.

Gluing Tip
If you intend to fasten the horse plaque out of doors—say, on a stable door—then make sure that you use waterproof PVA glue.

ROUGHING OUT THE HORSE

Once the glue is dry, remove the clamps (see 10–6), and then use masking tape to protect areas of ground that are at risk from tool-slip. Take the original tracing, align and fix it to the horse, and carefully pencil in the primary lines of the design—the tail, the mane, and the cross-over points of the legs. Shade in the areas that need to be lowered (see 10–7, top).

Using the reciprocating handpiece with the chisel blade, sink stop-cuts around the top of the neck/mane, at the point where the tail meets the body, and at the crossover points on the two legs. Make the cuts to a depth of about ¼ inch (see 10–7, bottom). Change to

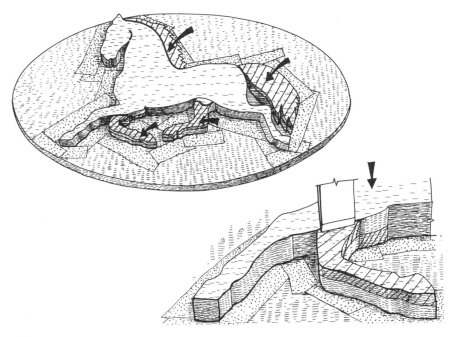

10-7 (Top) Shade in the areas that need to be lowered—the mane, the tail, and the two background legs. (Bottom) Use the chisel to make stop-cuts at the crossover points on the two legs. Run the cuts in to a depth of about ¼ inch.

the medium-size U-section gouge, and sink small stop-cuts at the back edge of the cheek.

Fit the small U-section gouge in the handpiece, and start very carefully to lower the waste areas. Lower the tail so that it slopes and tapers towards its end, lower and slope the mane, lower the neck so that the jaw/cheek stand in relief (see 10–8), lower the ears, lower the legs, and so on. And of course, if, when you have lowered such and such a detail, you need to deepen a stop-cut, then go back to using the small chisel.

Continue deepening a stop-cut here, shaping, rounding, and lowering a detail there, and so on, until the horse begins to take shape. You will need to lower the wood on the mane, tail, and "background" legs by about one-eighth of an inch. The tail and mane will need further reducing on the outer edges so that they slope and taper away from the body of the horse, and so that they finish up by being about ⅜ inch thick.

Power Carving Tip
Be very careful on areas of short grain—at the end of the tail and the points of the ears—that you don't split away the wood and spoil the image.

MODELLING THE DETAILS WITH THE ROTARY HANDPIECE AND THE HIGH-SPEED CUTTERS

Change to the rotary handpiece, and be sure to wear a dust mask or respirator to protect you from the fine-mahogany dust. Fit the high-speed inverted-cone cutter and start to define and crisp up the detail—the lines between the body and the tail and mane, and at the point where the body steps down to meet the legs. Switch to reverse rotation when you come to carving the tip of the tail (see 10–9, top).

When you have tidied up with the cone, change over to the small cylinder, and take the modelling a bit further by reducing the waste on the head, defining the ears and the mane, lowering the area between the cheek and the nose, and cutting in the mouth slot. When you have finished this stage, carefully peel and ease away the masking tape.

Power Carving Tip
When you come to modelling the eye and socket, leave the areas around the eye and the nostril as raised ridges. If at any point you are at all puzzled as to how such and such a feature might look when it has been carved, then take a little scrap of Plasticine and make a detailed maquette.

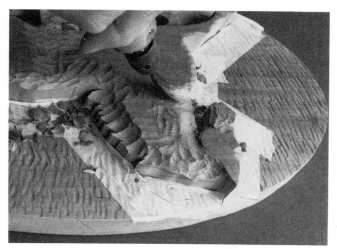

10-8   *Having protected the ground with strips of masking tape, use the U-section gouge to carefully lower the waste areas.*

When you have reduced the main bulk of the modelling with the high-speed cutters, then fit the flame ruby point, and work backwards and forwards over the horse, all the while gradually reducing and smoothing the surface. Don't try to achieve a sophisticated naturalistic image; stay with a form that is naively stylized.

Continue to carve—cutting the nostril and ear holes, rounding off the hooves and the legs, reducing the tricky little area between the front legs (see 10–9, bottom), rounding off the ends of the tail and separating the ears.

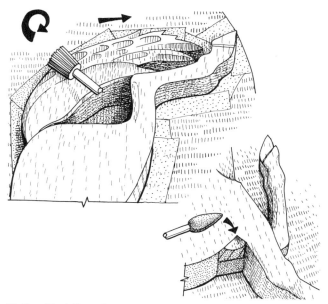

10-9   *(Top) Switch to reverse rotation and reduce the feathered tip of the tail. (Bottom) Use the flame ruby point to cut back the tricky little area between the front legs.*

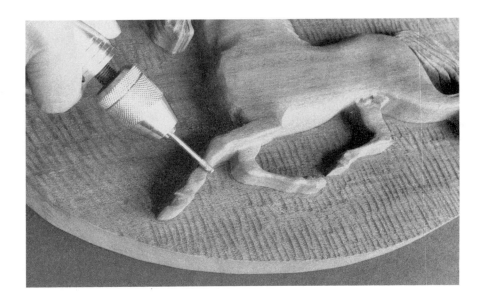

10-10 *Use the long-cylinder diamond point to model the leg muscles.*

CUTTING VERY FINE AND FINISHED DETAILS

Once the horse has been modelled and detailed using cutters and ruby points, then comes the pleasuresome task of using the diamond points to cut in the very fine and finished details. Of course, you could use the ruby points for this task, but for this project we favor using the diamond points, because not only do they "eat" the waste at speed, but, more than that, they leave the wood looking smooth and finished.

Use the large-cylinder point for modelling the mus-

cles on the legs and face (see 10–10), the large V-cuts on the mane and tail, and for the hoof ridges on the sides of the legs.

When you come to the final detailing and finishing, work through the selection of fine-taper diamond points. Hold the tool in one hand and steady it with the other (see 10–11). Then variously turn the workpiece and/or change your direction of approach so that the tool is always presented with the line of best cut. Working in

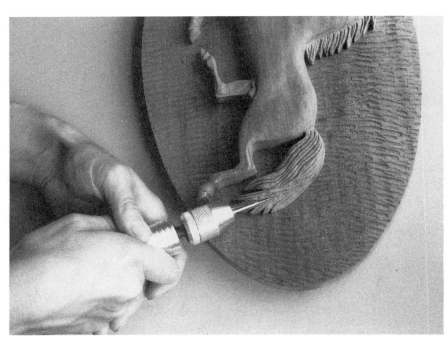

10-11 *Hold the tool in one hand, and steady it with the other.*

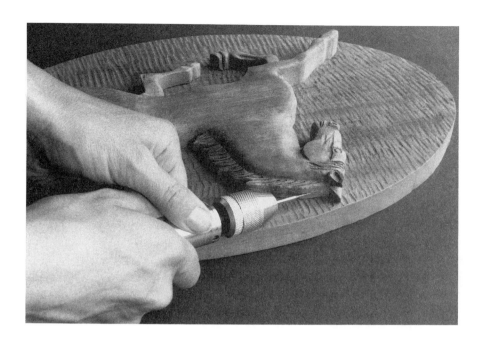

10-12 *With the mane facing towards your carving hand, draw the point slowly towards your body.*

this way, cut in the fine details of the eye, the mouth, the mane, and the tail. To carve the feathering at the top of the mane, position the workpiece so that the horse is running away from you, and so that the mane is looking towards your right hand (see 10–12). Then draw the point of the tool slowly from the neck and across the width of the mane so that the tool cuts a series of little furrows.

Power Carving Tip
To bring the wood to a good, smooth finish and to eliminate rough edges, cut the mane and tail furrows twice—once with the motor in forward rotation and then a second time with the motor in reverse.

Having rounded off the eyeball detail with the diamond point bud, use the fine-grit drum sander to bring the whole workpiece to a good finish. Work in the direction of the grain. Finally, use a small fold of sandpaper to tidy up all the little nooks and corners, brush off the dust, lay on the wax, burnish to a dull-sheen finish. The horse is ready for showing!

HINTS, TIPS, AND AFTERTHOUGHTS

- Don't try this project with a second-best piece of wood. If the wood looks to be in any way less than perfect—split, knotty, stained, sappy, or warped—then put it to one side and look for another piece.
- If you enjoy working on a small scale with thin-section wood, then I would say go for a scroll saw.
- If you are going to work with a rotary carver—especially when working with mahogany—then you must set yourself up with either a dust mask and a pair of goggles, or a respirator with a visor.
- When you are fitting a gouge in the handpiece, be very careful not to clench the head so tight that you strip the thread.
- If you plan to mount this project outside—over the stable door, perhaps—then leave out the wax polish and put on three or four coats of high-shine varnish to all surfaces—front, back, and edges.
- We textured our background—more to cover up flaws in the salvaged wood than for reasons of design. If you want to speed up the project some, then you can leave the background plain.

11

Carving a Treen Butter Stamp

Primary techniques—touch carving

11-1a and b   Project picture. The butter stamp—both ends—worked in boxwood, turned and touch carved.

The two Saxon words "treowen" and/or "treow"—meaning tree—have come down to us as the single word "treen," meaning specifically all the small functional wooden items that we have—or once had—in our homes and places of work. The key words being wooden, small, and functional.

I usually think of treen as being primarily all the items that we traditionally use in our kitchens, dairies, and storage rooms. Wooden bowls, plate racks, food boxes, kegs, clothes rollers, candle holders, food rollers and moulds, and perhaps most of interesting of all—from a woodcarver's point of view at least—butter stamps (see 11–1a and b).

Turned and carved in lime, sycamore, and boxwood, butter stamps are no more or less than little printing blocks that were/are used for pressing designs onto the surface of firm butter. Characteristically the stamps have a handle on one end and a design carved in reverse on the other end. In use, the firm butter is patted into a brick shape with a couple of treen "paddles," and then the stamp is dipped into cold water and carefully pressed into the surface of the butter to leave a design in crisp

relief. The design might be a family crest or a motto, a motif or a set of initials, a symbol of love or perhaps a date (see 11–2).

Materials
You need a six-inch length of two-inch by two-inch-square, hard, pale-colored wood such as lime, sycamore, apple, birch, or box.

We chose to use a piece of boxwood from our garden. While boxwood is generally a very good wood for this, our choice was guided more by sentiment than common sense. We had an old and stunted boxwood tree/bush that was blown down in a storm, and we were moving house and wanted to make a little keepsake heirloom that we could show our kids. We knew there was a good chance the wood was flawed, and—although we eventually discovered that it did indeed contain all sorts of undesirables from cracks and cavities to sappy areas, dark stains, and knots—it was also a beautiful cream/brown color and wonderfully smooth and dense in texture.

Tools and Equipment
- power carving system (see 11–3)
- sets of diamond-mounted points, ³⁄₃₂- and ⅛-inch-diameter shanks (see 11–4)
- accessories including vanadium-steel cutters, ruby carvers, mounted brushes with ⅛-inch shanks
- workbench with a D-vise (see 11–5)
- table, pillar, or bench drill press
- Forstner bits at 1⅜ inch and 1⅛ inch
- small woodturning lathe, as needed
- selection of woodturning tools, as needed
- pair of calipers
- small ball of Plasticine
- pencil and ruler
- one sheet each of tracing and workout paper—slightly bigger than the workpiece
- pack of graded sandpapers
- small quantity of vegetable oil and a clean cloth

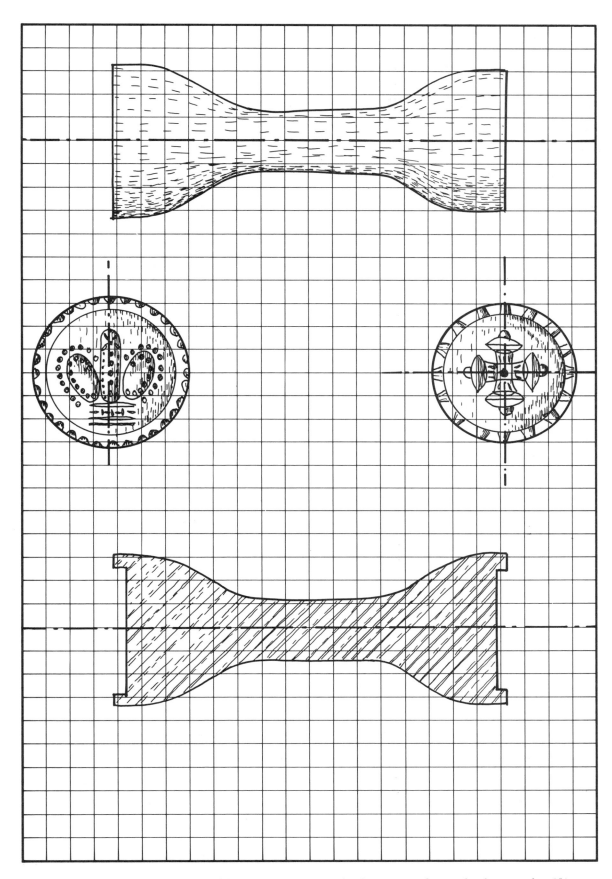

11-2 *Working drawing. At a scale of four squares to one inch, the stamp is four inches long, with a 1⅝-inch diameter at one end, 1½-inch diameter at the other—both ends are recessed about ⅛ inch.*

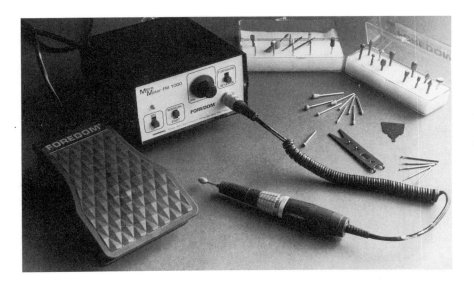

11-3 *The Foredom Micro Motor kit No. 1035/1045 is shown with its comfortable MH 1045 handpiece, FM-1000 control box, FC-1000 foot pedal, and a selection of tool bits. The system provides variable speeds with both a dial and the foot pedal. All switches are located on a single control panel, and the motor runs both forward and reverse with a 115/220-240 volt option. Tools can be fitted swiftly into the rotary quick-release collet (⅛ inch or ³⁄₃₂ inch). We also use this system for carving a found container in Project 2.*

Design Preparation Tip

If you have in mind carving a stamp with dates and initials, then don't forget to cut them in reverse!

Estimated Working Time

5–10 hours

DESIGN, STRUCTURE, AND TECHNIQUE CONSIDERATIONS

When you have gathered your tools and materials, have a look at the working drawing (see 11–2). See how, at a scale of four grid squares to one inch, the stamp is shaped like a dumbbell with the two ends at slightly different diameters, and with a flower motif on the smaller of the two ends and a traditional crown motif on

the other. That said, and remembering that our design was more or less dictated by our need to use a particular piece of wood, your design can satisfy your own needs by being bigger or even shaped and used like a roller, or whatever. Decide on the size and shape of the motif, consider the person for whom the stamp is being made, and then design the project accordingly.

Although we decided to use a lathe to turn an unpromising piece of branch wood down to the dumbbell shape, there's no reason why you can't either buy a

11-5 *The Dremel D-Vise.*

11-4 *Two sets of diamond-mounted points—with ³⁄₃₂- and ⅛-inch-diameter shanks needed for this project. These were supplied by Woodcarvers Supply Inc. We also use Foredom accessories including vanadium-steel cutters kits 30 and 65, ruby carvers kit HK 17, and mounted brushes kit 75 (⅛-inch shanks).*

ready-turned cylindrical blank or settle for having a square or an octagon section, or whatever takes your fancy. No woodturning is necessary if you would rather not.

TURNING THE BLANK

When you have studied the project picture and the working drawing, take the six-inch length of two-inch by two-inch-square section wood, and fix the end-centers by drawing crossed diagonals. This done, set the wood securely between the lathe centers; bring the tool rest up to the workpiece. Test the spin by turning the wood over by hand, read through your checklist, and then switch on the power.

Woodturning Tip

Bearing in mind that a lathe is potentially an extremely dangerous piece of equipment, always make sure that you are dressed for the task at hand—no flapping bits of hair/clothes/jewelry that can get caught up in the lathe. Even though I am what you might describe as an old hand at woodturning, I still read through a pre-switch-on safety checklist that I have pinned up over the lathe.

Having made sure that you and the lathe are in good order, take the round-nosed gouge and swiftly turn the wood down to a smooth, round cylinder that is slightly less than two inches in diameter. Use the parting tool, and establish the length of the dumbbell shape by sinking two channels 4⅛ inches apart (see 11–6, top). This done, sink a third channel halfway along the cylinder to set the diameter of the dumbbells' "waist." Next, go back to using the gouge, and reduce the ends of the 4⅛-inch-long cylinder until one end is 1⅝ inches in diameter and the other end slightly smaller at 1½ inches (see 11–6, middle). When you have cut in the various guide marks, take the small round-nosed gouge and turn the dumbbell to shape. Don't worry too much about the precise form, just go for a shape that is good to hold and pleasing to the eye (see 11–6, bottom).

Finally, use the skew chisel to turn the wood down to a good, smooth finish, and then take the parting tool and turn the dumbbell blank off from the lathe.

DRILLING THE ENDS AND SETTING OUT THE DESIGN

When you have achieved a good, smooth dumbbell form, move to the drill press and make ready for the task ahead. Bearing in mind that the workpiece needs to be stood and drilled on end—like a wine glass—decide

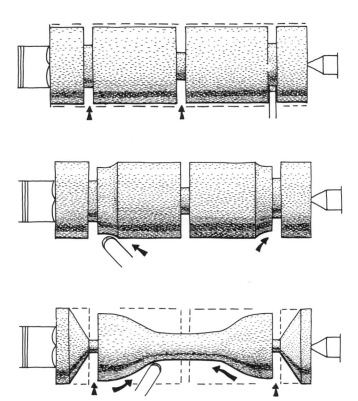

11-6 (Top) Use the parting tool to establish the total length and waist diameter of the dumbbell shape. (Middle) Reduce the ends of the cylinder with the round-nosed gouge. (Bottom) Working from high to low wood, turn the cylinder down to a looks-good-to-hold dumbbell shape.

just how you are going to support the wood while it is being worked. Are you going to clamp it between a couple of wooden V-blocks, or hold it in the Dremel D-vise or whatever? Having worked out a good safe way to hold the wood, set the drills one at a time in the drill chuck. Set the depth stop to one-eighth inch, and bore out the end of the dumbbell with the appropriate sinking. This procedure is easy enough as long as the drill is well centered, and as long as you take it very slowly.

With a nicely drilled-out ⅛-inch-deep recess at each end of the dumbbell, warm up the Plasticine and have a trial stamping. If all is well, the pressed mark should show a raised central disc enclosed by a deep ring or hoop. And, of course, if you would like the central area to be higher, then now is the time to bore the recess deeper.

Having bored the ends of the blank out to the required depth, draw the designs at full size—either our designs or ones of our own making—and make clear tracings. Finally, for one end and motif at a time, reverse the tracing, hold it in place with tabs of masking tape, and pencil-press transfer the lines of the design to the wood.

Drilling Tip

Just in case you don't know . . . a Forstner bit leaves a beautifully smooth flat-bottomed hole. Certainly such bits are more expensive than, say, flat spade-type bits, but then again, they can be used at a much lower speed, and they last longer.

CARVING THE PRIMARY CUTS ON THE CROWN MOTIF

With all the guide lines carefully drawn for the crown, take the Foredom vanadium steel cutter Kit 30 or equivalent, select the small ball cutter, and fit it securely in the power carver handpiece. Take a scrap of waste boxwood—a small bit left over from the turning—and spend a few minutes playing around. Try experimenting with various speeds and directions of stroke until you can confidently predict the cut.

When you are comfortable with the equipment, set to work with the carving. Start by using the ball-head cutter to run a deep trough down the center of the crown. Hold the wood in one hand and the handpiece in the other so that the tool is on its side and at right angles to the centerline of the crown—and lower the waste with two or three well-placed strokes (see 11–7, left).

With the central part of the crown nicely set in to a depth of almost ⅛ inch, select the round-cylinder cutter, and proceed to cut the "cushions" at either side of the crown. The procedure is much the same as already described, the only difference being that the tool is held at a low slicing angle over the work and drawn upwards towards your body (see 11–7, top right). If you are at all unsure as to how such and such a cut needs to be made, then go back to the piece of waste wood and have a couple of tryouts.

When you are happy with the initial cuts, then use the large and small ball ruby carver points, and clean up the three depressions with a delicate stroking action. Next, select the hollow-edged wheel, and remove the large scoop from the base of the crown. Grade the scoop, so that it runs in and out at a gradual angle, with the deepest part being at the center. To help steady and control the cut, rest your thumb on the edge of the work (see 11–7, bottom).

DECORATING THE CROWN

With the four primary cuts in place—the central area, the two side "cushions," and the deep hollow at the base of the crown—then comes the good-fun bit of cutting in all the little dots and dashes that go to make up the decoration.

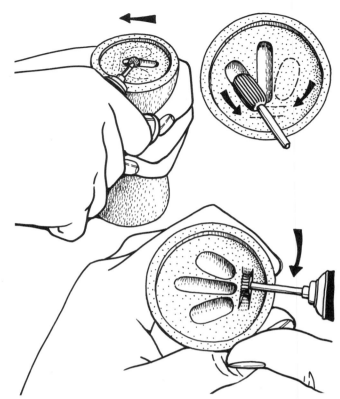

11-7   (Left) Use the small ball cutter to cut in a centerline channel—stroke towards your body. (Top right) Cut the two "cushions" with the round cylinder—hold the tool at a low slicing angle, all the while drawing the tool towards your body. (Bottom) Steady the cutter by resting your thumb on the edge of the work.

Start with the round-nosed cylinder fine ruby carver, and cut in the little scoops that go to make up the piecrust edging. Run the scoops around the outer ring. Bearing in mind that the cylinder is about ⅛ inch in diameter, set the touch cuts about 1/16 inch apart—⅛ inch, 1/16 inch, ⅛ inch, and so on all around the ring. Be ready to adjust the last six or so cuts so that the design fits.

When you have finished the piecrust rim decoration, take a ³⁄₃₂-inch shank knife-edge wheel diamond point and set to work cutting in the cross at the top-center point of the crown and the little dashes at the base (see 11–8). Next, fit one of the long, fine-tapered-cone diamond points, and cut the fine groove that runs from side to side at the very base of the crown (see 11–9).

Use one or other of the very small ball vanadium engraving burrs to touch-carve all the little "pearls" that decorate the edge of the crown.

Finally, when you are pleased with the carving, and when you have had several tryouts on the Plasticine (see 11–10) and maybe made one or two fine adjustments to the design, use a horsehair brush to bring the wood to a smooth finish.

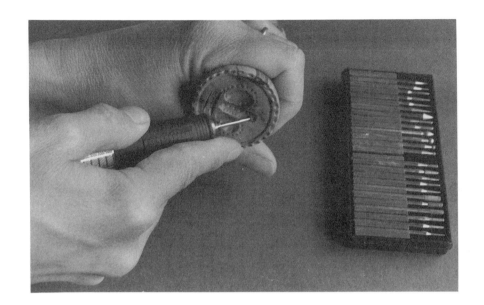

11-8 Use the diamond knife-edge wheel cutter to carve the cross at the top-center point of the crown.

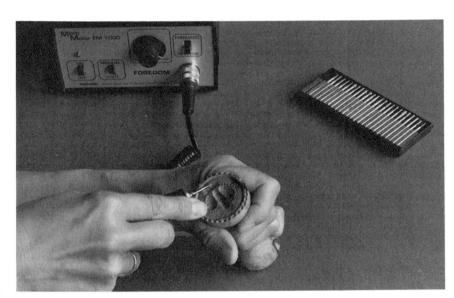

11-9 Use the diamond tapered cone to cut the fine groove at the base of the crown.

11-10 Have a tryout on a piece of Plasticine to check if any adjustments need to be made.

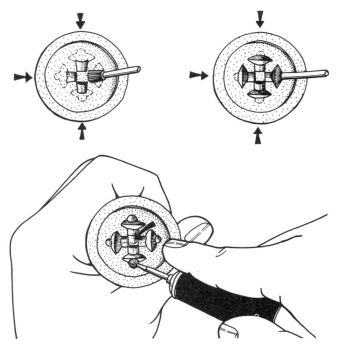

CARVING THE FLOWER AND FINISHING

After you have carved the crown, then all you do is go to the other end of the dumbbell, and carve the flower in like manner.

Order of Cutter Use Working Out from Center

- The inverted cone to make the four cuts that comprise the cross with the raised square at center (see 11–11, top left).
- The cone cap to cut the four outer petal shapes (see 11–11, top right).
- The small ball to sink the little half-bead shapes on the edge of each of the four petals and also to lower the center of the flower (see 11–11, bottom).

Power Carving Tip

If your hands are unsteady, then support the workpiece on the bench, and turn it so that the tool is presented and aligned with the line of the next cut.

Working with diamond points, use the cylinder point for the piecrust edge (see 11–12), the small ball point to cut the center bead, and the fine taper cylinder for the "stamens"—three to each petal (see 11–13).

11-11   (Top left) To cut the cross, turn the workpiece and approach in the direction of the arrow. (Top right) Use the cone cap to cut the four petal shapes. (Bottom) Use the small ball point to cut the four bead shapes and to lower the central square.

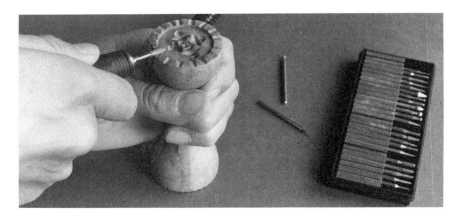

11-12   When you come to carve the edge design, space the cuts evenly by quartering and dividing the circumference—like a compass—north, south, east and west, northeast, southeast, and so on.

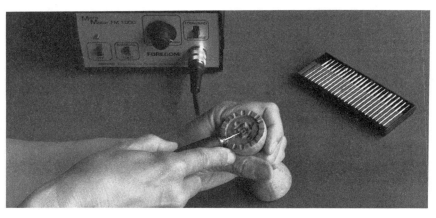

11-13   To cut the stamens, steady the tool by resting and bracing your fingers against the side of the workpiece.

Finally, when you have brought the work to a good finish with the horsehair brush (see 11–14)—as already described—wipe the carving over with vegetable oil. The stamp is ready to be used.

Finishing Tip
If the stamp still smells of Plasticine, wash it with liquid soap; let it dry, and then wipe it over with oil.

HINTS, TIPS, AND AFTERTHOUGHTS

- The diamond points make for a very swift and efficient cut, a cut so smooth that it doesn't need any extra finishing.
- With a project of this size and type, the choice of wood is all-important. The wood must cut smooth, must be close grained and pale in color, and, perhaps most important of all, must be nontoxic. Avoid toxic woods like yew!
- Although boxwood only comes in relatively small sections, I would say that it is after all the best choice for this project. If you get the chance, ask for English box and "engraving block" grade.

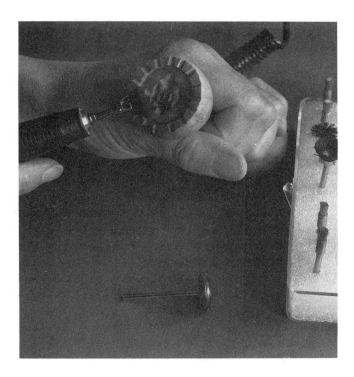

11-14   Use the horsehair brush to bring the wood to a polished finish.

12

Carving a Water Dipper Ladle in the Pioneer Tradition

Primary techniques—gouge carving

12-1 Project picture. The water dipper—gouge carved in pear wood.

A water dipper is no more, or less, than a long-handled wooden ladle used for scooping up liquid—usually water. Our dipper draws its inspiration from ones that were traditionally carved and whittled in a rural/pioneer environment by woodsmen and settlers (see 12–1 and 12–2).

Estimated Working Time
5–10 hours

Materials
You need a Y-shaped tree crotch, with the lower part of the Y being about six inches long and the upper part five to six inches in diameter, and with both of the upper spurs being about 14 inches long and at least 2½ inches in diameter. You will do best with a tight-grained fruit wood like apple or pear (see 12–3).

When you are choosing your wood—you might well be cutting it straight from a tree or, at least, using a piece that was cut the year before—look for a crotch that has a generous swelling or burl just below the junction of the Y. Before you make your choice, check that the wood is free from end splits, dead knots, rot, and worm. Our wood was left to season for about two years.

Tools and Equipment
- power carving system with gouges (see 12–4)
- ball-nosed cylindrical high-speed cutter
- ball-nosed cylinder tungsten carbide burr
- ½-inch ballhead tungsten carbide burr
- workbench with a vise
- band saw
- table, pillar, or bench drill press
- selection of Forstner bits of a size to suit your piece of wood
- pencil and ruler
- large black pencil or wax crayon
- one sheet each of tracing and workout paper—slightly bigger than the workpiece
- pack of graded sandpapers
- small quantity of vegetable oil and a clean cloth

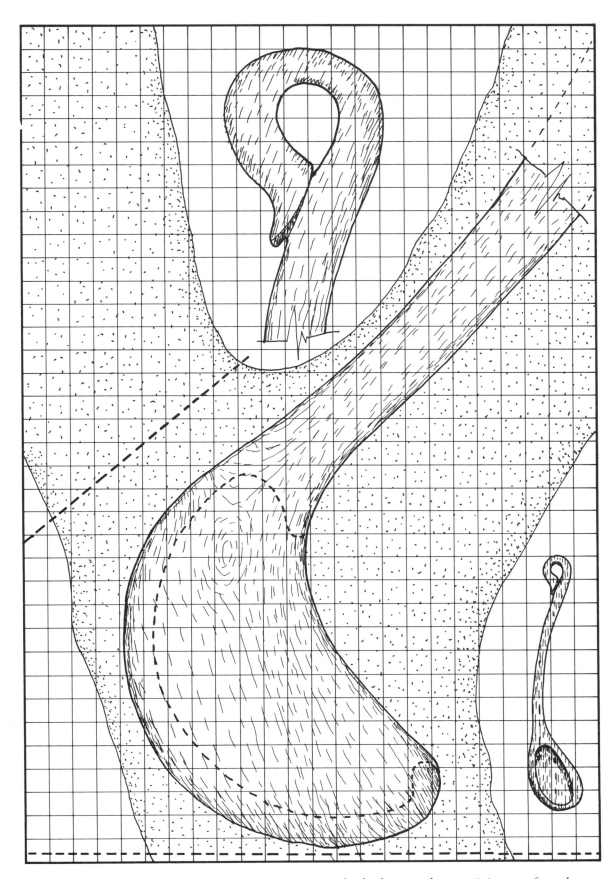

12-2 *Working drawing. At a scale of four squares to one inch, the dipper is shown as it is comes from the tree crotch with the handle detail at top and a reduced-size drawing in the lower right.*

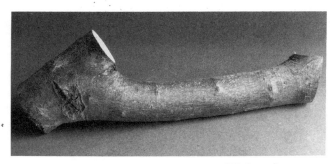

12-3 *The straight-from-the-tree piece of Y-shaped tree crotch wood.*

Wood Selection Tip

If you get the chance—say, you are cutting down a fruit tree or able to buy a good part of a tree—then it's always a good idea to keep a bit of choice wood for next time around. Apple and pear wood are particularly good for woodturning, making small toys, and for carving plates, bowls, and platters.

DESIGN, STRUCTURE, AND TECHNIQUE CONSIDERATIONS

When you have gathered your tools and materials, take a look at the working drawing (see 12–2). See how our finished dipper measures about 16 inches in total length, with a bowl or cup at about five inches long, 2¾ inches wide, and 2½ inches deep, and a pierced and

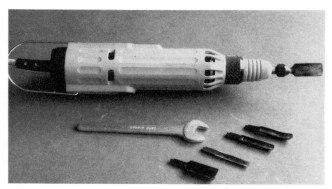

12-4 *The Tokyo Automach Handcraft wood carving system is shown with the reciprocating head, a selection of gouges, and a spanner. The unit accepts 100/120/220/240 volts, and also has a quick-change rotary head. The Handcraft wood carving system supplied by Woodcraft Supply Corp. USA is efficient, lightweight, and quiet as well as user-friendly. We also use this system to carve a sunflower panel in the American Colonial tradition in Project 4, to carve a gilt ribbon bow in the French tradition in Project 8, and to carve a mask in the American Northwest Indian tradition in Project 14.*

112

carved detail at the top end of the long curved handle. Note the way that the handle detail has been worked so that it looks as if the wood has been looped over.

Consider how the bowl of the dipper has been set within the crotch of the branch to take advantage of the extra-strong intertwining of fibres that occurs at this point. If you look at the dipper in plan view, you will see that we have used the natural curve of the upper branch to give the spoon a very individual right-handed function. That is, when the dipper is in use and being held in the right hand, the long handle curves in a delicate sweep, from the hand down and around towards the user.

Design Tip

If you want to make a very small miniature dipper—say, for a sugar sprinkler or some such—then you could use a small branch/crotch of boxwood and small tool bits.

SETTING OUT THE DESIGN

After you have studied the project picture and the working drawing, fit the broadest, shallowest U-curve gouge blade in the reciprocating head, and swiftly clear away all the bark. While you are clearing the bark, spend time getting to know how best to hold and use the tool. Try out different angles of approach, different speeds, the range of blades, and so on. Once you have cleared away the bark, draw the shape of the crotch at full size, and consider how the shape of the dipper can be modified and fitted to use the natural shape of your wood to best advantage.

For example, even though the bowl must occur below the fork of the Y—that is, within the body of the main branch—the handle has a choice of two stems. And, of course, if you want the bowl to be wider or longer—or wider or deeper—or if you want the handle to be longer, or whatever, then now is the time to play around with the design.

When you have achieved what you consider is a good design, draw the shape of the dipper at full size—meaning the shape as seen in side profile—and make a clear tracing. Cut the tracing into a template with a pair of scissors and carefully arrange the cutout on the crotch. When you are happy with the placing, hold the tracing paper template in place with a couple of thumbtacks, and draw around it with either a pencil or wax crayon. Don't worry too much at this point about being too finicky—just go for the big broad image.

Design Transfer Tip

If you are working with green wood—wood that is damp and slick under the bark—then you might need to draw the design with a water-based felt-tip pen.

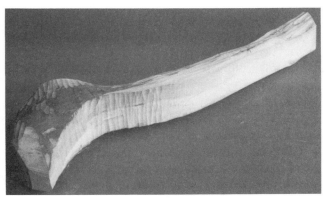

12-5 *The bark removed and the dipper cut out in side view profile.*

USING THE BAND SAW TO ROUGH OUT THE PROFILE

Having drawn the side profile on the wood and marked in clearly all the areas that need to be cut away, pin up all your drawings so that they are in view, and move to the band saw.

It has to be said at this point that, when you are working on the saw, you do have to work with great care and caution. Whereas it doesn't matter too much if you make a mess-up of the workpiece of even break the band saw blade, you can't take any chances with your hands. Always make sure that your fingers are well clear of the blade.

Band Saw Tip

When you are working on the band saw with "found" wood—meaning wood that is unpredictable—switch yourself into a defensive mode and be ready for the unexpected. So for example, be ready for the blade to twist when it hits a hard knot, and be ready for the work-piece to buck if the grain runs hard and then soft, and so on. Just be on your guard and then some!

Run through the usual pre-switch-on checklist, and then switch on the power. Position the crotch flat-down on the cutting table, and set to work cutting out the form as seen in side view.

Cut off the unwanted branch spur, trim away the main branch at the bottom of the bowl, and then slowly and carefully pare away all the waste. Cut well to the waste side of the drawn line (see 12–5). And, of course, if the cuts reveal hidden cavities, dead knots, splits, areas of exciting grain, or whatever, then be ready to modify the shape of the dipper to suit.

With the dipper roughed out in side view, draw the image on the top-of-spoon sawn face—the image as seen in top view—and repeat the sawing procedure as

12-6 *Fit the broad U-section gouge in the carver, and tidy up the rough-sawn profile.*

already described. The important thing to remember with a project of this character is that you do have to be ready for the unexpected.

Band Saw Tip

When you are working on the band saw, make sure that you have a spare blade at hand—just in case!

USING THE RECIPROCATING GOUGE TO SHAPE THE OUTSIDE FORM

Have roughed out the shape of the dipper on the band saw, take the carving tool—still fitted with the broad U-section gouge—and set to work cutting away all the sharp edges and corners (see 12–6). Generally bring the dipper to a good shape.

First cut off the sharp corners, and then tool the whole surface. Working in this way, you will soon be able to make judgments about the run of the grain and the quality of the wood. For example, after about two hours' work I found out that the bowl of my dipper was divided into two distinct areas—a dense, dark-colored, hard and difficult-to-carve wood to one side, and soft light-colored and easy-to-carve wood on the other.

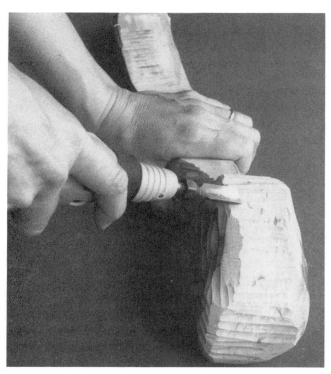

12-7 *Hold the workpiece firmly with one hand, and remove small scoops of wood with the gouge—work right around the profile image.*

Although the dark wood was difficult to carve, with lots of grain twists and small tight knots, the color was attractive, and the gouge left the dark wood looking crisply and cleanly tooled. The light areas on the other hand were a bit soft and crumbly. The same problem occurred at the end of the handle. When I came to shape the swelling at the end of the handle, I found that the wood was variously knotty and soft with a difficult-to-carve twisted grain. All you can do, if you come across such problems, is play it by ear and be ready to change the form to suit whatever occurs.

Continue running the gouge backwards and forwards over and around the workpiece until the dipper begins to take shape (see 12–7).

Power Carving Tip

Never be in a rush and try to dig the gouge too deep. Just go at it nice and easy, all the while removing small scallops of wood. If the grain cuts up rough, then sharpen the blade and/or change to a different angle of approach.

DRILLING OUT THE INSIDE-BOWL WASTE

Having cut the outside of the dipper to a rough shape, take a look at the working drawing again and see how the inside bowl measures about 1¾ inches wide, three inches long, and 1½ inches deep. This done, and having checked out the drill to make sure that it's in good order, fit a 1½-inch-diameter Forstner bit securely in the drill chuck and then go to work. With the depth-stop set at 1½ inches, hold the workpiece bowl face-uppermost on the worktable, and bore out the inside-bowl waste (see 12–8, top left). If need be, then clamp bits of wood to the drill table to help support and cradle the workpiece.

Although I was able to clear the bulk of the waste with just two side-by-side holes, you might need to use a small bit and go for more holes—or, perhaps, use a large bit and go for a single hole. It very much depends on the shape and size of your chosen piece of wood. Be very wary about drilling the holes too swiftly. The best procedure is to run the bit down about ¼ inch, then to lift it up and clear the waste. Then go down another ¼ inch, and so on, until you reach the required depth. Working in this way, you will minimize the chances of the workpiece bucking in your hands, and you will also be able to make timely decisions as to the depth of the hole and the thickness of the bowl bottom.

Finally, while the drill is at hand, take a ½-inch-diameter bit and bore out the hole at the end of the handle (see 12–8, right).

Drilling Tip

Have a piece of scrap wood under the workpiece so that the drill bit leaves a clean hole as it exits.

CARVING THE INSIDE OF THE BOWL

Take the power carver and—with the same gouge blade still fitted—start to shape the inside of the bowl and bring the rim of the bowl to a good finish. First enlarge the top of the drilled holes until the line of cut is a little to the waste side of the rim line (see 12–8, bottom). Then gradually start to lower the rest of the bowl waste. When you reach the bottom of the drilled hole, then change the angle of approach to run the gouge down-in-and-around in a single, smooth scooping action. As you are carving, aim both to undercut the side of the bowl and to run the inside profile in a smooth curve from the undercut rim down to the bottom of the bowl. Continue to carve, scooping down and around, down and around, much as you might use a spoon to scoop out a hard-boiled egg. It's all simple enough as long as you don't force the pace, and as long as you keep the tool sharp.

Power Carving Tip

Be very careful when you are undercutting the inside of the bowl that you don't lever against the rim and do damage.

114

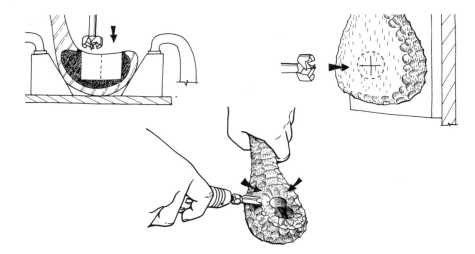

12-8　(Top left) With the drill's depth-stop set at 1½ inches, support and cradle the workpiece between a couple of pieces of scrap wood, and bore out the inside-bowl waste. (Right) Support the handle on a piece of waste wood, and drill out the ½-inch-diameter hole at the end of the handle. (Bottom) Enlarge the top of the drilled hole by gradually working outward towards the rim line.

USING THE ROTARY HEAD TO BRING THE SURFACE TO A GOOD FINISH

Having used the gouge to shape the outside of the dipper—and the drill and the gouge to shape the inside of the bowl—screw the rotary head on the power carver and fit the ball-nosed cylinder tungsten carbide burr in the collet. Start to bring all the surfaces to a good finish.

Power Carving Tip

Although tungsten carbide burrs are wonderfully efficient, they are also horribly dusty; so be sure to wear a coverall and a dust mask.

When you are using the burr, the most direct procedure is to start by going over the entire surface. Bearing in mind that you are aiming for a bowl wall thickness of about ⅜ inch and a handle that runs in a smooth curve up from the bowl, work backwards and forwards over the whole workpiece, gradually adjusting a bump here and a curve there until you have a pleasing form. You will find

that the process of "combing" the whole surface with the burr somehow brings all the individual dips and curves together and presents them as a unified whole (see 12–9, left). And, of course, the very act of running the burr over the surface—this way and that; over, under, and round—does ensure that the whole surface gets to be worked. Use the ballhead burr to work the inside of the bowl (see 12–9, right).

When you have scoured and combed all the surfaces, then fit the ball-nosed cylinder high-speed cutter, and set to work bringing the surfaces to a good finish. Use the cutter much as you might use a knife. That is, work with a slow, steady thumb-paring action, all the while trying to run the shapes and curves together. Aim for a natural form, one that looks as if it might have been worked on by the sea—like a piece of driftwood—or perhaps like a soft rock that has been scooped into shape by the action of the wind and water.

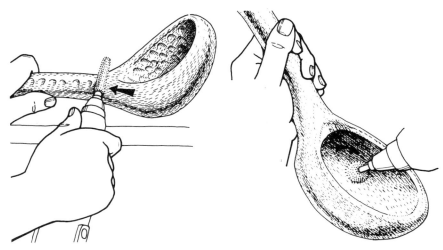

12-9　(Left) Use the ball-nosed cylinder burr to bring the whole workpiece to a unified combed finish. (Right) Use the ball-point burr to work the inside of the bowl.

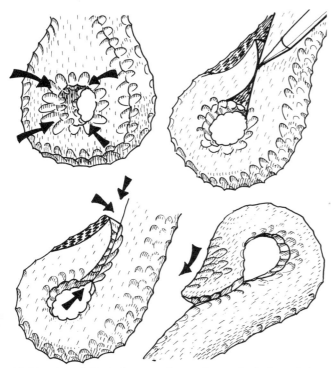

12-10 (Top left) Enlarge and round over the hole and the end of the handle. (Top right) Pencil in the guide lines and shade the waste areas that need to be cut away. (Bottom left) Make a stop-cut at the end of the curl, and then make further cuts down onto the stop-cut to achieve the curled form. (Bottom right) Lower the waste wood at the tail end of the curl.

FINISHING

When you have shaped the bowl and the handle, then refit the reciprocating head and the small gouge. Start to enlarge the drilled hole at the end of the handle (see 12–10, top right). Work around the hole on one side; then flip the workpiece, and work the hole on the other until the handle is more or less round in cross section—like a bone. When you come to make the looped-over join, first pencil in a guide line (see 12–10, top right), and then use the edge of the gouge to run a stop-cut down into the wood to a depth of about ¹⁄₁₆ inch, Now,

having marked the curled-over end of the handle with a stop-cut, run a cut around the stop-cut—that is, on the main part of the handle—so that the end looks as if it has curled over and just come to rest on the main part of the handle (see 12–10, bottom left). When you are happy with the illusion that the tail of the handle has been bent round, then lower the wood around the end so that the handle seems to run in a smooth curve (see 12–10, bottom right).

Finally, use the graded sandpapers to rub all the surfaces down to a smooth finish—in and outside the bowl, along the handle, in and around the loop hole, and around the decorative terminal—then rub the whole workpiece over with vegetable oil. Burnish it to a good finish, and tie on a leather hanging thong. The project is finished.

HINTS, TIPS, AND AFTERTHOUGHTS

- This is a beautifully flexible project in that the dipper can be cut and worked to suit your own particular whims and fancies. For example, if you want a dipper with a really big hooked handle—like a shepherd's crook—then all you have to do is to search around for just the right branch and crotch. Then adjust the working details to suit the wood.
- If you are in a hurry, then you could use flap sander wheels to bring the contours to a swift smooth finish.
- Part of the pleasure of carving a project of this type is that the "character" of the wood is hidden below the bark. You don't really get to know what you are up against until the bark has been stripped off and the carving is well underway. The wood might be richly colored, or contain wild burr patterns, and so on; there are any number of exciting possibilities. That said, you do have to accept that the wood might also be so seriously flawed that you have to abandon the piece and search for another branch and crotch or give up the project.
- If you are at all worried about green or half-seasoned wood splitting, then rub it over with a smear of mashed potato—seriously—to seal the wood.

13

Carving a Figure in the African Ashanti Tradition

Primary techniques—gouge and touch carving

13-1   Project picture. The stylized figure—gouge and touch carved.

Many traditional Black African societies were characterized by being well organized, with a stable feudal system. Within this system the various tribal groups were able to develop craft skills such as weaving, painting, and woodcarving. Of all the crafts, I think it fair to say woodcarving was one of the most important, if only because wood was an easy-to-find material and objects made from wood had so many practical uses. The wooden objects included masks, trays, headrests, stools,

pots, bowls, drums, screens, doors, pipes, full-size sculptural figures, and, of course, small figures.

Small wooden figures—called *"A'kua-ba"*—as traditionally carved by the Ashanti tribe in Ghana, are thought to have had a dual function (see 13–1). It is thought that they were no more, or less, than girls' dolls—as might be "played with" like a toy. Perhaps more significant, they were worn by young females as fertility or good-fortune-type charms. Measuring about 12 inches high with the discoid heads representing a mark of great beauty, the figures were carried by the Ashanti girls and young women in the small of the back—tucked into the waistband at the back of their skirts—in order, it is thought, to ensure that future children were well formed and beautiful.

Estimated Working Time
10–12 hours

Materials
You need a two-inch-thick slab of hard, smooth, dense-grained wood about 12 inches long and five inches wide, with the grain running along the length. It's best to go for a hard, uncomplicated close-grained wood like birch, maple, or sycamore. Authentic figures would no doubt be made of ebony.

When you are choosing your wood, look for a piece that is free from end splits, knots, sappy edges, and warps.

Wood Selection Tip
If you are going to let a very young finger-sucking child have the figure—I'm not, but you might like the idea—then it's most important that you avoid toxic woods like yew. If you have any doubts at all, then ask the advice of a specialist wood supplier.

117

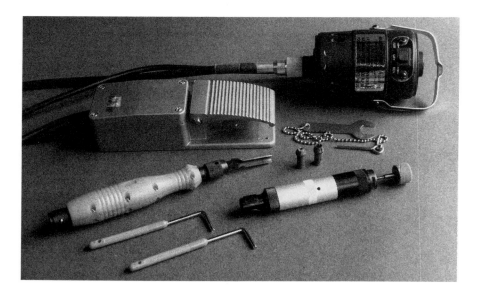

13-2 *The Wood Carvers Supply ABCD Mastercarver No. 797030 is shown with hang-up reversible motor unit, rugged foot pedal, wrenches, and both rotary and reciprocating handpiece options. The ¼ HP 115-volt unit is easy to use and efficient. We also use this sytem to carve a dough bowl in the American Folk Art tradition in Project 9.*

Tools and Equipment

- power carving system with gouges (see 13–2 and 13–3)
- set of tungsten carbide cutters including small cylinder, cone, and round cylinder shapes
- tapered-cylinder ruby carver point
- set of diamond points, including long tapered cylinder and large ball shapes
- ¾-inch-diameter fine-grade drum sander
- workbench with a vise, clamp, and bench stop
- band saw
- scroll saw with a 2-inch depth of cut
- pencil and ruler
- large black pencil or wax crayon
- one sheet each of tracing and workout paper—slightly bigger than the workpiece
- masking tape
- pack of graded sandpapers
- mask and goggles, or a respirator
- felt-tipped watercolor pens in orange, purple, brown, and grey
- wax polish
- cloth and brush for polishing

DESIGN, STRUCTURE, AND TECHNIQUE CONSIDERATIONS

When you have gathered your tools and materials, have a close look at the project picture (see 13–1) and the working drawing (see 13–4). Note how, at a grid scale of four squares to one inch, the figure stands about 10 inches high, four inches wide across span of the head, and a little under two inches in diameter across the width of the base. Consider how the head is a convex

13-3 *Set the blade in the handpiece chuck, and tighten with the wrenches.*

discoid—that is, it is more or less circular, with each side being domed towards the center—like an upside-down saucer. Note the way the back of the figure is completely plain, whereas the front is set out with the stylized features that are slightly raised in relief from the lowered ground. Study the details and you will see that the contours are rounded, the arms strongly carved, and the whole design considered so that there is little chance of the arms breaking away.

SETTING OUT THE DESIGN AND FIRST CUTS

After you have studied the project picture and the working drawing, draw the design at full size, and make a clear pencil tracing. Set the wood out with a centerline, and pencil-press transfer the traced profile image to one side of the wood. Label the best face "front." This done, turn the wood over, and use a pencil and ruler to set out the two-inch-wide side edges with the two straight lines that mark out the tapered shape of the figure as seen in "side" view (see 13–4).

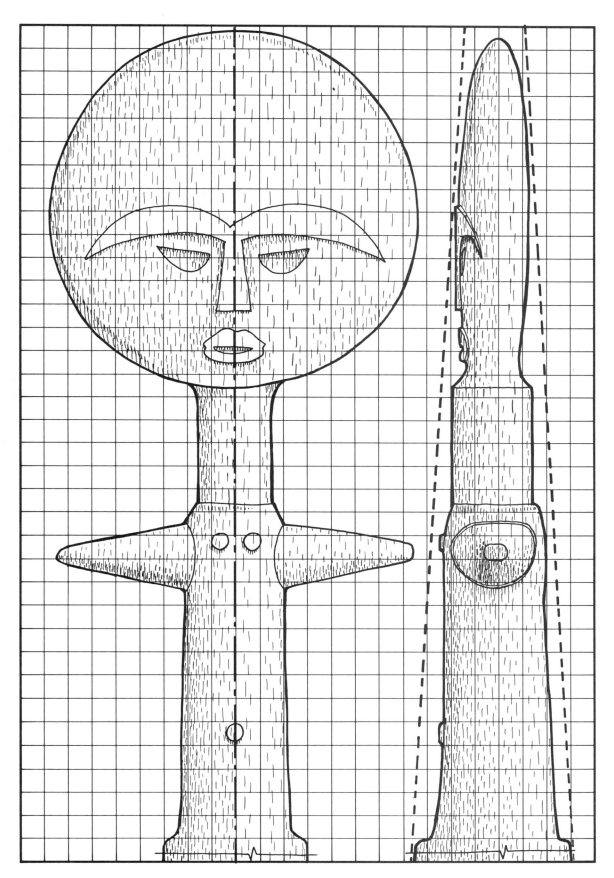

13-4 *Working drawing—front and side views. The scale is four grid squares to one inch. Note the center-line on the front view and the dotted cutting lines on the side view.*

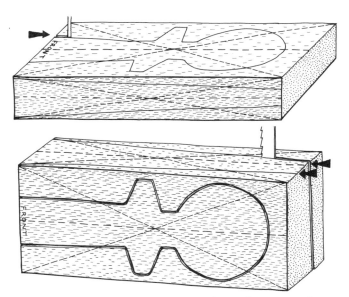

13-5 *(Top) With the workpiece set "front"-face-up on the scroll-saw table, run the line of cut a little to the waste side of the drawn line. (Bottom) With the fretted-out front view popped back into the surrounding one-piece block of waste, run the workpiece through the band saw to slice away the two wedge-shaped slivers of waste.*

Place the "front" face up on the scroll-saw table, and feed it through the saw so that you have a flat-faced, straight-sided doll—as seen in front view. Run the wood at a nice gentle pace through the saw, cutting a little to the waste side of the drawn line (see 13–5, top). Cut around the image so that the waste comes off as a single piece.

Once you have sawn right around the image, then comes the slightly tricky task of using the band saw to cut away the side waste. Pop the fretted-out front back in its surround of waste. Being mindful to use push sticks and to keep your fingers well away from the blade, run the total block side-edge-up through the saw to slice away the two wedge-shaped pieces of waste (see 13–5, bottom).

Cautions for Band Saw Use
The band saw is potentially a very dangerous machine, which needs to be used with great care and caution; but it is beautifully efficient if used properly.

- Familiarize yourself with the machine.
- Don't switch on without first making sure that it's in good working order.
- Look over the manufacturer's safety checklist.
- Don't wear flappy will-get-caught-in-the-machine clothes, hair, or jewelry.
- Make sure that the saw blade is correctly fitted and tensioned.

USING THE RECIPROCATING GOUGE TO ROUGH OUT THE FORM

Once you have fretted out the form and removed the bulk of the waste with the band saw, push the quick-change reciprocating handpiece onto the shaft, and fit the deep U-gouge blade. Draw center guide lines on all faces of the figure—down and around the side views, down the front view, down the back, across the span of the arms, around the head, and so on.

Power Carving Tip
Since it is most important that the figure be symmetrical in both front and side views, you will need to constantly refer to the centerlines. If, in the process of carving, the lines are obliterated, then pencil in fresh ones.

With the workpiece clamped face-up on the bench, and being sure to cut across and at an angle to the grain, set to work gouging away all the sharp edges and corners of waste. Work from center to side, all the while being careful that the "arms" and "hands" don't split away across the short grain (see 13–6). Don't forget that the front face needs to be slightly thicker to allow for the depth of the abstracted details of the face and body—eyebrows, nose, mouth, and breast and navel "buttons." Shape both sides of the figure.

When you have cleared the bulk of the waste with the deep gouge, change over to the shallow gouge, and rework the whole carving (see 13–6, bottom). It's always a good idea at this stage to keep pencil-labelling the front face just so that you don't make a mess-up and overlook that the front face needs to be slightly thicker.

Power Carving Suggestions
- Don't try to remove too much wood at a single stroke.
- Keep the gouge blades razor sharp.
- Don't overwork any single area in isolation.
- Stand back from your work and assess your progress.
- Don't run the tool towards your body.
- Keep repositioning the workpiece so that you are always presented with the best angle of cut.

Troubleshooting Tip
If the wood starts to cut up rough—and assuming that the wood is dry and free from dead knots—this is an indication that you need to change the angle of approach to make a smooth cut, and/or resharpen the blade.

Continue to carve, trimming off a whisk here, slicing off a little more there, standing back to see if the overall "feel" is right, shading in wood that needs to be cut away, and so on.

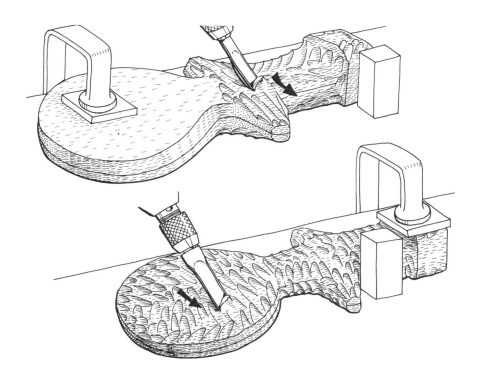

13-6 (Top) Work from center to side, all the while being careful not to slice away the short-grained "arms" and "hands." (Bottom) Being mindful that the front face needs to be slightly thicker, use the shallow gouge to rework the surface.

USING THE ROTARY CARVER TO MODEL THE DETAILS

When you have taken the gouge carving as far as it can go, then change over to the rotary handpiece and fit the large tungsten carbide cylinder burr. Start the swift task of working the gouge-worked surface to a smooth and rounded "combed" finish (see 13–7). It's a dusty business, so make sure that you are wearing either goggles and dust mask or, better still, a respirator.

Power Carving Tip

If you decide to hold and support the workpiece on your lap, then make sure that you are wearing a stout, smooth-surfaced leather or plastic apron—meaning one that won't get snagged up in the rotary point. It's also a good idea to tie your hair/whiskers/jewelry back out of harm's way!

Work from center to side, that is, so that the strokes made by the spinning point runs towards the edge of the figure. Along the way you might well need to change the direction of rotation to suit a particular cut. For example, if you are holding the figure by its body in your left hand, and if you are working the right-hand side edge of the face, then you will find it that much easier if you switch the motor to reverse (see 13–8). Best advice is to take it as it comes. If the cut feels a bit awkward, or less than easy, or you keep getting a face full of dust, then try switching the motor into forward/reverse and/or angling the tool to travel in another direction.

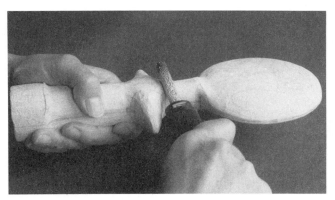

13-7   Use the large, structured-tooth carbide bit to work the whole surface to a combed finish.

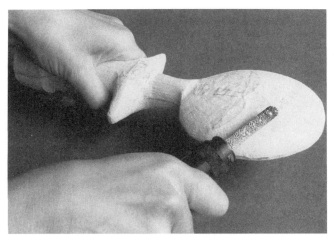

13-8   When you come to work the right-hand side of the face, switch the motor to reverse rotation.

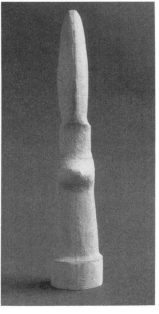

13-9 *The roughing-out completed. (Left) Front view. (Right) Side view.*

When you are ready to start modelling the features, first draw a line around the top of the eyebrows, and then use the carbide burr to lower the top of the forehead by about ⅛ inch (see 13–9). The roughing-out stage completed, fit the small-cylinder tungsten carbide cutter, set the tool at a low angle to the wood, and make stop-cuts or V-trenches to the waste side of the drawn lines—at the eyebrows, nose, and mouth, and at the neck, arm, "foot" (see 13–10), and around the "buttons" (see 13–11).

Having outlined the feature details with stop-cuts, change over to using the tungsten carbide cone cutter, and trim back the wood around the V-trenches—at the arms and neck, and around the features that need to be

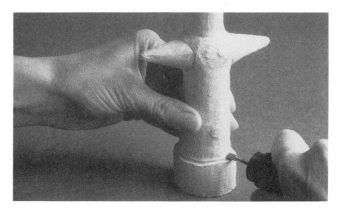

13-10 *Use a cylinder or inverted cone cutter to cut the stepped ridge around the base. Have your hand supported on the bench, and turn the workpiece in a counterclockwise direction.*

left in relief. This done, change over to the round-ended-cylinder cutter, and lower and smooth the remaining ⅛-inch skim of waste. And just as before, if the need arises, switch the motor to reverse rotation. Continue until the "buttons," mouth, nose, and brows are left standing proud by about ⅛ inch.

Power Carving Tip
When you are modelling the details with the rotary handpiece, be careful that the spinning chuck does not rub on the wood and make burn marks. To avoid this problem, you might need to support the tool with both hands—one guiding and the other supporting. If this doesn't work, try protecting areas at risk with strips of masking tape.

MODELLING AND SANDING

When you have achieved a well-balanced, symmetrical figure—one that stands upright—use a pencil to draw in the shape of the eyes. Fit the tapered-cylinder ruby point. Being very careful not to damage surrounding areas and edges, hold the tool at a shallow angle, and lower the eye and mouth waste on the inside of the drawn line (see 13–12, top). While the tool is at hand, hold the ruby point so that it is directed over the eye and looking towards the underside of the brow, and then very carefully lower the wood so that it slants and cuts into the underside of the brow and to either side of the nose (see 13–12, bottom)

Fit the large-tapered-cylinder diamond point and rework the cuts left by the ruby point. Aim to leave all the surfaces looking smooth and well worked. Concentrate your efforts on cleaning up all the stepped details and rounding the ends of the arms. Use the large-ball diamond point to remove the waste and to tidy up inside the eye sockets (see 13–13). Don't worry if you can't reach all the areas in and around the face details, because you will be able to tidy up when you come to sanding.

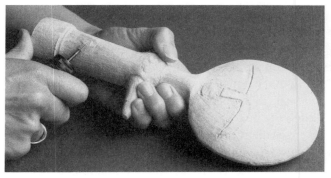

13-11 *Work with a thumb-supported paring grip.*

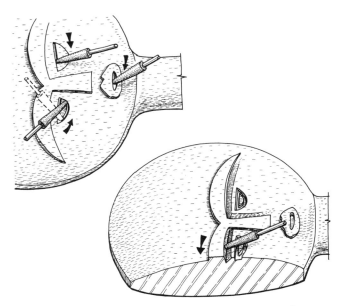

13-14 When you come to sanding the bottom edge, switch the motor to reverse so that the spinning bit has a smooth runoff.

13-12 (Top) Use the tapered-cylinder ruby point to lower the waste on the inside of the mouth and eyes. (Bottom) Use the ruby point to slant and cut in the underside of the brow.

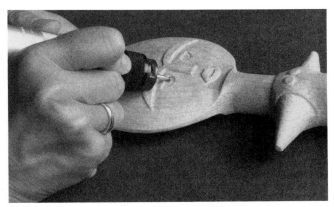

13-13 Use the large-ball diamond point to tidy up inside the eye socket.

When you have what you consider is a well-worked, nicely detailed carving, then fit the ¾-inch-diameter fine-grade sanding drum, and go over the whole carving, bringing it to a smooth, clean finish. And just as before, when you come to running the tool off the end and edges of the base and off the sides of the face—and this will depend on whether or not you are right- or left-handed—switch the tool over to the rotation that best fits the task (see 13–14).

Power Sanding Tip
Having rubbed it down with the rotary drum sander, hold the figure up to a side light and use a soft pencil to mark in any ripples or blemishes that still need to be cut back.

Finally, take a sheet of fine-grade sandpaper and, being careful to only work in the direction of the grain, rub the whole workpiece down to a smooth finish.

STAINING AND FINISHING

If like us you have used a piece of light-colored wood and want to stain it dark—and this is optional—take the large watercolor felt-tipped pens and—working in the order orange, purple, brown, and grey—lay one color on top of another until the figure looks to be a rich mahogany finish. When the ink is completely dry, take a sheet of superfine sandpaper, and rub off the fine nibs and whisks of wood. Finally, give the whole figure a generous coat of wax polish, and burnish it to a dull-sheen finish.

HINTS, TIPS, AND AFTERTHOUGHTS

- Don't try this project with a second-best piece of wood. If the wood looks in any way to be split, knotty, damp, or stained, then put it to one side and look for another piece.
- When you are fitting a gouge in the handpiece, be sure to clench the chuck up with the two wrench tools—not so tight that you strip the thread—just tight enough to stop the blade moving in its slotted housing.
- Traditionally, some Ashanti figures have additional decorative rings around the neck—you could build this feature into the design.
- If you decide to go for a light-colored wood, then be sure to arrange the figure so that it uses the grain to the best decorative advantage.
- If you find that the figure wobbles around on its base, then scoop out the underside of the base slightly.

14

Carving a Mask in the Pacific Northwest Native American Tradition

Primary techniques—gouge and touch carving

14-1　Project picture. The mask—gouge, touch carved, and painted.

American Indians of the Pacific Northwest stand out as a culture that produced extraordinary wood carvings and sculptures displaying exquisite craftsmanship. Their rich tradition of woodcarving seems to have drawn its nourishment from an active relationship with spirits, myths, and legends. This combined with ample time that came from such an abundance of sources of food that just a few months were needed to store enough for the rest of the year. The Native Americans not only carved the largest wooden sculptures in the world—totem poles well over 70 feet high—they also made and carved steam-bent wooden boxes that could hold water,

lived in huge communal houses made of carved wood, and carved massive one-piece canoes. Just about everything they used, from dishes and masks to furniture and fixtures, was made from carved wood. They even wore hats and masks (see 14–1, 14–2, and 14–3) made from carved wood.

The Indians of the Northwest lived in a woodcarver's paradise! They were literally surrounded by huge forests of easy-to-carve, fine-textured, straight-grained wood. Just about everything was sculpted from wood, and then further detailed with carved and painted motifs that proclaimed lineage and prestige entitlements related to hereditary myths and the name of the clans, as well as their relationship with the spirits.

Estimated Working Time
2–3 working days

Materials
You need a 60-inch length of prepared, easy-to-carve wood that is three inches by three inches square. We have used jelutong, but you could just as well use lime or another such bland easy-to-work wood.

Although it doesn't matter too much what type of wood you use—since it's going to be painted—just make sure that it's easy to carve, straight-grained, and free from knots. If you have any doubts, make contact with specialists in wood supply and see what they have to offer.

Wood Selection Tip
By "specialists" we mean suppliers who sell wood to carvers, turners, furniture makers, and such. Be wary of wood intended for rough tasks like building sheds and fences. Such wood tends to be green, hard-grained, full of termite holes, sappy, and loaded with dead knots!

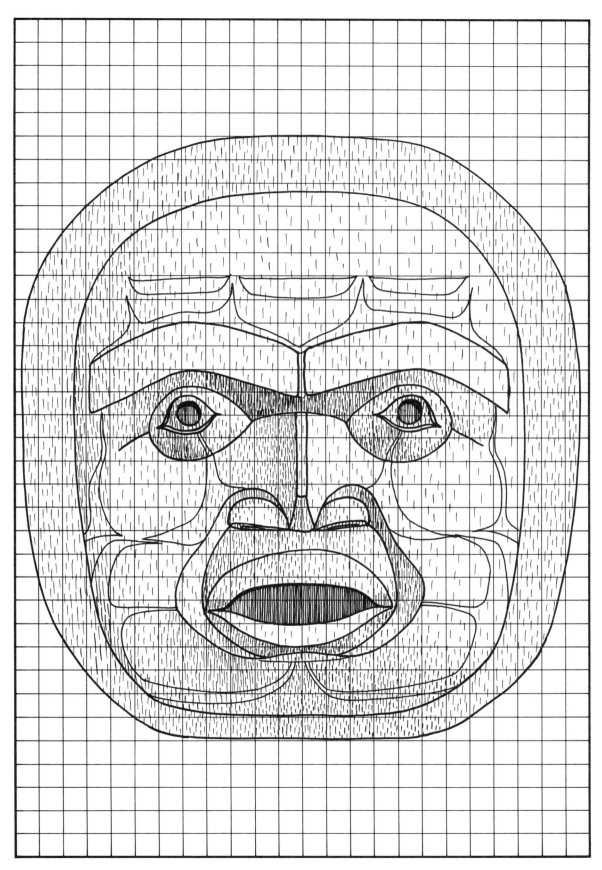

14-2   *Working drawing—front view—the scale is three*
grid squares to one inch.

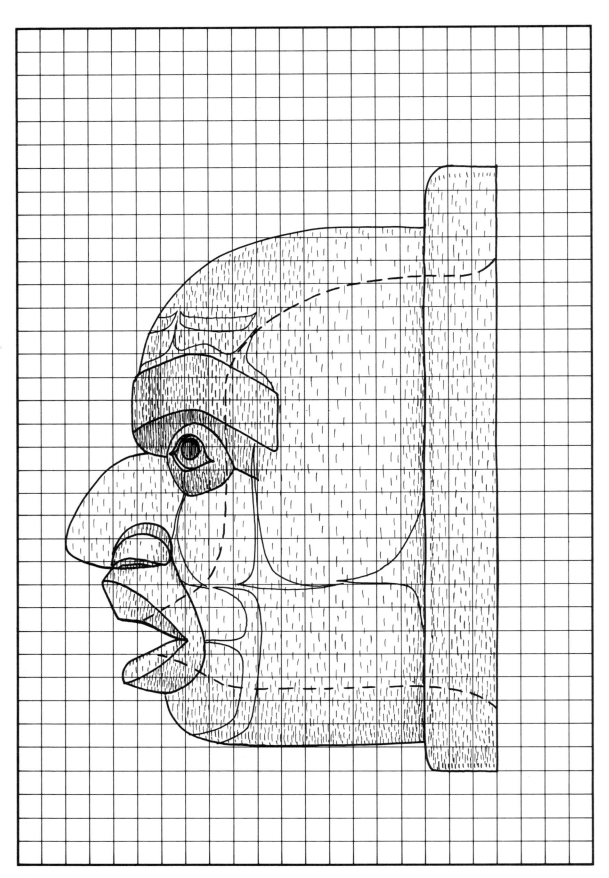

14-3   Working drawing—side view—the scale is three grid squares to one inch. Note the dotted line that marks out the inside shape of the mask.

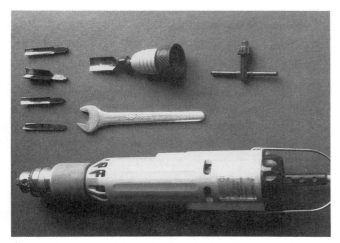

14-4 *The Tokyo Automach Handcraft self-contained, handheld carving system is shown with the reciprocating and rotary carving headpiece options. The unit accepts 100/120/220/240 volts, and it includes a set of five gouge blades. The Handcraft woodcarving system supplied by Woodcraft Supply Corp. USA is efficient, lightweight, and quiet as well as user-friendly. We also use this system to carve a sunflower panel in the American Colonial tradition in Project 4, to carve a gilt ribbon bow in the French tradition in Project 8, and to carve a water dipper ladle in the American pioneer tradition in Project 12.*

Tools and Equipment

- power carving system with gouges (see 14–4)
- set of vanadium-steel cutter bits
- set of tungsten carbide cutters
- set of diamond-mounted points
- set of ruby carver points
- workbench with a vise
- general-purpose saw
- band saw
- pencil, ruler, and square
- block of Plasticine as big as the envisaged mask
- pair each of dividers and calipers
- large soft black pencil or wax crayon
- generous amount of tracing and workout paper
- good quantity of PVA wood glue
- acrylic matt prints in the colors red, white, and black
- two soft-haired watercolor brushes—a broad- and a fine-point
- couple of large clamps
- pack of graded sandpapers

DESIGN, STRUCTURE, AND TECHNIQUE CONSIDERATIONS

When you have gathered your tools and materials, take a look at the working drawings (see 14–2 and 14–3). See how, at a scale of three grid squares to one inch, the mask is made up from six lengths of three-inch by three-inch square sections of jelutong. The wood is cut into 10-inch lengths and laminated in a six-block stack so that three lengths face front and two face sideways.

The reason for using this size wood in this rather unusual manner is simple enough—the wood was at hand, and the three-inch by three-inch section nicely fit my band saw. My band saw best cuts relatively small sections, and fretting out the primary nose-and-mouth profile speeds up the carving process; so I opted for cutting the central three-inch by three-inch section, and then gluing the block together—a great time-saver!

Alternative Wood Selection Tip

If you have a large band saw—one that can cut a nine-inch thickness—and if you can get hold of a nine-inch by six-inch section of easy-to-carve wood, then there's no reason why you can't leave out the gluing-up stages and go straight into the carving.

Have a look at the painting stages, and consider how this project draws its inspiration from a characteristic ancestor mask that was carved and painted by the Bella Coola Indians in the mid-nineteenth century. Note the "U" form motifs that suggest facial painting.

MAKING THE MAQUETTE

Draw your own working drawings to size, and then use a hand-sized paddle of wood to knock the Plasticine together so as to make a mask-sized lump. Now, with one eye on the working drawings, use the calipers and a modelling tool to sculpt the Plasticine to shape and size. Model the stylized mask—the beak-nosed profile, the open mouth, the eyes, and so on. When you have roughed out a swift image, use the dividers to transfer step-off measurements from the working drawings to the Plasticine.

Continue, adding a bit here, taking a bit there, reworking the mouth, standing back to assess the work, reworking a detail in the light of your assessment, and so on. Once you have achieved what you consider is a fair image, use the dividers and the calipers to map out the primary points with matchsticks as markers. For example, you might place matchsticks at the center of the eyes, at the corners of the mouth, on the tip of the nose, at the meeting of the eyebrows, and so on all over the mask. Once the markers are in place, further refine and define the details to triangulate the whole image—making step-offs between markers, say, from the tip of the nose to the center of both eyes, from eye to eye, from nose to chin, to adjust measurements—ensuring that the image is balanced and symmetrical.

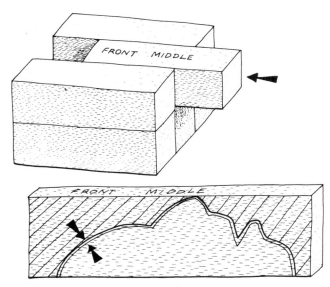

14-5 (Top) Set the best three lengths of wood at the front, and pencil-label the middle block "front middle." (Bottom) Draw the cutting line ¼ inch to the waste side of the transferred line, and shade in the waste area that needs to be cut away.

14-6 Set the wood together in the original six-block stack so that the "profiles" block is at center front.

SETTING OUT THE DESIGN, USING THE BAND SAW, AND GLUING UP

After you have achieved a crisply modelled Plasticine maquette, first use the pencil ruler and square to set the wood out into six 10-inch sections, and then cut it to length. Make sure that the six lengths fit nicely together to make a block 10 inches high, nine inches wide, and six inches deep; try various arrangements so that the best three lengths are set to the front. Pencil-label the middle block "front middle" (see 14–5, top).

Make clear tracings of the front view and the side section profile. This done, take the side profile and the middle block, and carefully press-transfer the imagery to the "side" face. Draw the "line of cut" about ¼ inch to the waste side of the drawn line. Shade in the waste so that you know exactly what needs to be cut away (see 14–5, bottom).

When you are happy with the drawn imagery, and when you have made certain that the band saw is in good order, switch on the power and set to work cutting out the profile.

Band Saw Tip

Be warned that the band saw is potentially a very dangerous machine. Always make sure that you are dressed for the task at hand and that the machine is in good order. If you have any doubts, read through the manufacturer's literature, and have several tryouts on scrap wood before starting the project.

Run the wood through the machine, cutting a little to the waste side of the drawn line. As needed, cut the waste away in a little-by-little manner—that is, make repeated slices or passes until you have a faceted face that more or less follows the curve of the profile.

Set the wood together in the original six-block stack so that the "profile" block is at front center, and make a few pencil guide marks so that you know what goes where. Finally, smear glue on all mating faces and clamp up (see 14–6).

Clamping Tip

If you are a bit short on clamps, but do have a large, strong workbench vise, then you could secure the six-stack in the vise and, at the same time, pull it together with the clamps.

USING THE RECIPROCATING OPTION TO ROUGH OUT THE IMAGERY

After you have roughed out the front middle profile on the band saw and glued up the six-block stack, take the reciprocating carving tool, and fit the broad U-section gouge. With the block secured face-up on the bench, switch on the power and clear the waste away from the other two front blocks. Working from the central block—the one that has been cut on the band saw—gouge out-and-around towards the two front-side edges. Carve and lower the face of the blocks so that they slope down from the middle profile out towards the side edges (see 14–7 and refer to 14–9, top left).

14-7 *Carve and lower the faces of the side blocks so that they slope down from the centerline towards the side edges.*

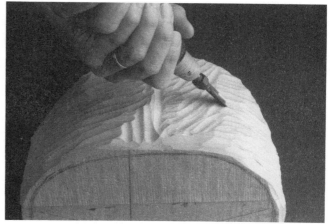

14-8 *Gouge away the corners and sides of the block.*

With the bulk of the waste cleared from both side cheeks, draw the total back-of-mask shape on the back of the block, and gouge away the corners and sides (see 14–8 and 14-9, top right). When you have achieved the round-cornered form, run a pencil guideline around the whole side of the face—around the top, bottom, and sides' edges—so that it is about 1¼ inches up from the back of the mask. Fit the V-gouge in the handpiece, and run a deep stop-cut to the waste side of the pencil line—that is, between the pencil line and the front of the face (see 14–9, left). Carve the stop-cut progressively deeper and deeper until you have an overall all-around-the-face trench at a depth of about ½ inch.

With a deep V-section stop-cut in place, refit the U-section gouge, and lower the whole side area between the stop-cut and the front of the face so that the mask steps in by about ½ inch (see 14–9, bottom right). Slice this area away to the depth of the stop-cut to achieve the step. While you are cutting the step, you can also tidy up the shape and generally work towards a more pulled-together image (see 14–10).

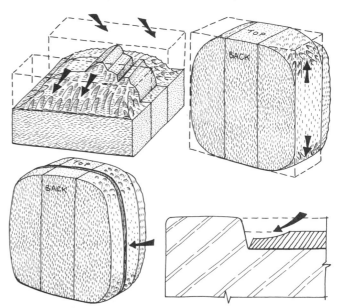

14-9 *(Top left) Clear the waste away from both side cheeks. (Top right) Draw the total back-of-mask shape out on the back of the block, and gouge away the corners and sides. (Bottom left) Run a deep stop-cut to the waste side of the pencil line. (Bottom right) Use the U-section gouge to lower the whole area between the stop-cut and the front of the face.*

USING THE RECIPROCATING GOUGE TO ROUGH OUT THE FEATURES

Having chopped out the broad shape of the face and carefully studied the maquette and the working drawings, take the pencil and draw a guide-line grid over and across the surface of the mask. Draw a line that runs down the center of the face, lines that set out the mouth and the eyes, lines that set out the top of the brows, and so on. Draw in as many guide lines as you think necessary (see 14–11, next page).

Having marked in the primary features—and taking into account that the position of the details will change

14-10 *Tidy up the shape and round off the sides.*

129

14-11 *Draw in the centerline, set out the lines for the nose, eyes, and mouth, and draw out the top of the brows.*

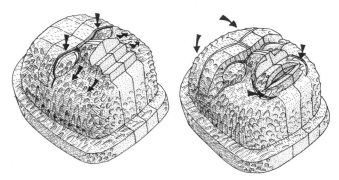

14-12 *(Left) Cut away the wood on either side of the nose and mouth, and sink the wood around the ball of the eye. (Right) Continue to remove small scoops of waste so that the features are revealed and left standing in relief.*

14-13 *Remove the layers of waste so that the features are left standing proud.*

14-14 *Use the vanadium-steel bud cutter to carve the nose and mouth creases.*

as you cut down into the body of the wood—take the gouge and start to lower the waste on either side of the cheeks, at the eyes, at either side of the nose, and so on (see 14–12, top). Being very mindful not to cut too deep, gradually work backwards and forwards over-and-around the mask until the details begin to stand out in relief. When you have chopped out the main areas, change over to a smaller gouge and concentrate your efforts on secondary details.

It's all simple enough as long as you take it easy, and as long as you keep checking your progress by taking caliper readings from the maquette. For example, if you mark in on the wood the total width of the nose—either side of the nostrils—and if you also mark in the depth, and if you then lower the wood so that the whole nose area stands out in relief, then there is no reason why you should chop away too much wood. That said, you do have to bear in mind that as you cut deeper and deeper into the wood, you will have to be ready to modify your angle of cut in the light of the direction of the revealed grain.

Continue to carve, cutting away the wood at either side of the nose, sinking the wood around the ball of the eyes, rounding the forehead, lowering the wood around the mouth (see 14–12, bottom), cutting back the wood from under the chin, and so on. Take note as you are working that carving is not so much a process of completing a single detail and then moving on to the next, but rather one of working the piece as a whole, all the while checking off various details against each other. Working in this way, layers of waste are gradually removed, lowered, and modelled so that features are revealed and left standing in relief (see 14–13).

Power Carving Tip
Never be in a rush and try to dig the gouge too deep. Just go at it nice and easy, all the while removing small scoops of wood. If the grain cuts up rough, then sharpen the blade and/or try a different angle of approach.

USING THE ROTARY CARVER TO MODEL THE DETAILS

Having said that carving is a little-by-little process, there comes a time when you will have to start the delicate make-or-break task of modelling the details. When you come to the point where you consider that the gouge is too broad a tool for the job at hand, then fit the rotary head. Fit variously the vanadium-steel bud cutter (see 14–14), the round-cylinder cutter (see 14–15), and the long tree-point burr (see 14–16). Set to work carving the details—the eyes and mouth. Use the burr to comb the whole surface of the mask to a unified finish.

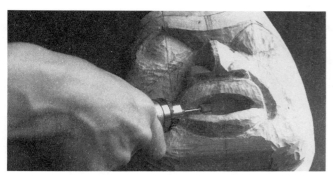

14-15   Use the vanadium-steel round-cylinder cutter to deepen the inside of the mouth.

14-16   Use the long tree-point burr to comb the whole surface of the mask.

Power Carving Tip

Although tungsten carbide burrs are wonderfully efficient, they are also horribly dusty; so be sure to wear a coverall and a dust mask.

The combing process is one of pulling everything together so that the carver can see whether or not the carving is going in the right direction. That is to say, the act of combing somehow or other shows up the problems.

Power Carving Tip

If, at the combing stage, you see that there are still large areas of waste to be cut away, then be ready to go back to using the reciprocating gouge option.

Once you have used the burr to comb the entire surface of the wood to a unified whole, then pick up your pencil, calipers, and dividers. Draw in a whole new set of guide lines. Shade in areas that need to be deepened—for example, the crease around the mouth, the hole inside the mouth, and the eye socket at each side of the nose (see 14–17).

I find that the best way of working at this stage is to pencil in the details that need to be cut away; cut them in with one or other of the cutters and burrs; brush away the dust and debris; have another look at the maquette; pencil in a few more guide lines; clear a little more waste with the appropriate shaped bit; and so on.

When you decide that you have gone as far as you can go with one type of tool, then change over to using smaller and finer bits and points. You might use a carbide cylinder cutter for the lips (see 14–18), the small, pointed long-tree burr for the crease around the mouth, the small ball burr for the eye holes and for the mouth, a long ball-nosed steel cutter for shaping the cheeks, and a long tapered diamond point for the crease around the lips. Don't worry if there comes a time when you are spending more time selecting and fitting points

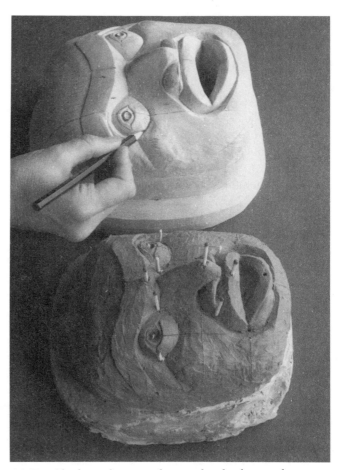

14-17   Shade in the areas that need to be deepened.

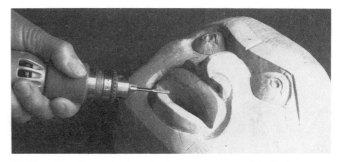

14-18   Use the carbide cylinder cutter to model the lips.

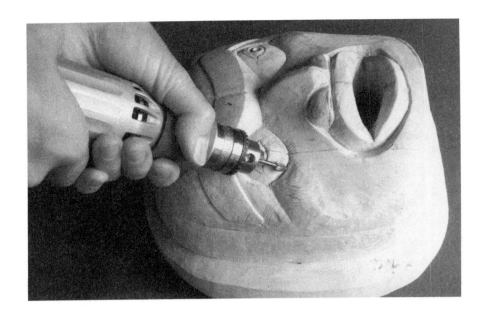

14-19 *Use the flame cutter to shape and define the moats around the eyeballs.*

than actually carving. The time spent pays off once the correct shape point is fitted, since the carving moves along at a much swifter pace.

Continue, using the flame high-speed cutter to shape and define the sides of the nose and the moats around the eyeballs (see 14–19), a ball cutter for sinking the pupils, and a slender carbide tree-radius cone cutter for generally shaping and smoothing the surface (see 14–20). When you get close to the finished image, rub the whole workpiece down with the sandpaper. Stand back and check the carving against the maquette.

Power Carving Tip
If at this stage you consider that the carving needs extra work, then simply draw in more guide lines, shade in

more areas that need to be sharpened up and defined, and go back to using the best tools for the job.

Turn the mask over so that it is face-down and supported on an old cushion. Use the reciprocating gouge to scoop out the waste from inside the mask. Working in much the same way as you might carve a bowl, cut from the side rim to the middle to sink deeper into the wood. Once you have cut through to the mouth hole, go back to using the rotary handpiece—fitted with the burrs and the cutters—and work the mouth hole so that it runs in a smooth curve, from the sharp line of the outer lip through to the inside of the mask. Use the dashed line in the working drawing side view as a guide (refer to the working drawing side view, 14–3).

14-20 *Finally, use the slender carbide cone cutter to generally sharpen up the creases.*

PAINTING AND FINISHING

Once you consider the mask finished—and this might take anything from a couple of days to a couple of weeks, depending on your skill and speed—take the graded sandpaper and, being careful not to blur the sharp edges left by the points, rub the surface down to a smooth finish. Pay particular attention to the lips, the nostrils, the eyebrows, and the forehead. Brush off the dust, and, if necessary, use a fine diamond point or a knife to sharpen up the details. For example, when I had used the smallest ruby point to cut and define the whites of the eyes, I then took my smallest and sharpest penknife and further worked the details to leave all the lines looking crisp and clean.

Continue, rubbing down with the graded sandpaper, trimming with a knife, using a smaller and finer rotary tool, reworking smaller and more detailed guidelines with a pencil, perhaps using the edge of a small cutter to sharpen up the edge of the eyebrows, until you consider the carving finished.

Power Carving Tip

If there comes a time when you can't "see" the carving for dust, debris, and doubt, then I suggest it's time to take a break, clean up the workshop, and ask your friends around for a viewing. Study the mask; ask yourself if it has gone as far as it needs to go; study the maquette; and generally be super-critical. If I have a problem, I usually let the carving be for a few days, and then come back with a fresh eye.

When at long last you are truly pleased with the carving, brush off all the debris, and move to the dust-free area that you have set aside for painting. Carefully study the working drawings' details again; take a sharp-pointed pencil and draw on the mask all the lines that go to make up the design. Consider how some of the details are pretty straightforward—because they follow the carved shapes—while others, such as the U-motifs on the cheeks, cut right across smooth areas.

With the details nicely set out, first take the fine-point brush and the white paint, and painstakingly line in the deep crease around the mouth, the outer lips, the whites of the eyes, and the U-motifs on the chin, cheeks, and forehead. Next, repeat the procedure with the red paint—only this time, line in the outer corona that rings the mask, the lips, the nostrils, and the details that run up to the eyes. Don't worry too much if the paint bleeds a little over the drawn lines, because you can make good with the black. First use the fine-point brush to define the edges of the details, and then block in the remaining areas with the broad brush.

Painting Tip

If you make a bit of a mess-up with the black paint, and, say, spoil such and such a line, wait for the paint to dry; then correct the mistake by reworking the red and white motifs.

When you have followed through a procedure of gradually adjusting and defining the details until you are happy with the overall effect, take a small piece of the finest-grade sandpaper and cut through the colors at the main "wear" points: the ridge of the nose, the ridge of the eyebrows, the curve of the cheeks, and the outer edge of the corona. Try to achieve the effect that the colors have worn through over a period of time.

Finally, apply several generous coats of wax polish. Let it soak into the wood, and then burnish the whole mask to a dull-sheen finish.

HINTS, TIPS, AND AFTERTHOUGHTS

- If you are in a hurry, then you could use a flap sander wheel to bring the contours to a swift, smooth finish.
- It's most important that your gouges are razor sharp. Every five minutes or so, fit the little aluminum oxide grinding cylinder in the rotary head, and swiftly bring the bevel of the gouge blade to a keen edge.
- Be very careful, when you scoop out the nostrils and the mouth, that you don't lever the tool on the edge and damage the fragile rim.
- Always be ready, in the light of changing grain conditions, to change over to different tools and to approach the carving from another angle. For example—if, after bringing a detail to a beautiful finish with a fine cutter, you feel that the detail needs a bit of drastic reshaping, then be prepared to go back through the tool range and modify the carving.
- When you are painting, allow for bleeding and running of the paint along the grain of the wood. For maximum control, paint the edge of the design first—the light colors—and then cut back and block in with the dark paint.
- If you are going to hang the mask on the wall, there's no reason why you shouldn't leave it solid, and do no more than bore out the eye and mouth holes.
- When the carving is nearing completion, watch out that the edge of the chuck doesn't rub and abrade the surface.

15
Carving a Duck Decoy

Primary techniques—gouge and stroke carving

15-1 Project picture. A stylized merganser duck decoy—gouge and stroke carved.

Decoy ducks are imitations—usually made of wood—that have traditionally been used to lure wild fowl (see 15–1 and 15–2). In use, the woodcarved and painted ducks were anchored in a body of water, and the hunters settled down in a blind or a boat. Passing flocks of wild fowl saw what they thought were ducks and so came down to settle on the water. At this point, the hunters started shooting the birds. I use the past tense, because by about 1920 or thereabouts, the U.S. Congress put a ban on large-scale shoots, and the whole practice of using duck decoys more or less came to an end.

In the context of woodcarving, duck decoys are particularly exciting in that, because they were usually made by the hunters themselves, the forms are swift, basic, bold, and at the same time, built with the minimum of waste. Traditionally, the bodies were shaped with a knife and axe, the heads were pegged and glued into the bodies, and then the whole form was brought to a good finish and painted.

With the passing of the years, duck decoys have come to be considered examples of American folk art, with collectors prepared to acquire a single decoy at great expense.

Estimated Working Time
10–15 hours

Materials
You need a 48-inch length of prepared, vigorously grained wood 10 inches wide and 2½ inches thick. A piece of timber salvaged from a building site, or an off-cut from a beam or joist, would be perfect. I went for a length of pitch pine even though I knew at the outset that the carving was going to be hard going. But then again, I also had a pretty good idea that hidden away within the unpromising bulk there was a beautifully grained duck.

If you do decide to use a piece of difficult-to-carve wood—because you like its color, form, or whatever—you still have to avoid any piece that contains end splits and dead knots. Traditionally, the decoys have been cut from very ordinary wood—usually pine.

Tools and Equipment
- power carving system with gouges (see 15–3 and 15–4)
- long ball-nosed high-speed cylinder cutter
- long ball-nosed tungsten carbide burr
- medium-size abrasive flap wheel
- workbench with a vise
- three large G-clamps
- pencil and ruler
- one sheet each of tracing and workout paper
- wax crayon for drawing on the wood
- craft knife
- band saw
- bench plane
- white PVA glue
- old copper flathead nails and hammer
- pack of graded sandpapers
- set of artist's watercolor paints
- couple of paintbrushes—a broad- and a fine-point
- wax polish and a brush

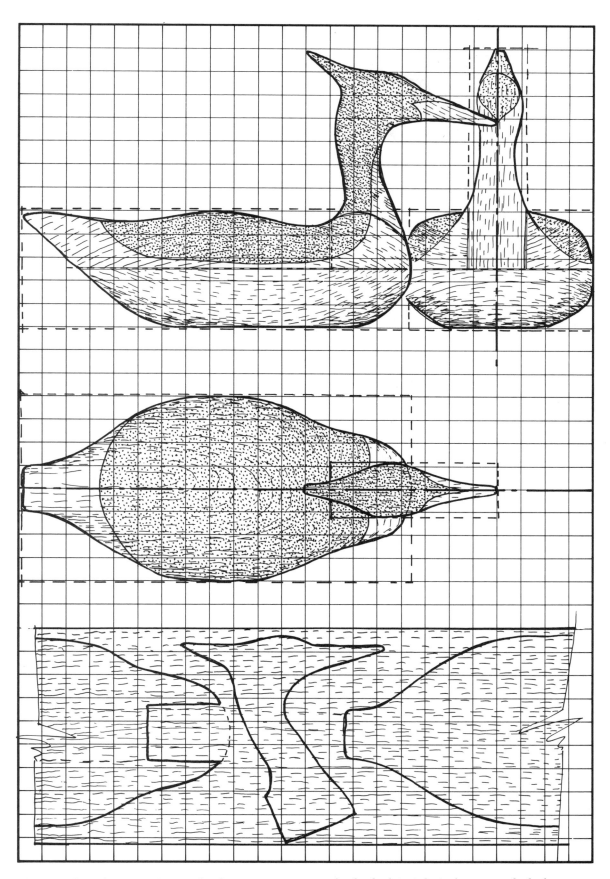

15-2 *Working drawings. At a scale of one square to one inch, the duck is eight inches across the body, 12 inches from the base to the head crest, and 17 inches from tail to bill.*

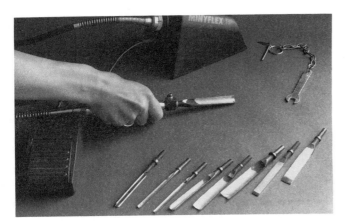

15-3   *The Hegner Moviluty Minyflex woodcarving system is shown set up for the reciprocating option. Also shown are the heavy-duty foot pedal, a selection of gouges, and a spanner. The rotary option is shown in 15-3. The reciprocating option is efficient and smooth with the gouge blades removing wood at an amazing pace. The blade only starts to move when it is in contact with the wookpiece, so it is safe and easy to control. We also use this system to carve an American Folk Art rooster in Project 3 and to carve the cigar-store figure of "Captain Jinks" in Project 16.*

DESIGN, STRUCTURE, AND TECHNIQUE CONSIDERATIONS

Before you put tools to wood, stop and consider just how you want your decoy to be worked. Do you, for example, want to go for the stylized merganser type as illustrated, or would you prefer a more detailed image? Will you be using a band saw, or are you going to use a handsaw? . . . and so on. It's important, right from the start, that you be clear in your own mind as to the tool and materials implications of a project of this character.

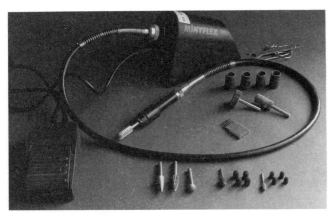

15-4   *The Minyflex carver is shown with the rotary option, a selection of cutters, a flap sander, and various drum and cap sanders. The abrasive flap wheel can sand a large sculptural form very quickly. The wheels can also be formed to fit tight curves.*

When you have gathered your tools and materials, take a look at the working drawings (see 15–2). See how, at a grid scale of one grid square to one inch, the decoy measures about eight inches across the width of the body, 12 inches high from the base line to the top of the head, and nearly 17 inches long from the tip of the tail to the breast.

Note the way the decoy is built from three 2½-inch-thick units or components—the head and two body slabs (see 15–5, bottom). The two body slabs are identical, apart from the upper slab having a notch or mortise for the neck. Take a look at working drawings again, and see how important it is that the head be cut from the plank so that the grain runs along the length of the head—that is, from the tip of the plume to the point of the bill.

SETTING OUT THE WOOD

When you have a good, clear image in your mind's eye of just how you want the decoy to be—and when you have made your own research drawings and spent as much time as possible studying existing decoys in museums and galleries—pin your studies up around your working area and arrange your tools so that they are comfortably at hand. Set out the power-carver unit, and fit the shaft with the reciprocating handpiece. Set your wood out on the workbench, and give it a last looking over just to make sure that there aren't any flaws that are going to mess up the project.

Take a good tracing from the working drawings, and then pencil-press transfer the traced lines to the working face of the wood. Spend time making sure that the profiles are arranged for best effect. For example, if you think that there is a subtle twist of grain or a small knot

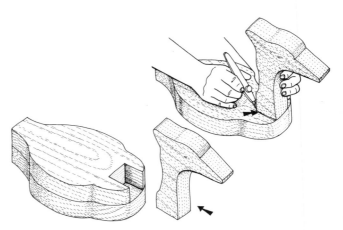

15-5   *(Top) Using the neck width as a guide, mark the mortise slot out on the body slab. (Bottom) If all is well, the neck should be a good tight push-fit.*

that might enhance the duck's head, then see to it that the head profile is arranged accordingly. Once you have transferred the tracing, go over the transferred lines with a soft pencil.

FIRST CUTS, GLUING, AND CLAMPING UP

Having first made sure that you are familiar with the power-carving unit, and having checked that you are safely dressed—your tie/ribbons/cuffs/hair are tied back out of harm's way—then run the wood through the saw, cutting out the three profiles. Don't, at this stage, cut out the neck mortise in the topmost body shape, and don't try to achieve anything like a finished form. Just settle for a line of cut that is about ⅛ inch to the waste side of the drawn line.

When you have achieved the three cutouts, take the head-and-neck profile to the bench and give the bottom half—meaning the neck end that is to fit in the body mortise—a swift run over with the plane to leave the two sides and the back smooth; remove as little wood as possible.

Having studied the working drawings to see how the head slots into the body mortise, take what you consider is the best of the two body slabs, and mark out the position of the mortise. Bearing in mind that the end of the neck will now measure something less than 2½ inches in width, use the neck width as a guide (see 15–5, top). This done, take the body slab back to the band saw and remove the waste. Have a tryout to assess how much

wood needs to be cut away, and then trim back to a good, tight push-fit (see 15–5, bottom).

Cutting the Mortise Tip
If the neck is a loose, sloppy fit, this will show up at a later stage as a gap or hole that will need filling; so spend time at this stage getting it right.

Finally, having made sure that the neck tenon is a good tight push-fit in the body mortise, smear PVA adhesive on all mating faces—the underside of the top body slab, all around the base of the neck, and in the body mortise. Then bring the three pieces of wood together and clamp up (see 15–6, top).

REMOVING THE MAIN AREAS OF WASTE AND WORKING THE BODY

When the glue is dry, remove the clamps. Set the rough-sawn blank out on the work surface, and then have a good long look at the working drawings, and at any sketches and inspirational illustrations that you have gathered along the way.

Having noted how the duck needs to be shaped, take a large soft pencil, or better still a wax crayon, and mark on the blank all the areas of waste that need to be cut away. For example, there is a large angle of waste underneath the tail, waste on either side of the bill and crest, and so on. Mark out the wood; draw in a bill-to-tail centerline; and generally establish in your own mind just how much waste needs to be removed.

Having made sure that the carving machine is in good order, screw the shaft on the unit. Push the reciprocating handpiece on the shaft; fit the large U-section gouge (see 15–7). Tighten the allen screw and the locknut, and make ready for the really exciting task of roughing out the primary shape.

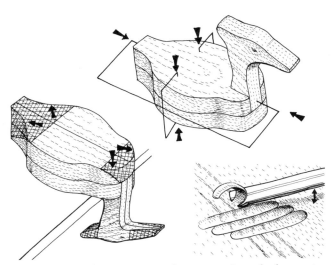

15-6 (Top) Clamping up—the arrows show the best point of contact for the clamps. (Bottom left) Work the underside of the duck from center to side—remove the two large areas of waste. (Bottom right) With the tool held at a low, shallow angle, remove a series of crisp curls of waste to leave the wood looking dappled and shiny.

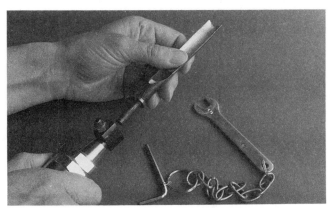

15-7 Having fitted the large U-shaped gouge, carefully tighten the allen screw and the lock-nut.

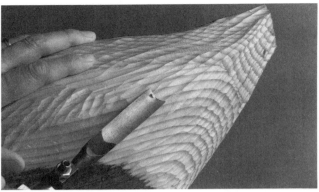

15-8 *Carving the underside of the tail—the waste should come away as a series of crisp curls, leaving the wood nicely dappled.*

15-9 *Use a crayon to carefully mark in the areas that need to be wasted. Hold the workpiece firmly with one hand and the tool in the other.*

Bearing in mind that pitch pine is just about one of the hardest, most resinous woods that you are likely to come across, start by clearing away the large wedge of waste from the underside of the tail. With the duck upside down on the bench—either handheld or clamped in place—work from center to side (see 15–6, bottom left). Holding the tool at a low, flat angle to the wood, work from the middle of the base out and down towards the tail and side. If you find that the motor fades or that the wood cuts up rough, then try variously using a small U-section tool, a higher speed, or sharpening the blade. If all is well—meaning the blade is good and sharp, and the wood is dry—the waste should come away as crisp, hard curls, leaving the wood nicely dappled and shiny (see 15–6, bottom right).

Continue scooping away the areas of waste, then mark out more areas in reference to the wood already removed. Cut away more waste, and so on, all the while getting closer and closer to the envisaged form that is "hidden" within the wood.

Power Carving Tip
It's all pretty straightforward, as long as you never dig the tool in too deep, never point the tool at your body, and never run the tool straight into end grain. If you stay with these basic rules of thumb, then the going will be easy and uncomplicated.

Continue carving, running the gouge backwards and forwards across and around the body, until the form begins to take on a round-ended duck-like characteristic (see 15–8). For the moment, stay away from the head and neck, and concentrate your activity on the body. Note that the whole form has a very low center of gravity, with the main body bulge being below the water line. Continue, looking at the working drawings, scooping away a little more waste (see 15–9), marking out the

15-10 *Stand back and consider your progress, and then mark out the next areas to be worked.*

15-11 *The large, high-speed ball-nosed cylindrical cutter fitted and ready to go.*

shape with the crayon, skimming off a little more waste, and all the while getting gradually closer and closer to the envisaged duck form (see 15–10).

CARVING THE HEAD AND THE BODY WITH THE HIGH-SPEED CUTTER

Before you do anything else, fit the rotary shaft and the large, ball-nosed cylindrical high-speed cutter (see 15–11). Tighten up and generally check that all is correct.

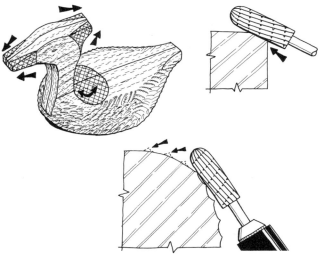

15-13   *Keep moving both the tool and the workpiece to achieve the best angle of cut.*

15-12   *(Top left) Use the crayon to shade in the areas that need to be worked—the arrows show the best direction of cut. (Top right) Hold the high-speed cutter at a low, flat angle and carve away the sharp corners. (Bottom) Cut away the sharp peaks left by the gouge.*

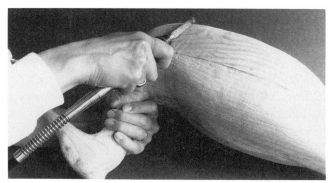

15-14   *Using the ball-nosed cylinder carbide burr, hold the duck on its side and carve the underside edge.*

Have another look at the working drawings. Note how the bill and the head crest relate to the bird's neck and how the dip of the body runs in a smooth, deep curve up into the back of the neck. Use the crayon to shade in the areas that need to be wasted (see 15–12, top left). Support the duck in your lap or on the work surface and set to work with the high-speed cutter. Use the tool much as you would a knife. That is to say, grasp the handpiece as if you were going to peel or pare an apple—hold it at a low, flat angle so that the length of the cylindrical cutter is in contact with the wood—and draw the tool towards you in an easy, stroking motion. Don't try to dig away great chunks of wood; just let the tool slice away delicate scooped curls at its own pace. Run the tool around the rough-sawn head. Settle, in the first instance, for doing no more than cutting away the sharp corners (see 15–12, top right). With one eye on the working drawings, and the other on the run of the grain, round over the bill, the head crest, under the neck, the back of the head, and so on. When you have removed the corners and angles, then mark with the crayon the next area to be wasted, and continue carving.

Once you have carved what you consider is a fair head and neck shape, stay with the high-speed cutter, and start shaping up the body. The procedure is more or less the same as for the head—the only difference this time being that you are cutting a surface that has already been worked with the gouge. Start by cutting off all the little sharp peaks that were left by the gouge (see 15–12, bottom). Then continue until the whole surface—from bill to tail—runs into one smooth, undulating plane.

CARVING WITH THE TUNGSTEN CARBIDE BURRS

When you have removed the bulk of the waste with the high-speed cutters, fit a ball-nosed cylinder carbide burr into the handpiece, and set to work bringing all the forms together. Bearing in mind that the burrs are able to remove wood at an amazing pace, be very cautious that you don't cut too fast and/or too deep. Start by going lightly over all surfaces, this way and that, until the decoy takes on a rough-filed appearance. Try as far as possible to cut with or across the grain, rather than into end grain (see 15–13 and 15–14).

When you have reduced the whole surface to a matt finish—so that you can see the workpiece as a single form—then once again stand well back and try to figure out your progress. Look at the duck from all angles—side, front, back, and plan. Study the shapes and curves, and try and decide in your own mind whether or not you have taken the carving as far as it needs to go. This final assessment isn't easy, because, after all, beauty really is in the eye of the beholder—but do your best.

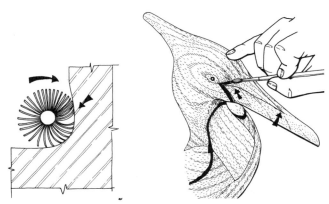

15-15 (Left) With the tool run at high speed, deform the flap wheel sander so that it fits the curve. (Right) Work a little to the color side of the drawn line so that, if and when the paint bleeds, it stops short at the drawn line.

SANDING

When you have brought the whole surface of the decoy to a nicely burred finish, then comes the dusty task of sanding. Fit the abrasive flap wheel in the handpiece, and tighten up. The procedure is simple enough; all you do is run the tool backwards and forwards over the whole surface until it's smooth to the touch (see 15–15, left). Try, as you are working, too criss-cross the surface to avoid making score marks.

You will notice, that the action of the flap wheel on the hard-soft-hard grain tends to cut back the soft wood so that the hard grain stands proud, leaving the whole surface beautifully rippled. If you feel that such and such a grain detail is particularly attractive, then it's a good idea to concentrate on the soft areas to exaggerate the ripple. Continue sanding a little, identifying blemishes, sanding back to remove the blemishes, cutting back soft wood to draw attention to attractive runs of hard grain, and so on.

Finally, hammer the copper nails into the body to draw attention to what you consider is an attractive run of grain.

PAINTING AND FINISHING

When you have taken the carving as far as you feel it needs to go, wipe it clean with a slightly damp cloth, and move to the dust-free area that you have set aside for painting. Bearing in mind that the painting can make or break the carving, have another good long look at the project picture and the working drawings. See how we have gone for a stylized image. That is to say, after studying photographs of merganser ducks, we decided that rather than try to pick out every detail, we would use a single color to suggest the imagery.

Take a soft pencil, and draw on the decoy the area that you want to block in with color. Don't fuss around, just go for a big, bold smooth-lined shape that follows the form. And of course, if you think that such and such a run of grain would make a good line to follow through with the paint, then so much the better. Have a tryout with a piece of scrap wood. Mix the desired color—we used a mixture of deep blue, green, and yellow—and lay it on as a medium nonrunny wash; no so thick that it sits on the surface, nor so thin that it bleeds into the wood.

When you have a good color, take a fine-point brush and a thick paint mix, and outline the area that you want to block in. Work a little to the color side of the drawn line so that if the paint does run and bleed, it stops short at the pencil line (see 15–15, right). Having edged the color area, then fill in the whole area with paint.

After the paint is good and dry, take a sheet of fine-grade sandpaper, and rub the painted area down, cutting through the paint on the hard-grain areas. The exciting thing is that, because the paint soaks into the soft grain rather than the hard, when you rub the wood down in the direction of the grain, you will easily be able to cut through the color on the lines of hard grain. The overall effect, of a smoothly rippled surface, with the ripples being alternately green and the dark brown color of the hard grain, makes for a beautiful "water" effect—like dappled sunlight on still waters.

Wipe away the dust with a dry cloth, and give the whole duck a generous coat of wax polish. Finally, burnish the decoy to a high-sheen finish. It is ready for showing!

HINTS, TIPS, AND AFTERTHOUGHTS

- There's no denying that pitch pine is very hard going—it's a tricky, difficult wood to carve. This being so, you have to decide whether you want to try the project with pitch pine and risk making a mess-up or to go for an easy option—making the duck from jelutong and covering the bland grain with paint. Then again, pitch pine is such an exciting, vigorous wood, I think it's worth taking the risk!
- If you work in such a way that the carving-tool shaft is tightly kinked or bent, you will soon find that the handpiece will heat up. Arrange yourself so that the shaft bends in an easy curve between the motor and the handpiece.
- It is most important that you use a well-seasoned length of wood. I say this because if it is in any way unseasoned, then there is a good chance that it will shrink across its width and split along its length. If you are at all worried, then seal the wood before waxing.

16
Carving a "Captain Jinks" Cigar-Store Figure

Primary techniques—gouge and stroke carving

16-1   Project pictures. Captain Jinks—gouge and stroke carved.

In the context of American folk art, cigar-store figures are carved and painted wooden figures—some life-size and others small enough to be stood in a window or on a counter—that were used in the nineteenth century by tobacco shops as advertisements for cigars, snuff, and related products.

"Captain Jinks of the Horse Marines" characterizes cigar-store figures, in that he is eye-catching and gener-

ally a figure of fun (see 16–1). Our particular "Captain Jinks"—and there are many such figures—draws his inspiration from a carving circa 1875 that once stood outside a certain "Feary's" cigar store in Newark, New Jersey.

As to who Captain Jinks was—we have it that he has to do with either "Captain Jinks of the Horse Marines"—a popular Civil War song—and/or he was a bandmaster of the early nineteenth century. You might think that his uniform would give us a clue as to his origins, but I've seen "Captain Jinks" figures with green jackets that look like German bandsmen, with red jackets like English soldiers, with decorative frogs and ribbons on their jackets, and with high hats like Russian hussars.

To my mind, Captain Jinks has to do with the saying "high jinks"—meaning lively enjoyment. Then again, he looks a bit like a dancer and a bit of a dandy; maybe he does draw his inspiration from a real music-hall character of the early nineteenth century. If you find out, please let us know!

Estimated Working Time
3–4 working days

Materials
You need a two-inch-thick slab of prepared, easy-to-carve wood 12 inches wide and 24 inches long with the grain running down the length, and with the "heart" face being planed to a smooth finish. We have gone for a piece of lime/linden/basswood, but you could just as well choose a piece of jelutong or similar wood. As long as the wood is easy to carve, smooth grained, and generally free from knots, then the type—the color and the grain especially—aren't too important. I say this because the wood is going to be painted.

141

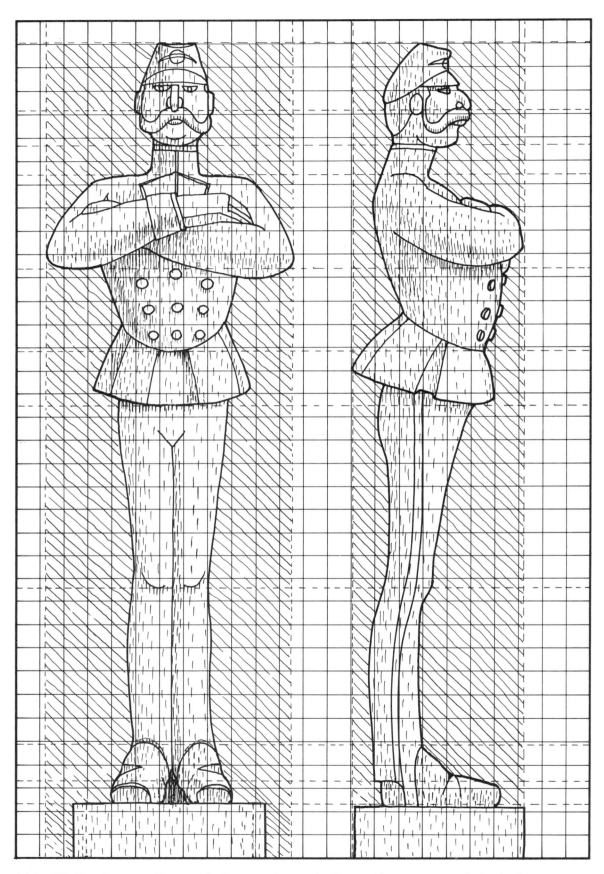

16-3 *Working drawings. Front and side views. At a scale of two grid squares to one inch, the figure measures about 19 inches in total height.*

Tools and Equipment

- power carving system with gouges (see 16–2)
- large and small high-speed cutters
- carbide cutters and burrs
- diamond cutters
- abrasive bobbins
- workbench with a vise
- three large G-clamps
- pencil and ruler
- one large sheet each of tracing and workout paper—as big as the wood
- dividers and calipers
- wax crayon for drawing on the wood
- craft knife
- large block of Plasticine
- band saw
- white PVA glue
- graded sandpapers
- mask and goggles, or a respirator
- set of acrylic paints in the colors blue, red, black, antique white, "flesh" pink, and gold
- couple of paintbrushes—a broad- and a fine-point
- tin of clear varnish

DESIGN, STRUCTURE, AND TECHNIQUE CONSIDERATIONS

When you have gathered your tools and materials, have a good look at the project pictures and the working drawings (see 16–3). See how the finished figure stands about 19 inches in total height—meaning from the bottom of the base to the top of the hat. Note that the figure is a bit of a caricature in that all his features—his broad shoulders, skirted jacket, and slender legs—are exaggerated in proportion. Consider how the imagery is both naive and bold.

Have a look at the way the initial block, or blank, is made by slicing the 12-inch-wide slab down its length (see 16–4, left) and then gluing the two slabs together so that the "heart" wood is at the center.

SAWING, GLUING, CLAMPING, AND SETTING OUT THE WOOD

When you have a clear understanding of how the figure needs to be blocked up and worked, take the two-inch-thick slab and pencil-label the heart face with the word "glue." Draw a centerline down the length so that the slab is divided into half. Run the wood carefully through the band saw along the centerline. If all is well, you should have two pieces of wood at two inches thick, six inches wide, and 24 inches long.

16-2 The Hegner Moviluty Minyflex woodcarving system is shown set up with the reciprocating option. Also shown are the heavy-duty foot pedal, a selection of gouges, and a spanner. The system is also capable of rotary cutting action. The reciprocating option is efficient and smooth with the gouge blades removing wood at an amazing pace. The blade only starts to move when it is in contact with the workpiece; so it is safe and easy to control. The rotary and reciprocating shafts are swiftly interchangable. The handpiece can be gripped like a knife and used at a low angle in a paring right-to-left action. We also use this sytem to carve an American Folk Art rooster in Project 3 and to carve a duck decoy in Project 15.

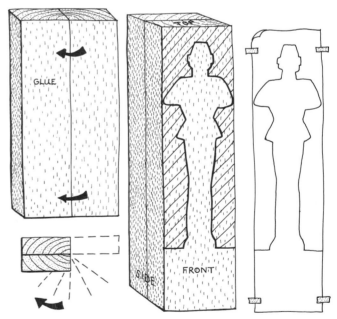

16-4 (Left) Close the two halves together—like a book—so that the two glued heart faces are touching. (Right) Press-transfer the figure outline to the wood.

Having smeared a generous amount of PVA glue over the "glue" face, close the two halves—like a book (see 16–4, left). Rub the two mating faces side-to-side and end-to-end to press out air pockets and excess glue; then clamp and put to one side for about twenty-four hours.

16-5 Front and side views—use the band saw to clear away the bulk of the waste.

Take the glued-up block and pencil-label the best end "top," one six-inch by 24-inch face "front," and one of the four-inch by 24-inch faces—meaning the face showing the glue joint—"side." Having double-checked that you haven't made a mess-up, draw the design up at full size. Make a tracing of the outline of the figure as seen from the front view, and press-transfer the imagery to the wood (see 16–4, right).

16-6 Front and two side views—after using the gouge to rough out the basic figure, start to set out—to carve—the broad forms.

When you are happy with the drawn image, set to work on the band saw to carefully cut out the front view profile. Don't try to run the sawn line around the image in one continuous cut; rather, make several cuts from the edge of the block to the drawn line, and then saw away the waste in a series of "bites."

Once you have roughed out the figure as seen in front view, then draw the side imagery on the band-sawn side face—up, down, and over all the sloped contours—and repeat the procedure in much the same way as already described. I say "much," because you will, at times, be cutting through thicker sections such as the six-inch elbows. Depending on the depth of cut of your band saw, you might have to settle for only cutting the waste away from around the head and the legs. If this is the case, then you can use a coping saw—or a straight saw and a chisel—to chop out the waste. Don't worry too much, at this stage, about trying to get close to the drawn line; just do your best to clear away the bulk of the waste (see 16–5).

BUILDING A PLASTICINE MAQUETTE

After you have roughed out the blank, clear away all the dust and debris, and pin up your drawings. Start with the Plasticine to model what you consider are the most complex details—the details that you can't see in your mind's eye. For example, although I was happy with the legs, I couldn't "see" how the arms and hands were set in relation to each other. Consequently, I settled for modelling the torso. Have a friend model, if possible, and then modify the image from life. Using the drawings as a guide, try as far as possible to make the maquette the same size as your workpiece.

USING THE RECIPROCATING GOUGE— FIRST CUTS

Having first had a good tryout with the power-carving unit and with all the various wood-removing options, fit the reciprocating head and one or other of the shallow U-curve gouges. Set to work carving out the image as seen in front view. The procedure is pretty straightforward; all you do is keep one eye on the working model, and then systematically cut away the waste through the whole four-inch thickness of wood.

When you have achieved a roughed-out "front view," then take a pencil or crayon and mark on the wood all the areas that need to be cut away and/or rounded. Then get back to work with the gouge. Don't get too disheartened if, at this stage, the workpiece looks all hacked about and not at all like the carving that you see in your mind's eye (see 16–6).

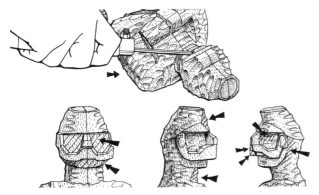

16-7 (Top) As you progress, use a smaller gouge to make smaller cuts. (Bottom left) Reduce the wood at the cheeks and chin. (Bottom center) Cut back the waste on the hat and neck. (Bottom right) Reduce the wood at the lips and behind the ears.

As you get closer and closer to the figure "within" the wood—and when the form becomes more rounded than square—then you will have to be more cautious and take smaller and smaller cuts (see 16–7, top). Draw a centerline on the head and hat, and define the nose, brows, and whiskers. Note the slope of the neck. Take the gouge and cut down into the wood—to the waste side of the drawn line—to make stop-cuts. Do this around the nose, along the brow, and at the peak of the cap. Reduce the waste to leave the nose and whiskers standing proud (see 16–7, bottom left). Repeat this procedure, all the while gradually reducing the waste, redrawing guide lines, and cutting back to the lines. Aim to reduce the head to a series of steps (see 16–7, bottom center and right).

USING THE ROTARY HANDPIECE AND THE LOW- AND HIGH-SPEED CUTTERS

Fit the rotary shaft and handpiece to the power unit (see 16–8). Slide the tapered ball-nosed cylinder or the large ball-nosed cylinder high-speed cutter in the handpiece, and tighten with the allen key and spanner.

Support the workpiece on your lap or on the work surface, and begin with the high-speed cutter. Use the tool much as you would a knife. That is to say, grasp the handpiece as if you were going to peel or pare an apple—hold it at a low, flat angle so that the length of the cylindrical cutter is in contact with the wood—and draw the tool towards you in an easy, stroking motion. Don't try to dig away great chunks of wood or to apply too much pressure; just let the tool slice away small scooped wisps at its own pace. Run the tool up, down, and around the figure, all the while cutting away the little "peaks" as left by the gouge (see 16–9).

16-8 The rotary option—with the handpiece, spanner, and a selection of tool bits.

16-9 Being careful not to apply too much pressure, draw the tool towards you with an easy stroking action.

With the workpiece held upside down on your lap, clean out some of the sharp angles. Deepen V-cuts with the pointed cutter—sharpen large steps and angles with the cylinder, define stepped cuts with the inverted cone, and use the small cylinder to define the smaller stepped details. Generally run the cutters around the waist, around the neck, between the legs and the feet, in the angle between the chest and the top of the arms, in the angle between the body and the underside of the arms, and so on around the rest of the figure (see 16–10).

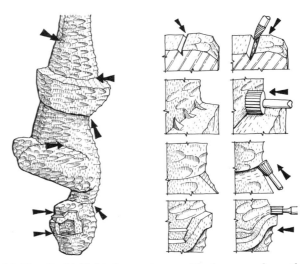

16-10 (Left) Hold the carving upside down, and use the various points to model the primary steps and angles that go to make up the design. (Right top-to-bottom) Cut the narrow slot between the legs, the underside of the jacket, around the neck, and over the whiskers. The arrows show the best angle of approach.

145

16-11 *Use the tapered cylinder carbide burr to lightly work and comb all the surfaces.*

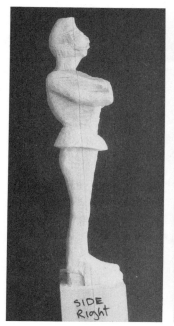

16-12 *Front and side views—comb the whole surface until you can see the figure as a single pulled-together image.*

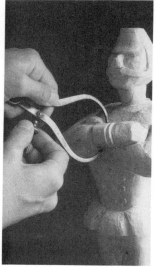

16-13 *Take caliper readings from the Plasticine maquette, and use them to help size the carving.*

CARVING WITH THE TUNGSTEN CARBIDE BURRS

After you have removed the bulk of the waste with the high-speed cutters, fit a long-taper carbide burr in the handpiece, and set to work bringing all the forms together. Bearing in mind that the burrs are able to "eat" wood at an amazing pace, be very cautious that you don't cut too fast and/or too deep. Start by going lightly over all surfaces—this way and that, over and around all the curves—to "comb" all the forms and surfaces together. Be very wary about running the tool into end grain (see 16–11).

Continue until you have reduced the whole surface to a matt finish—so that you can see the workpiece as a single form—then once again stand back and be super-critical. Look at the figure from all angles—side, front, back, and plan (see 16–12). Try to decide in your own mind whether or not you have removed the main areas of waste and are ready to bring the figure to a final finish. If, on reflection, you think that such and such a detail needs to be dramatically reworked, then mark the area with a crayon and go back to using the high-speed cutters. For example, when, after "combing" our figure with the burr, we realized that both arms were oversize, we first had to cut them back with the gouge and then reduce them with the cutters. Finally, use a small gouge to shape and texture the base block.

MODELLING THE DETAILS WITH FINE CUTTERS, DIAMOND CUTTERS, AND ABRASIVE BOBINS

As you work, try to think of the finished carving as being a figure that is hidden away just below the surface of the wood—like a precious archaeological underwater artifact hidden away in the middle of an encrusted lump. With this in mind, don't try to gouge off all the concealing layers in one great thrust, but rather, gently pare away until you feel that the lines of the form are revealed.

When you reach a point when only one thin layer needs to be removed, then—using the Plasticine model and the calipers to check sizes and form (see 16–13)—fit variously the tungsten carbide cutter, the very small high-speed cutters, and the small abrasive bobbins in the rotary handpiece, and set to work carving all the fine details.

Continue working the stepped details around the boots, the hands, the cuffs, the top of the collar, the hair line, the bottom of the hat, and all the rest (see 16–14). To round off the folds on the jacket, use the cylinder cutter and work with a delicate stroking action (see 16–15).

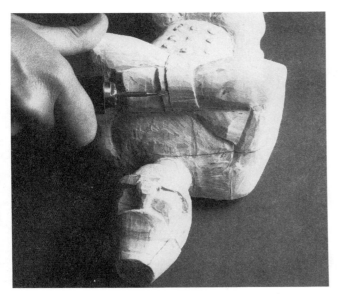

16-14   Use the small cylinder to define the stepped areas.

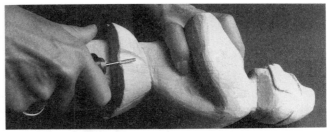

16-15   Use a stroking, paring action to round off the sharp edges on the folds of the jacket.

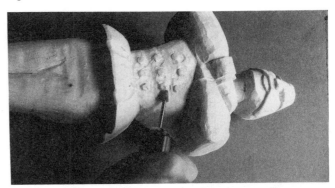

16-16   Lower the wood to leave the buttons standing proud.

When we came to work the nine little dots of wood that go to make the buttons, we found it was not so much a case of "carving" the buttons, but more a task of lowering the ground wood so that the buttons were left in high relief. We worked through the whole range of tools, using the small cylinder high-speed cutter to rough out the little circles, a long, thin tapered-cylinder tungsten carbide cutter to define the buttons, a little tree-radius cutter to lower the wood between the buttons (see 16–16), a diamond cutter to shape the top of the buttons, and then the abrasive bobbins to tidy up.

Finally, use a fine-point tool and a delicate stroking action to achieve the hair effect on the whiskers.

SANDING, PAINTING, AND FINISHING

When you have taken the carving as far as you feel it needs to go, then use the fine-grade bobbin sanders and the sheets of sandpaper to rub the work down to a smooth finish. We used a fold of sandpaper to clean between the legs and fingers and under the whiskers—and the smallest bobbin sander to finish the pleats around the bottom of the jacket and the eye socket hollows.

Are You Finished Carving?

If you are unsure as to whether or not the carving is finished, put it to one side for a day or two—or even a week or two—and then come back to it with a fresh eye.

When you have taken the carving as far as you want it to go, then vacuum it thoroughly; wipe it clean with a slightly damp cloth and move to the dust-free area that you have set aside for painting. Start by giving the whole

figure—from the head to the top of the base—a coat of matt white. While the paint is drying, have another good long look at the project picture and the working drawings, and see how we have gone for good strong colors and a caricature image.

Aim for stylized details rather than naturalistic realism. When the ground colors are dry, add a small amount of pink "blush" to the cheeks and a small amount of blue/grey shadow around the nose and eyes.

When the painting is finished, take a sheet of fine-grade sandpaper, and selectively rub the figure down to cut through the paint on the "wear" areas.

Finally, once you consider the project well and truly finished, complete the "antiquing" by mixing a small smear of brown oil paint in with the clear varnish and giving the whole workpiece several generous coats.

HINTS, TIPS, AND AFTERTHOUGHTS

- This carving is tricky in that there is no single and easy way of working. Choose the best wood for the job, keep your tools sharp, keep trying the various rotary and reciprocating options, and don't be in a rush to finish.
- If by chance you do happen to split off a part, don't panic; make repairs with Super Glue and a piece of wood set at the same grain angle, and then go back to work.

17
Carving a Miniature Lidded Box and Decorating It with a Shell Motif

Primary techniques—stroke and touch carving

17-1 *Project picture. Lidded box with shell motif—two views—stroke and touch carved.*

There is something awe-inspiring about a woodcarving that is so tiny and fragile that it can be held in the palm of one hand. Like a jewel, or a bird, or a flower, such a delicate object is almost beyond our understanding. If the object has been created and fashioned by human hands, then it is held in especially high regard.

Traditionally the woodcarver's love affair with miniatures found—and still finds—expression in Japan with the carving of netsuke—often intricately carved, small toggles used to fasten a small container to a kimono sash—in Switzerland with the carving of figures, in Germany with the carving of pipes, in England and America with the carving of various small boxes, buttons, printing blocks, buckles, rattles, dolls, toys, and so on. There is something particularly special about a small lidded box (see 17–1 and 17–2)—it's almost as if it is asking to be picked up, held, and nestled.

Estimated Working Time
10–12 hours

Materials
You need a 1⅜-inch-thick piece of hard, smooth, dense-grained wood about two-inches by two-inches square, with the grain running from side to side across the two-inch face. Make your first choice English or European boxwood; failing that, you could use top-quality holly.

Bear in mind that boxwood only comes in relatively small pieces, and these tend to have end splits and stains. In the context of this project, the stains aren't too much of a problem—because the wood is going to be colored black—but the stains sometimes do indicate that there are cavities hidden within the wood. If you have any doubts, then ask the advice of a specialist wood supplier.

Tools and Equipment
• power carving system with cutter bits (see 17–3)
• set of high-speed cutters
• set of tungsten carbide cutters
• sanding disc with mandrel to fit
• workbench with a vise
• pencil, ruler, and compass
• ball of Plasticine that is as big as the box
• modelling tools such as penknives and spoons
• large black felt-tip pen or spirit marker
• one sheet each of tracing and workout paper
• roll of double-sided adhesive tape
• scroll saw with a selection of blades
• couple of rubber bands/elastic bands
• penknife
• pack of graded sandpapers
• hand drill with a ¹⁄₁₆-inch-diameter bit
• single brass/steel panel pin
• Super Glue, wax polish, and a brush

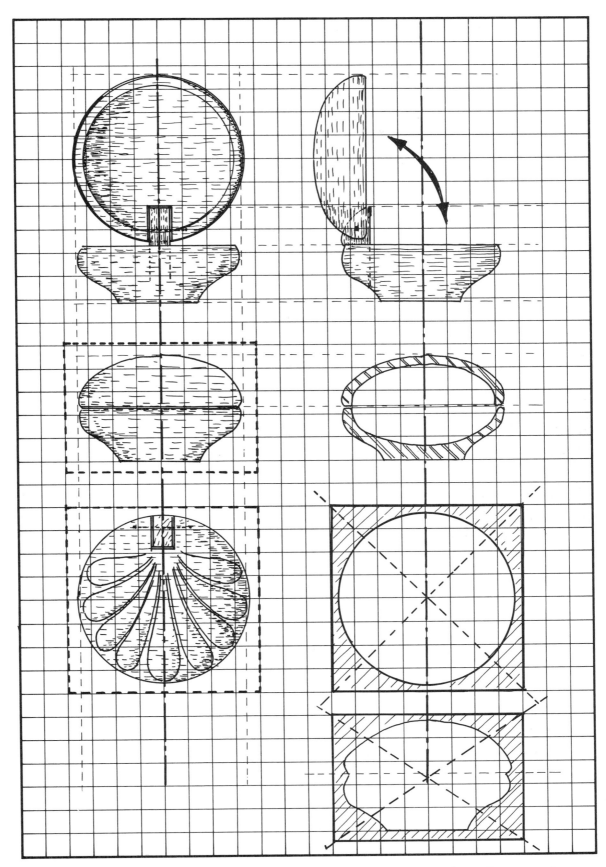

17-2   Working drawings. At a scale of four squares to one inch, the box is 1½ inches in diameter and 1¼ inches high. Note the pin-hinge-post detail and the cross sections showing wall thickness.

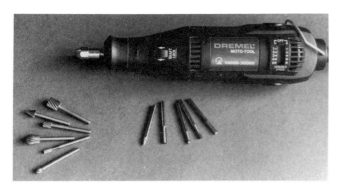

17-3 *The Dremel Moto-Tool woodcarver No. 395/396 is shown with cutter bits. The handheld motor unit uses 120/220 volts and has a variable-speed finger-controlled switch. The Moto-Tool features a quick-change ⅛-inch-diameter collet and a collet wrench. The grip is comfortable, allowing a carving action similar to the usual strokes used when carving with a knife. We also use this system for decorating the found box with incised carving in Project 1 and in part to carve an Icelandic knot roundel in Project 6.*

DESIGN, STRUCTURE, AND TECHNIQUE CONSIDERATIONS

When you have gathered your tools and materials, take a look at the working drawings (see 17–2). See how, at a grid scale of four squares to one inch, the little box measures a little over 1½ inches in diameter and not quite 1¼ inches high. Note the way the top of the box is pin-hinged on a little post, with the post being cut, fitted, and glued into the bottom of the box. The stylized shell motif fits the top of the lid and is aligned with the hinge post.

The project is a bit tricky in that the box is first carved in the round, then sawn in half and hollow-carved, then hinged, and finally decorated with a carved motif. Of course, you could change the order some—decorate the lid before you hollow-carved, for instance—but, because there is a danger of the whole thing going wrong during the high-risk hinge-fitting and hollowing stages, I recommend that you only start the final decorative carving after the box is made. Or put another way, it would be a great pity to carve the box complete with the motif, cut it in half, and then make a mess-up with the hollow-carving or with fitting the hinge.

When you have studied the project, made decisions as to whether or not you want to modify the design—the shape of the box or the lid motif—draw the design at full size, and make a good clear tracing.

Finally, take the ball of Plasticine, and build a full-size working model of the box. And, of course, if you don't quite understand how the hinge is fitted, or whatever, then this is the time to sort out such details.

SETTING OUT THE DESIGN AND FIRST CUTS

Once you have made a full-size working model of the box, and you have a clear understanding of how you want it to be—its size, the shape of the inside, the way the hinge is fitted, and so on—put the model in view, but out of harm's way.

Take the two-inch by two-inch square block of wood; mark the top and bottom faces, and establish its center by drawing crossed diagonals on all six faces. Next, run a centerline from the centers across the face of the wood and down and around the sides. Do this in two directions and across all faces so that the two-inch by two-inch square block is quartered. Most important of all, run a "bottom of lid" line around the block (see 17–2, bottom right). With all the guide lines in place, take the tracing of the side profile, and set it on the side faces of the wood so that all guide lines are aligned. Then pencil-press-transfer the profile image to the wood (see 17–4, top left).

When you are happy with the way the wood is marked out, take it to the scroll saw and set to work cutting out the form. It's all pretty straightforward; just make sure the blade is well tensioned, the saw is in good working order, and you are completely familiar with all the safety procedures. Feed the wood into the saw so that the blade is always presented with the line of next cut, and so that the cut is a little to the waste side of the drawn line.

The suggested order of work is to cut out the box as seen in one side view; use the double-sided sticky tape to fit the block back together; and then cut the box out as seen in the other side view.

Sawing Tip

The only thing that you do need to bear in mind in the context of this project is that boxwood is very hard and dense. You may have to slow down the rate of feed—or you might say the speed of the cut—so that you don't break the blade and/or scorch the wood. Just use your common sense—if the blade looks to be stressed, or the wood starts to smoke, then slow down the action.

CARVING IN THE ROUND

After you have cut out the basic profile on the scroll saw—a profile with angled shoulders (see 17–4, top right)—then move to a comfortable corner of the workshop, and settle yourself down with the power carver. As

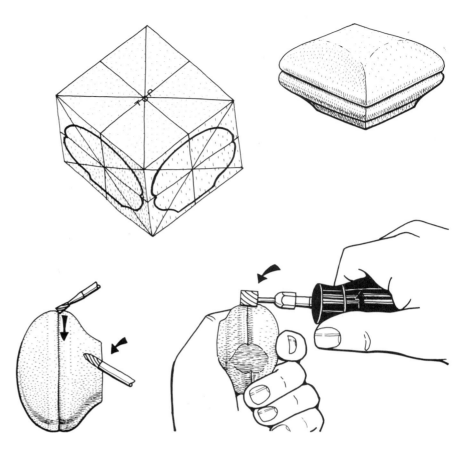

17-4 (Top left) Label the block "top" and "bottom," and draw crossed diagonals and the line that marks out the bottom of the lid. Trace the side face profiles onto the two sides of the block. (Top right) The profile with angled shoulder, after the waste has been removed. (Bottom right) Use a stroking, paring action to remove the unwanted corners. (Bottom left) Use the inverted-cone cutter for the rim line, and the tree-point cutter for the underside concave curve.

with the other projects, equip yourself with goggles and dust mask, and set out the tool selection so that everything is comfortably at hand. It's always a good idea at this early stage—especially if you are a beginner—to take a piece of scrap wood (the same type used in the project) and to have a tryout with the tool and the bits.

When you have decided on the best cutter/bit for the job, fit it securely in the power carver, and set to work rounding off the workpiece. We tended to favor three high-speed cutters—the large ball-nosed cylinder, the tapered ball-nosed cylinder, and the small inverted cone. The working action is to take the wood in one hand and the tool in the other, holding the tool much as you would hold a knife, and then run the cutter over the wood in a gentle, right-to-left paring stroke (see 17–4, bottom right). The main thing to bear in mind is that it is the side of the cutter that does the work, not the end.

Continue cutting away the waste and turning the wood—cutting and turning, cutting and turning—until the little piece of wood takes on the envisaged rounded shape.

Power Carving Tip

The control is so good that there is very little danger of doing real damage to your hands. Of course, there is always a chance that you will nip and abrade your fingers a wee bit—and that's perhaps to be expected when you are working on a small carving of this character. We found that holding the workpiece in one hand and the tool in the other increased our control. If you are at all worried about nipping your fingers, then secure the workpiece in the jaws of the vise.

You will soon discover as you are working that you have to keep changing the cutters to suit the task at hand. For example, you might use the large cylinder bit for the general shaping, the long tree-point carbide cutter for the concave underside curve, the edge of the inverted-cone cutter for the rim line (see 17–4, bottom left)—the line between the lid and the base—and so on. The good news is that when you are working on a material like boxwood, you don't have to worry too much about the direction of the grain. Just about every cut, no matter the direction of the stroke, will leave the wood looking smooth and crisp.

Once you have achieved what you consider is a good box form, use the full range of sanders—power sanding discs and sheets of graded sandpaper—to bring the wood to a good finish. Work through the grades from medium to fine until the wood feels smooth to the touch.

HOLLOW-CARVING

With a new heavy-duty coping-type blade fitted and tensioned in the scroll saw, run the little box edge-on through the saw to cut the lid from the base. There is no foolproof way to do this. And worse still, since you only get one shot, it's got to be right the first time around. Have a tryout with a piece of scrap just to make sure the blade is correctly tensioned, and then to do no more than go at it slowly and carefully, all the while checking that the line of cut stays true and doesn't wander. If you are a bit unsure of yourself, then you could use a handsaw to do the cutting.

Separating Lid from Base Tip

You could, perhaps, change the working order around slightly, and cut the wood along the lid line before you start shaping up the profile—it's a thought!

When you have successfully cut the box in two, then comes the good fun bit of hollow-carving the inside of the base and the lid. Fit the tapered ball-nosed cylinder high-speed cutter in the power carver. Again, you can secure the workpiece in the vise or hold it in your hand; the choice is yours. Holding the wood seems natural because the close contact lets the work be "felt" in progress. The working action is to run a pencil around the inside rim to establish the thickness of the box—about ³⁄₁₆ inch is right—and then run the cutter from side to center to dish, and lower the waste in successive stages (see 17–5, top left). Don't be tempted to try to burrow into the wood with a single thrust; just go at it nice and slowly.

When you have lowered the waste by about ⅛ inch, you can change the carving action so that the tool "wipes" around the inside curve (see 17–5, top center). Run the cutter around the inside of the hollow just as if you are spooning out a hard-boiled egg—or maybe wiping your finger around the inside of a small pot of cream. Try with each stroke to do two things: make the hollow a little bit deeper, and tidy up the inside curve.

Continue stroking around the inside of the hollow, and then digging a little deeper—stroke, dig, stroke, dig—until you decide that the hollow has gone as far as it needs to go. Go through this hollowing process for both the base and the lid. Finally, fit one of the flat sanding discs to the tool, and rub the inside of the hollows down to a smooth finish (see 17–5, top right).

FITTING THE HINGE

Once you have hollowed out the little box, have a look at the working drawings (refer to 17–2, top), and see how

the hinge post is fitted. Note how it is let into a slot that cuts about ⅜ inch into the side of the box. See also the way the hinge post is glued into the bottom of the base of the box, and pinned to the lid. Fitting the hinge is decidedly not easy. If the slot is too wide or too deep, or if you twist the blade and the wood splits, then the box is going to be a mess-up.

Fit the two halves of the box back together so that the grain matches. Strap it up with an elastic band, and use a pencil to mark on the lid the position of the slot. Make the slot about ³⁄₁₆ inch wide, about ⅜ inch deep—from the side towards the center—and aligned on the centerline. With the slot clearly marked, and with the box still strapped up with the elastic band, go back to the scroll saw. Fit and tension a fine blade, and then to work.

Set the box on its base, and run the blade into one side of the slot, across the end, and then out the other side so that the ³⁄₁₆-inch-wide slice of waste falls away. Cut slightly to the waste side of the drawn line (see 17–5, bottom left).

Sawing Tip

As the blade bites through the side of the box and into the hollow, it will jump forward—be ready for it!

With the box slotted, cut a 1¼-inch-long rod of boxwood about ½-inch by ¼-inch in section. Trim it down so that it is a tight push-fit in the slot—not too tight, just a nice, neat fit. This done, dribble a small amount of Super Glue into the bottom-of-box slot, and fit the hinge post in place (see 17–5, middle). If all is well, the post should fill the slot and run right through the box so that it sticks out at both top and bottom. When you are happy with the fit, check that the glue-fix is secure. Then use one of the small cylinder cutters to trim the rod back so that the top, bottom, and back edges are flush with the profile of the box. If you have made a good job of it, you should hardly be able to see the join between the rod and the box.

When you are happy with the fit, remove the top of the box, and use a small round-nosed cutter to cut the inside of the rod back so that it is flush with the inside curve of the box. Don't worry too much about the inside top of the rod; just round it over a bit so that the sharp corner doesn't get in the way of the lid as it opens. Strap the lid of the box back in place. Check that it's aligned; grip it in the jaws of a muffled vise; and then fit the ¹⁄₁₆-inch bit in the drill, and run a pivot hole in from one side of the lid through the hinge post and out through the other side (see 17–5, bottom right). Inspect the lid and the hinge post, and, if all is well, push the pivot pin in place, trim it to length, and glue-fix it with a drop of Super Glue.

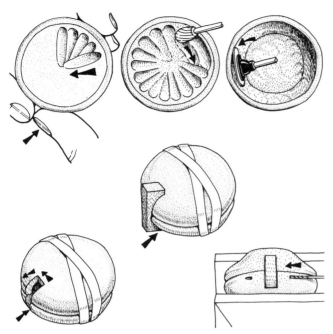

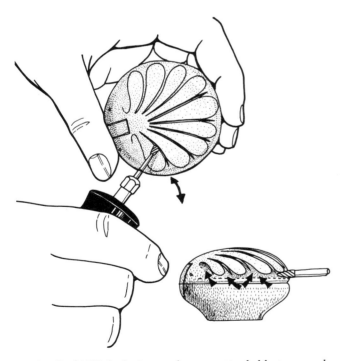

17-5 (Top left) Use the tapered ball-nosed cylinder cutter to lower the inside waste—bracing your hand with your thumb. (Top center) Remove the inside edge waste. (Top right) Use the sanding disc to rub down to a smooth finish. (Bottom left) Cut a 3/16-inch-wide slot for the hinge post. (Middle) Glue the hinge post in place. (Bottom right) Use the 1/16-inch bit to drill the pivot hole.

17-6 (Left) With the inverted-cone cutter held at an angle to the work, stroke along the guide lines, and make shallow incised cuts. (Right) Use the tree-point cutter to lower the wood around the motifs and around the front rim of the box.

CARVING THE DECORATIVE MOTIF

When you have hinged the lid to the base, take the black felt-tip or spirit pen, and color the whole box black—inside and out, top and bottom—every single surface. Wait a while for the ink to dry. Having traced off the shell motif on a small disc of paper cut to size, align the tracing with the hinge post and the centerline, and fix it in place with a couple of tabs of masking tape. Use a hard pencil to press-transfer the traced lines to the top of the lid. The image should show up against the black surface, as a slightly indented silver-grey line.

With the inverted-cone tungsten carbide cutter fitted in the power carver, set in the drawn guide lines with shallow incised cuts. Sink the lines in to a depth of about 1/16 inch (see 17–6, left, and 17–7). Note that although by this stage the box has been dyed black, we have drawn it white for the sake of clarity of detail.

Fit the long tree-point cutter, and lower the area between the rounded front edge of the motif and the front rim of the box (see 17–6, right). Continue, gradually cutting in the lines of the design and lowering the area around the motif, until the shell design begins to stand up in high relief. Don't cut too much away from the edge of the lid, but rather, slice an angled cut from the rim and up into the edge of the motif to create the illusion that the area around the motif has been deeply lowered. Work around the whole edge of the shell, and through the incised cuts that separate the round-ended petal shapes.

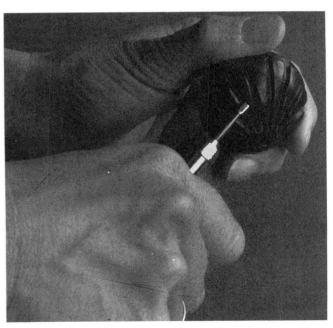

17-7 Take the inverted-cone cutter, and set the drawn lines in with an incised cut.

17-8   *Use the fine-grade sanding disc to rub the workpiece down to a super-smooth finish.*

As you variously define and edge here, and deepen a detail there, so the cuts will break through the black stain and show up as the yellow of the boxwood. When you are satisfied that such and such a detail or cut has been successfully accomplished, then use the felt-tip to reblacken the whole box. Stand back and weigh your progress. Ask yourself—is the shell motif more or less symmetrical? Are the curved ends of the shell nicely rounded? Does the back edge or face of the hinge post follow in a smooth curve the profile of the box? Does the hinge open without putting stress on the lid slot? and so on. Look at the box this way and that, hold it in your hand, set it on a shelf for a couple of days, and generally spend time looking, thinking, and feeling.

17-9   *Buff the surface to a high-shine finish.*

Self-Evaluation Tip

If you have mixed feelings about a project—is it finished? Does it need throwing away? or whatever—then it's always a good idea to put it on hold for a few days and later go back to it.

FINISHING

Once you have taken the project as far as you think it needs to go, first use the chip-carving knife to clean out the sharp incised lines, and then use the fine-sanding disc to rub the whole workpiece down to a smooth finish (see 17–8).

Power Carving Tip

Run the edge of the sanding disc around the edge of the motif while at the same time rolling it over the sharp shoulders of the area in relief. This rolling action produces a nicely defined and rounded curve.

When you have a well-finished, nicely considered box, then give go over it with the black felt-tipped pen. Finally, when the ink is completely dry, give the whole work a generous coating of wax polish. Buff it to a high-shine finish (see 17-9), and give it to your best friend!

HINTS, TIPS, AND AFTERTHOUGHTS

- This is one of those projects that can easily come to complete grief at a couple of high-risk stages along the way. For example, if the lid splits when you are fitting the hinge post, or if the tool pierces the box wall, then the project is totaled. It follows that it is sensible to organize your progress so that you only attempt the decorative carving when the high-risk stages are past.
- Don't try this project with a second-best piece of wood; if you do, then you are just increasing the chances of failure. As it was, when we started cutting into our piece of boxwood, we found that it was pocked with cavities. Fortunately, the cavities were in the wood that needed to be cut away.
- When you are fitting a cutter, always be sure to unplug the tool from the power supply.
- Since the project is so small, you could use an aluminum oxide white point to finish the box—instead of sandpaper.
- The lid design could be improved by having a location hole and pin on the front lip.

Glossaries

General Purpose Tools

Band Saw A power-operated tool consisting of an endless metal band running over and driven by wheels—a good tool for cutting out large thick-section blanks. If you aim to do a lot of power tool woodcarving, then you need a band saw.

Bench A woodcarver's bench might be anything from a carefully designed carpenter's bench to an old table. All that is required is that it be strong, stable, and solid enough to take a variety of clamps, vises, and holdfasts.

Brushes Brushes come in all shapes and sizes. I always use good-quality artist's brushes, meaning brushes that are variously small, soft, and long-haired. Wash them immediately after use, and store them bristle up.

Calipers A two-legged compass-like instrument used for stepping off or gauging measurements/diameters—usually consists of two C-shaped legs that are pivoted at the crotch, or two S-shapes that are crossed and pivoted.

Chisel In the context of power tool woodcarving, a chisel is a flat-bladed cutting tool as used in a reciprocating carving system.

Clamps and Cramps Screw devices for securing wood to the bench or for holding two or more pieces of wood together—they are variously called clamps, cramps, G-clamps, holdfasts, and hold-downs.

Clasp Knife Just about any fold-up pocketknife might be termed a clasp knife—I favor the use of small penknives.

Compass or Compasses Two-legged instruments used for drawing out circles and arcs—best to get a long-legged screw-operated type.

Coping Saw A frame saw used for cutting small-section wood. The G-shaped frame allows the thin, flexible blades to be swiftly fitted and removed. A good saw for clearing out and piercing "windows" of waste. If you aim to do a lot of power tool woodcarving, then get a scroll saw and/or a band saw with a fine blade.

Cushion A leather or canvas bag loose-filled with sawdust, sand, or old rags. In use, the workpiece is nestled, cradled, or supported by the cushion—good for carving small, round-based, lap-supported pieces such as bowls, dishes, and spoons.

Forstner Bit A large-diameter drill bit used for drilling out flat-bottomed holes—sizes range from ⅜-inch to 3½-inch diameter. A good tool for clearing out large/deep areas of waste.

Gouges In the context of power tool woodcarving, the gouge is a curved-sectioned blade, as used in conjunction with a reciprocating carving system. All such tools—whether the blade be shallow-curved so as to be almost flat, or deeply U-sectioned—are termed gouges. In the context of this book, gouges are named by the shape of the cutting edge, rather than by any number or code. For example, a gouge might be described as a "shallow-curved straight gouge" or as a large "U-sectioned scoop gouge" and so on. The "large" refers to the width of the blade/cutting edge, the "deep U-sectioned" describes the shape or cross section of the cutting edge, and the "straight" or "bent" refers to the shape of the shaft.

Holdfast Of all the wood-holding tools such as the vise and the clamp/cramp, I think, in the context of this book, the bench holdfast is the most useful. In use, the shaft is fitted into a hole in the bench, the swivel-arm pad is set on the workpiece, and the screw thread is tightened. The mechanism allows for the swift release of the workpiece.

Masking Tape A general-purpose tape used to secure various parts while they are being glued, pegged, sawn, or otherwise worked. Also used to fix paper to the drawing board and tracing paper to the wood. Avoid using clear plastic adhesive tape—it's too sticky and sometimes leaves a mess.

Measure Might be a wooden ruler, a tape measure, or a steel ruler—best to use a steel ruler, because it can also be used as a cutting/scoring guide.

Skew Chisel In the context of power tool woodcarving, this is a pointed blade, used in conjunction with a reciprocating carving system, where the cutting edge is set at an angle of less than 90 degrees to the side edge of the blade. A good tool for cutting V-section trenches and for clearing difficult-to-get-at areas of waste.

Vise A bench-mounted clamp—they come in all shapes and sizes—engineer's vises, carver's chops, and so on. A vise needs to be strong enough for the job at hand.

Recommended Woods

Alder A sapwood tree common in low-lying damp areas—a good wood for carving bowls and such—a wood traditionally used by North American Indian carvers.

Apple A hard, dense close-grained wood—comes in small sizes, carves well, and takes a good polish.

Ash A long-grained, tough wood. Not suitable for beginners.

Beech A heavy, pleasant-to-carve, inexpensive wood—has a yellow sapwood and reddish heart—a good wood for carving.

Box A beautiful, pleasant-smelling, butter-smooth wood with a hard, dense grain. Can't be bettered for small, special carvings.

Canary (American Whitewood) A yellowish soft wood, even-grained and knot-free—easy to carve.

Cherry A close-grained, pleasant-to-work, red/brown wood—good for small projects. Carves well—can be brought to a high-shine polished finish.

Chestnut Brown in color—rather like English oak in that the grain is firm and compact. It carves well.

Holly A beautiful close-grained, ivory-white wood—it carves well and takes fine details. A good wood for small, delicate carvings.

Lime (American Linden and Basswood) A close-grained, knot-free easy-to-work wood that can be cut and carved in almost any direction. The perfect wood for beginners.

Oak (English) A strong, heavy wood varying from being straight-grained, easy-to-work, and beautiful to being knotty, twisted, tool-breaking, and horrible.

Pear Pinkish brown in color with a close grain and satin finish. It cuts in just about any direction. A good wood to carve.

Pine There are many varieties—most of them being stringy, knotty, and difficult to work. However, for large, bold carvings, pine can be used to good effect, with the knots and grain shining out and enhancing the carving.

Plum A beautiful pink-brown wood—pleasant to carve, with a tight grain and a hard, smooth finish.

Sycamore A hard, light-colored wood—it has a firm, compact grain, and it carves and finishes well. A traditional, nontoxic, low-taint wood used for dairy, storage, and kitchenwares.

Walnut Dark to light brown—a good wood for both small and large pieces. It carves well and takes a good polish.

Yew A fine wood, yellow/brown in color. Although it cuts cleanly and takes a polish, it tends to be full of cracks and dead knots. Yew is **toxic**, and so must be used with caution—**not** to be used for toys or kitchenwares.

Timber Faults

There is no such thing as a perfect piece of wood or a guarantee that your chosen length or block is sound and workable throughout. Certainly the wood might look and smell good, and it might even be described as being the best of the best—and it may even cost you a small fortune—but there is no saying that once the wood is opened, you won't come across a split, or cavity, or a piece of shapnel, or who knows what! The best the woodworker can do is to look out for problem indicators and symptoms—pointers and clues—and then to try and spot the flaws at an early stage and work around them.

There are a great many faults to be on the lookout for—foreign bodies within the wood, hidden cavities, cup shakes, unwanted wane, sappy edges, unexpected grain twists, and so on. Always double-check your wood before you start carving, and if you have any doubts as to its quality, put it aside and look for another piece.

Blemishes Meaning that, sometimes, after cutting, the wood changes to an uncharacteristic color, and/or that the wood can actually be stained by, say, rust, grease, oil, and such. Either way, if the stain/color is unwanted, then it's a blemish. Although some stains are desirable, others indicate rot and decay. If possible, select another piece of wood.

Checks If a board or plank is cracked or split, then it is termed as having a "check." Since the defect is an indicator of possible problems, my advice is to look for another piece of wood.

Decay If a piece of wood looks in any way to be uncharacteristically colored or textured or if it shows signs of decomposition—sponginess, an odd sugar-sweet smell, or stains—then it is likely to be unsuitable for carving. If you find evidence of decay, you can either cut out the bad wood, or better still, find another piece.

Knots Knots are termed dead, hollow, loose, spiked, encased, and so on. They tend to be difficult to carve, so avoid them if possible.

Shakes and Splits Separations that occur throughout the length of a log are termed "shakes" and "splits." For example, star shakes are cracks that show up on the edges of log end-sections as splits, and heart shakes are cracks that show up on the log end-sections as open cavities at the center. Shakes and splits are acceptable if the wood is offered as a gift; but if it's going to cost money, then look for a better piece.

Woodcarving Terms and Techniques

Beeswax A yellowish or dark brown wax secreted by honeybees—the perfect wax for polishing and burnishing. It can be purchased in solid or paste form.

Blank A block, slab, or disc of prepared wood—a piece of wood that has been prepared for carving.

Blocking In To draw the lines of a design onto the face of the wood and to establish the primary details of the pattern or form. Sometimes blocking in means to paint—in the sense that a design has been painted and blocked in.

Burnishing The act of taking a piece of woodcarving to a hard, high-shine finish. Burnishing is best achieved using oil and/or beeswax, a brush, a fluff-free cloth, and lots of "elbow grease." Some carvers might use a tool such as a spoon or bone to rub the wood to a burnished finish.

Carved in the Round A three-dimensional carving—a piece that needs to be worked and seen from all sides such as a doll, a mask, a duck decoy, and a cigar-store figure (Projects 13–16).

Close-Grained Wood that has narrow annual growth rings—such woods usually carve well.

Constructed or Built Up A carving that is constructed or built up from a number of blocks, layers, elements, or parts. For example, if you examine the mask project (number 14), you will see that it is built up from six blocks of wood that have been glued together.

Deep Carved   In the context of power tool woodcarving—cuts that are deep rather than shallow. The mask (Project 14) and dipper (Project 12) are deep carved, whereas the motifs on the surface of a box would be described as being carved in shallow relief.

Designing   Working out a structure, pattern, or form by making sketches, outlines, and models and/or making prototypes that relate to museum originals.

Drilling Holes   In the context of power tool woodcarving—it's best to use, whenever possible, a good-size drill press and a range of Forstner drill bits.

Elevations   In drawing, the views of an object. So a particular view might be described as "top," "end," or "side" elevation.

End Grain   Cross-section grain at the end of a piece of timber. End grain is difficult to carve, and so needs to be approached with care.

Finishing   The act of scraping, rubbing down with sandpaper, detailing with with a rotary point, painting, waxing, burnishing, and otherwise enhancing the appearance of a project.

First Cuts   Meaning the very first stages in the carving after the initial designing, drawing, and transferring has been done.

Found Wood   Taken to mean wood that can be found, beach-combed, or salvaged. In the context of this book, you might use log wood, old building joists, fallen trees, etc. If the wood is sound, then it's good for carving.

Glues and Adhesives   Although there are all manner of glues and adhesives—everything from animal glues to instant glues and resins—the best in the context of this book is PVA glue, meaning polyvinyl acetate. Such glue is easy to use and can be washed off when wet—it's not smelly or wasteful.

Grain   Meaning the annual rings that run through the wood—all the lines, colors, and textures that characterize a piece of wood. Woodcarvers spend most of their time trying to angle the thrust and direction of their tools so as to cut the grain to best advantage. Ideally the woodcarver cuts either across or at a slight angle to the run of the grain. That said—and depending upon the wood type—many sharp-bladed reciprocating power carvers are able to slice at just about any angle through the wood.

Green Wood   Wood that still contains sap—unseasoned wood that is worked before it has dried out.

Gridded Working Drawing   A scaled, square grid placed over a working drawing—in use the object illustrated can be reduced or enlarged simply by changing the scale of the grid. For example, if the grid is described as "one square to one inch," and you want to double the scale, then all you do is read off each square as being equal to two inches. When you come to transferring the drawing to the wood, you just draw out a grid at the suggested size and directly transfer the contents of each square. At one square to one inch you draw out a full-size one-inch grid—at one square to two inches you draw out a full-size two-inch grid, and so on.

Grounding or Wasting   The act of cutting away the wood in and around the main design and taking it down to a lower level so that the design is left in relief. A good example is the sunflower panel (Project 4).

Hardwood   Botanically speaking, hardwood comes from broad-leafed deciduous trees. Hardwood isn't necessarily harder to work than a soft wood, but rather it is a term that describes general characteristics.

Hollow-Carved or Dished   Meaning areas that have been lowered and modelled so that the resultant cavity is curved and dish-like in form.

Knot   These are termed as dead, hollow, loose, spiked, encased, and so on. Knots are unpredictable; so do your best to avoid them.

Laminating   The act of gluing, pegging, or screwing together several pieces or layers of wood prior to carving.

Lowering   Meaning to cut away background wood to leave the design in high relief. This can also be termed grounding or wasting.

Maquette   A working model—could be made of clay, Plasticine, or scrap wood. For most projects, we favor drawing the design up to size, making a working model from Plasticine, and then using the model to step measurements/proportions through to the carving.

Marking Out   Using a sharp-pointed pencil to make crisp, clear, smooth-curved guide lines.

Moats   In the context of North American Indian carving—a shallow U-section trench around "eye" and "joint" motifs. Moats are important features that characterize the work. A good example is the mask (Project 14).

Modelling   The act of carving a design to completion—the carving process of shaping the wood.

Modifying   Changing and redesigning a project so that it is smaller, bigger, worked from thicker or thinner wood, or whatever—changing details to suit your own needs.

Off-Cuts   Small pieces of usable wood that are left over after you have made the project.

Outlining   Meaning to take a V-section reciprocating tool and incise the drawn lines of the design.

Paints and Painting   Before painting, always clear away bench clutter, wipe up dust, and carefully set out your tools and materials so that they are conveniently at hand. We prefer to "lay the colors on" as thin matt washes rather than as solid gloss colors. It is best to use acrylics or even watercolors, and then to rub down with a fine sandpaper and lay on a coat of wax polish.

Pencil-Press Transferring   The act of tracing a master design and then pressing the tracing onto the workpiece so that the lines of the design are transferred to the wood.

Piercing   To drill, fret, or cut wood away so that only a tracery remains.

Plateau Wood   When the ground wood in and around a design feature has been cut away and lowered, the resultant remaining high-relief flat-topped feature might be termed a plateau. Many woodcarvers use geographical or topographical terms to describe various features—valleys, peaks, cliffs, beds.

Profiles   A form, blank, or cutout might be called a profile—this is also used to describe the flat, silhouette, or side view just after the waste has been cleared and just prior to modelling.

Prototype   The initial model, workout, or mock-up made prior to buying and cutting your wood—you might use Plasticine, clay, or inexpensive throwaway wood.

Pulling together Meaning to actually assemble various components, or to assess the work in progress and critically rethink the design.

Reciprocating Power Carving System A power carving tool that imitates the thrusting/pushing action of a mallet and gouge.

Rotary Power Carving System A power carving tool that uses fast-spinning points and bits to variously drill, bore, scrape, abrade, and otherwise cut the wood to shape.

Roughing Out The act of swiftly clearing away the bulk of the waste with saw or large reciprocating gouge—the carving stage prior to modelling.

Rubbing Down To rub the wood down with a series of graded sandpapers/glasspapers so as to achieve a smooth, ready-to-paint finish. In the context of power tool woodcarving, the rubbing down can be achieved by running through the various grades of rotary tool bits/points. For example, you might clean up with a coarse ruby point, then work to a smoother finish with a fine ruby, and so on—all the while using finer and finer points.

Sanding The act of using an abrasive sandpaper/tool to rub the wood down to a good finish. Sanding is a pleasuresome but dusty task that is best managed well away from the painting and designing area. In the context of power tool woodcarving, we always wear googles and a dust mask, or a power respirator.

Scale The ratio between the working drawing and the carving to be made. In use, you read off the scale—for example, "one grid square to one inch"—then you draw up a full-size one-inch grid and transfer the contents of the working drawing squares to your full-size squares.

Seasoned Wood Wood that is considered to have a low and workable moisture content. One woodcarver's seasoned wood could well be another woodcarver's useless over-dry scrap.

Setting In Meaning to cut in along the design line and to separate the ground wood from the relief design. A design might be set in either after or before cutting the V-section trench—it all depends on the character of the work. So you might cut a V-section trench to the waste side of the drawn line, then set in on the line, and finally clear away the small amount of waste between the set-in line and the trench—or you might set in on the drawn line, then cut the V-section trench and finally remove the small amount of waste.

Setting Out The act of transferring the traced lines to the wood and generally preparing the wood, the tools, and the working area prior to carving.

Shallow Relief Carved Areas that have been wasted and lowered to a shallow depth. A design that travels over the surface of a carving without changing the primary shape of the piece.

Sharpening One of the secrets of power tool woodcarving is knowing just how to keep your reciprocating blades razor sharp. Sharpening is not a problem with flat chisel blades; you simply set them in a little wheeled cradle (as sold by most tool manufacturers), run the cradle backwards and forwards over the lightly oiled stone, and then—apart from a couple of swift strokes with the strop to remove any burrs—the job is done. Gouge blades are rather more tricky. We recommend holding the blade up to the light in your left hand—so that you can peer closely at the cutting edge—and then take a rotary handpiece fitted with a small, aluminum oxide cylinder point and strokes the bevel of the gouge to a good shape and finish. By seeing the shape of the bevel up against the light—and by seeing the light shine between the blade and the point—the woodcarver can adjust the angle of the tool and/or blade, so as to sharpen the cutting edge to best effect.

Short-Grain Meaning areas of wood where the structure of the grain is such that the wood is fragile and liable to split.

Stop-Cuts An initial cut straight down into the wood—a cut into which secondary cuts are made. A stop-cut defines the length of subsequent cuts and acts as a brake; it literally stops the cut.

Tooled Finish Meaning a finish that is textured with the marks left by the tools. It can either be a positive part of the procedure, in that the surface is worked with a punch, or it can be the unintended or intended finish as left by the tools. In the context of power tool woodcarving, the individual blades and points all leave their own characteristic mark.

Tracing Paper A strong translucent paper used for tracing. We usually work up a good design, take a tracing with a soft 2B pencil, line in the reverse side of the tracing, and then press with a hard pencil to transfer the lines of the design to the working face of the wood.

Undercutting The act of sinking the waste to make a plateau, and then to gouge out a cavity from the side of the plateau to achieve an overhang or undercut.

Vegetable Oil This can be just about any plant oil that you might use to protect and burnish the wood—corn oil, nut oil, soya oil, etc. It is best to lay on a couple of coats, let it soak in, give the wood a swift rubbing down, and then burnish with a brush and cloth.

Waste Ground The areas in and around the design that need to be lowered, wasted, and otherwise cut away.

Working Drawing A scaled and detailed drawing—one that shows sizes, sections, details, etc. Never cut the original drawings; always take a tracing, and keep the drawing as a master.

Working Face The best side of the wood—the side on which you have drawn the shapes—the front of the panel; the outside panels of the box—the face that is in full view.

Workout Paper Inexpensive paper such as might be used for initial roughs and workout drawings—it is best to use slightly matt white paper.

Workshop Although, in the context of power tool woodcarving, your workshop might be just about anything from a spare room to a lean-to shelter out in the garden, the noise, dust, and debris associated with power tools need to be carefully considered.

Index

Metric Conversion

Inches to Millimetres and Centimetres

MM—millimetres   *CM—centimetres*

Inches	MM	CM	Inches	CM	Inches	CM
⅛	3	0.3	9	22.9	30	76.2
¼	6	0.6	10	25.4	31	78.7
⅜	10	1.0	11	27.9	32	81.3
½	13	1.3	12	30.5	33	83.8
⅝	16	1.6	13	33.0	34	86.4
¾	19	1.9	14	35.6	35	88.9
⅞	22	2.2	15	38.1	36	91.4
1	25	2.5	16	40.6	37	94.0
1¼	32	3.2	17	43.2	38	96.5
1½	38	3.8	18	45.7	39	99.1
1¾	44	4.4	19	48.3	40	101.6
2	51	5.1	20	50.8	41	104.1
2½	64	6.4	21	53.3	42	106.7
3	76	7.6	22	55.9	43	109.2
3½	89	8.9	23	58.4	44	111.8
4	102	10.2	24	61.0	45	114.3
4½	114	11.4	25	63.5	46	116.8
5	127	12.7	26	66.0	47	119.4
6	152	15.2	27	68.6	48	121.9
7	178	17.8	28	71.1	49	124.5
8	203	20.3	29	73.7	50	127.0